After In-Yer-Face Theatre

"Twenty-five years after the premiere of *Blasted* at the Royal Court Theatre, *After In-Yer-Face* offers a timely and myth-busting reassessment of In-Yer-Face Theatre—its genesis, influence and legacy. Featuring essays from an international array of contributors, the cutting-edge scholarship in this collection examines the plays, institutional contexts, and global reach of In-Yer-Face Theatre. This is a welcome intervention that delivers fresh new perspectives on an extraordinary theatrical phenomenon."
—Chris Megson, *Royal Holloway, University of London, UK*, Author of *Decades of Modern British Playwriting: the* 1970s (2012)

"Informed by twenty years of scholarship, this new collection offers an incisive analysis of In-Yer-Face theatre, its original contexts and its lasting cultural significance. In particular, it helpfully explodes a number of myths surrounding the Royal Court and its role in developing this reliably controversialist generation of British playwrights. It also offers fascinating glimpses into the international impact of those playwrights and their work. It will doubtless prove invaluable to scholars and students alike."
—Trish Reid, *Kingston University, London, UK*, Author of *The Theatre of Anthony Neilson* (2017)

William C. Boles
Editor

After In-Yer-Face Theatre

Remnants of a Theatrical Revolution

palgrave
macmillan

Editor
William C. Boles
Rollins College
Winter Park, FL, USA

ISBN 978-3-030-39426-4   ISBN 978-3-030-39427-1 (eBook)
https://doi.org/10.1007/978-3-030-39427-1

© The Editor(s) (if applicable) and The Author(s), under exclusive licence to Springer Nature Switzerland AG 2020
This work is subject to copyright. All rights are solely and exclusively licensed by the Publisher, whether the whole or part of the material is concerned, specifically the rights of translation, reprinting, reuse of illustrations, recitation, broadcasting, reproduction on microfilms or in any other physical way, and transmission or information storage and retrieval, electronic adaptation, computer software, or by similar or dissimilar methodology now known or hereafter developed.
The use of general descriptive names, registered names, trademarks, service marks, etc. in this publication does not imply, even in the absence of a specific statement, that such names are exempt from the relevant protective laws and regulations and therefore free for general use.
The publisher, the authors and the editors are safe to assume that the advice and information in this book are believed to be true and accurate at the date of publication. Neither the publisher nor the authors or the editors give a warranty, expressed or implied, with respect to the material contained herein or for any errors or omissions that may have been made. The publisher remains neutral with regard to jurisdictional claims in published maps and institutional affiliations.

Cover illustration: Science Photo Library / Alamy Stock Photo

This Palgrave Macmillan imprint is published by the registered company Springer Nature Switzerland AG.
The registered company address is: Gewerbestrasse 11, 6330 Cham, Switzerland

For my family
The North Carolina Crew: Penny, Carl, and Christine
and
The Florida Crew: Leslie, Emma, and Leslie

Acknowledgements

Putting together this volume was an effort of many and they deserve recognition for their contributions.

My travels to London over the last twenty-years-plus have been made possible by the Ashforth Grant at Rollins College, which provided me with funds to visit archives and the London theatre. More recently, support from Grant Cornwell, President of Rollins College, and Susan Singer, Provost at Rollins College, via funds associated with the Hugh F. and Jeannette G. McKean Chair, was essential in wrapping up the final elements of the volume.

Laura Snyder and the Board of the Comparative Drama Conference encouraged me to create a mini-conference on In-Yer-Face in Baltimore, Maryland. The initial contributors to those sessions and the ensuing conversations helped to shape the direction of this book. In addition, the hard work and insight of all the contributors have been greatly appreciated as well as their patience with this first-time editor.

My colleagues in the English Department have been supportive throughout and, even as I finish writing this introduction a few weeks away from the deadline, I appreciate the drop-ins by my colleagues as they check on the progress of the book.

My students in the classroom and on the field study trips to London have been essential sounding boards on the power of these playwrights to create physically evocative, emotionally wrenching, artistically challenging, and completely unforgettable theatre.

Finally, my wife, Leslie, and daughter, Emma, have been the biggest supporters of my work on the In-Yer-Face authors and have, on innumerable occasions, sat through some uncomfortable, depressing, and violent theatrical experiences (except for Martin McDonagh, whom they both love), when they could have been attending a musical instead ("When are you gonna write a book on *Anything Goes?*" I am often asked). For their continued support and presence with me in the dark as we watched these worlds that aimed to be "in-our-faces," I thank them with great love and affection.

Contents

1 Introduction: Reflections on In-Yer-Face from the Other Side of the Atlantic   1
William C. Boles

Part I   Re-assessing the Movement   19

2 "In the Pursuit of New Writers": The Royal Court Young Peoples' Theatre and the Development of First-Time Playwrights in the 1990s   21
Nicholas Holden

3 "A Shop Window for Outrage": Harold Pinter's *Ashes to Ashes*, In-Yer Face Theatre and the Royal Court's 1996 West End Season   37
Graham Saunders

4 "The Last Rolo": Love, Conflict and War in Anthony Neilson's *Penetrator*   57
Rachael Newberry

5 Mark Ravenhill's Dialectical Emotions: In-Yer-Face as Post-Brechtian Theater   71
Anja Hartl

Part II A Movement's International Influences   87

6 Undressing Sarah Kane: A Portuguese Perspective on
   In-Yer-Face   89
   Cátia Faísco

7 Russian "In-Yer-Face Theatre" as a Problem or a Process   103
   Elena Dotsenko

8 Surfing the Wave of In-Yer-Face Theatre on Australian
   Shores   121
   Sandra Gattenhof

Part III A Movement's Aftermath   137

9 The Hidden Dialogue Between Sarah Kane and Edward
   Bond: The Dramaturgy of Accident Time and Ethical
   Subjectivities   139
   Chien-Cheng Chen

10 From "In-Yer-Face" to "In-Yer-Head": Staging the Mind
   in Martin Crimp, Sarah Kane, and Anthony Neilson   153
   Solange Ayache

11 Philip Ridley: Still In-Yer-Face   171
   Thomas A. Oldham

12 Tales from the East End: Dialogic and Confessional
   Storytelling as Therapy (?) in the Plays of Philip Ridley   185
   Cath Badham

13 Joe Penhall's Fatherhood Plays: Escaping the Influence of
   Sam Shepard and the Lad   201
   William C. Boles

14 "Experiential, not speculative": Love In and After In-Yer-Face 217
Korbinian Stöckl

15 The Echo Chamber: Theater in a "Post-Truth" World 231
Shane Kinghorn

Index 247

Notes on Contributors

Solange Ayache (Sorbonne University, France) is a senior lecturer in the Faculty of Arts and Humanities. She teaches English as a Foreign Language and Second Language Teaching at the Graduate School of Teaching and Education of Paris. She defended her PhD thesis on contemporary British drama from the University of Paris-Sorbonne and the University of Sheffield in Paris in 2017. Her research primarily focuses on the dramatic representation of mental space, the emergence of a theater "in-yer-head," and the use of science in the staging of the mind. Her interests also include children's literature, youth theater, and drama in education.

Cath Badham (University of Derby, United Kingdom) is Lecturer in Technical Theatre. She is completing her PhD at the University of Sheffield, examining the work of playwright Philip Ridley. She is using her experience as a professional stage manager (as Cath Booth) to inform her research. Stage management work includes Sheffield Theatres, Nottingham Playhouse, The Royal Exchange Theatre, Manchester, The Stephen Joseph Theatre, Scarborough and the Royal Shakespeare Company. She has had book reviews published in *Performing Ethos* and *Platform* and has written a short essay for the forthcoming *Cambridge Companion to British Playwriting Since 1945*.

William C. Boles (Rollins College, United States) is the Hugh F. and Jeannette G. McKean Chair of English. He is the author of *The Argumentative Theatre of Joe Penhall* (2011) and *Understanding David Henry Hwang* (2013). His most recent publications include: theatrical depictions of climate change in Steve Waters' *The Contingency Plan*, an interview with Simon Stephens, the presence of death in Martin McDonagh's *In Bruges*, and the theatricalization of the London housing crisis. He is the director of the annual Comparative Drama Conference.

Chien-Cheng Chen (Taipei National University of the Arts, Taiwan) lectures in the Department of Theatre Arts. He has a PhD in Drama, Theatre and Dance from Royal Holloway, University of London. His doctoral thesis examined Edward Bond's theory, later plays and their productions. His project focuses on the discourses and dramaturgy of violence in contemporary British theater.

Elena Dotsenko (Ural State Pedagogical University [Yekaterinburg], Russia) is Professor of Literature and teaches European and American literature, British drama and fiction, and theory of criticism. Her fields of research are Samuel Beckett's plays, comparative studies, and contemporary British drama. She has written *S. Beckett i problema uslovnosti v sovremennoj angliiskoj drame* [*Samuel Beckett and the Problem of Convention in Contemporary English Drama*] (2005) and has edited *Sovremennaya britanskaya drama: Stoppard, Churchill, Ravenhill* [*Contemporary British Drama: Stoppard, Churchill, Ravenhill*] (2018).

Cátia Faísco (University of Minho, Portugal) is a PhD student in Theatre Studies and researching sexual desire in contemporary British dramaturgy under the supervision of Rui Pina Coelho at the University of Lisbon. Said research is financially supported by the Portuguese FCT institution. Furthermore, Cátia Faísco's research interests include sexuality in theater, Sarah Kane, and memory as an artistic creative process. Since 2013, she has been teaching playwriting and dramaturgy and is a researcher in the GIEP (Research Group in Performance Studies) at the University of Minho. Cátia Faísco is a playwright at coletivoCASA and writes a monthly chronicle on theater for *RUA magazine*.

Sandra Gattenhof (Queensland University of Technology [QUT], Australia) is an associate professor and the director of Research Training in the Creative Industries Faculty. Previously she has been discipline leader—Dance, Drama, Music (2017) and head of Drama (2010–2016) and is the founding leader of the Creative Education and Creative Workforce theme in the Creative Lab at QUT. Sandra specializes in postdramatic theater, theater for young audiences, arts education advocacy, and arts and cultural evaluation. Most recently, Sandra's research engagements have established her as an Australian leader in the field of arts and cultural evaluation.

Anja Hartl (University of Konstanz, Germany) is a lecturer in the Department of Literature. In her PhD project, which is supported by a scholarship from the German National Merit Foundation (*Studienstiftung des deutschen Volkes*), she focuses on post-Brechtian aesthetics in contemporary British theater. She is the assistant to the review editor of the *Journal of Contemporary Drama in English* (*JCDE*). Her publications include articles on contemporary British theater and Brecht, book reviews, and performance reviews.

Nicholas Holden (University of Greenwich, United Kingdom) is Lecturer in Drama. His research interests lie in modern and contemporary British theater and playwriting pedagogy, and he has had works published internationally in these areas. He is the co-convener of the International Playwrights' Symposium: a biennial conference that brings academics, practitioners, and students together to discuss the work of a living playwright. He is writing a monograph on the Royal Court and its historic and contemporary practices for and with young people, and co-editing a collection of essays on the stage and television works of Dennis Kelly.

Shane Kinghorn (Manchester Metropolitan University, United Kingdom) is Senior Lecturer in Drama and Contemporary Theatre. He has previously worked in London as a director and dramaturg. His teaching practice has focused on the practice and application of dramaturgy, examining the relationship between dramatic and contemporary performance trends. His performance work, shown in various international festival contexts, informs his specialist research area: documentary and verbatim theater practice in the United Kingdom and Europe, the subject of several international publications.

Rachael Newberry (Goldsmiths College, University of London, United Kingdom) is a lecturer in the Department of Theatre and Performance, where she teaches across a range of specialisms from Shakespeare, critical theory and theater history through to post-war British theater, and postmodern and avant-garde dramatic texts. She is the director of the degree program Drama and Theatre Arts, chair of Learning and Teaching, and coordinator of the Teaching Excellence Framework pilot study. She is a champion of teaching excellence and widening participation. Her research interests are in the fields of gastro-criticism, eco-criticism, the body, and themes of consumption and self-denial.

Thomas A. Oldham (Texas A&M University-Corpus Christi, United States) is Assistant Professor of Theatre. His research involves onstage representations of violence in English/British drama, including Elizabethan and Jacobean tragedy, in addition to In-Yer-Face Theatre. Tom has also served as dramaturg in a variety of professional and educational theatres from Nebraska to New York, and his past teaching experience includes positions in Colby College and Indiana University. His writing has appeared in *The Routledge Companion to Dramaturgy*, *New England Theatre Journal*, *Ecumenica*, and *Theatre Journal*, along with the forthcoming collection *British Literature and Technology, 1600–1830*.

Graham Saunders (University of Birmingham, United Kingdom) is the Allardyce Nicoll Professor in the Department of Theatre and Drama Arts. His books include *Love Me or Kill Me: Sarah Kane and the Theatre of Extremes* (2002), *About Kane: the Playwright and the Work* (2009), *Patrick Marber's Closer* (2008) and *British Theatre Companies 1980–1994* (2015). He is co-editor of *Cool Britannia: Political Theatre in the 1990s* (Palgrave, 2008) and *Sarah Kane in Context* (2010). His latest monograph—*Elizabethan and Jacobean Reappropriation in Contemporary British Drama: "Upstart Crows"*—was published by Palgrave in 2017.

Korbinian Stöckl (University of Augsburg, Germany) is a lecturer and the chair of English Literature. He studied English, History, and Social Sciences at the University of Augsburg, graduating in 2014. His PhD project, "Concepts of Love in Contemporary British Drama," investigates historical continuities and contemporary peculiarities in treatments of love in British drama since the mid-1990s.

CHAPTER 1

Introduction: Reflections on In-Yer-Face from the Other Side of the Atlantic

William C. Boles

In the mid-to-late 1990s as a recently hired, tenure track professor at a small private liberal arts college just one town north of Orlando, Florida, my personal interactions with London theater were limited to the occasional research trips and annual study abroad field studies with students to see plays and visit museums. My first trip with students was in January 1997. A quick glance over the list of productions we attended that year reflects the stereotypical choices that a dramatic literature professor would select. Not surprisingly, some of the most important dramatic figures, plays, and theaters were represented: Harold Pinter's *The Homecoming* at the National Theatre, Tennessee Williams' *A Streetcar Named Desire* featuring Jessica Lange on the West End, William Shakespeare's *A Midsummer Night's Dream* at the Almeida Theatre, Anton Chekhov's *The Cherry Orchard* on the West End, and the Albert Finney-led cast of Yasmina Reza's West End hit *Art*. However, two works by two new playwrights provided a theatrical experience far different than those canonical pieces listed above, and, in turn, *Shopping and Fucking* by Mark Ravenhill and *The Beauty Queen of Leenane* by Martin McDonagh (both Royal Court on

---

W. C. Boles (✉)
Rollins College, Winter Park, FL, USA
e-mail: WBoles@Rollins.edu

© The Author(s) 2020
W. C. Boles (ed.), *After In-Yer-Face Theatre*,
https://doi.org/10.1007/978-3-030-39427-1_1

the West End productions) were to be instrumental touchstones for the trip and would set me on the eventual path to the creation of this book twenty years later.[1]

Ravenhill's play, at the Royal Court Upstairs, generated the most pre-performance eagerness for the students, driven, obviously, by the title and the warning on my syllabus that audience members had to be eighteen years old because of explicit material. The prurient nature of what might happen onstage only fomented the excitement for my students, especially considering that they attended a school surrounded by a conservative, well-heeled Central Florida community that had attempted to ban our college's production of Peter Shaffer's *Equus* only a decade earlier due to its graphic nudity. Our arrival at the theater revealed an energy more apt for a rock concert than a West End play by a previously unknown writer. Many of my students successfully pressed forward through the crowded lobby in order to be first into the theater, since it was a general seating arrangement. Techno music played as we entered and giddy excitement abounded as they set about trying to find the best place to enjoy what would be the most non-traditional show we would view. It did not disappoint. In the first few minutes a character vomited, releasing the floodgates that followed: male and female nudity, a hand job, a blow job, rimming, numerous explicit sex stories, drugs, and one of the funniest retellings of *The Lion King* committed to the stage. All leading to the penultimate scene, where Gary, a rent boy, was bent over a table and roughly, anally penetrated by first Robbie and then Mark. Sitting in the front row, mere feet from this violent gang rape was a group of five of my female students.

In-Yer-Face indeed.

The next play was McDonagh's *The Beauty Queen of Leenane*, a far different theatrical experience than Ravenhill's play. There was no pent-up excitement on the part of my students, and the first scenes seemed to fit more comfortably within the type of plays we saw by Pinter, Chekhov, and Williams. Relying on only one set, the action built slowly, following a traditional dramatic structure. However, in the midst of this familiar form were little moments that announced that while the play may share similar DNA with canonical writers, it also was not that far removed from Ravenhill's play. A full chamber pot was casually emptied over dirty dishes in a kitchen sink, generating loud groans of disgusted laughter from the audience. Madness and brutality were casually hinted at with a dash of overhanging menace. A comedic character was fascinated with the heft of a poker and whether it would be heavy enough to attack police officers. Characters could not agree on the correct pronunciation of the local priest's last name. And then it happened. In the penultimate scene the elderly, nagging Mag sat rocking in her chair, as she had done throughout the play, but this time as the chair slowed in its rocking, Mag silently collapsed onto the floor, as part of her skull came away. The earlier groans of disgust were replaced by screams from the audience.[2] Needless to say, screams do not happen in Ibsen or Chekhov or Williams. McDonagh's play, like Ravenhill's, was something different. These experiences for my students were like taking a theatrical version of Ecstasy, as they enthusiastically embraced Ravenhill and McDonagh's plays and, in turn, fashioned an artistic standard against which all other plays and performances during our trip would be measured.

At the end of those two performances I realized that I had unknowingly exposed myself and my students to a new theatrical movement that would not only prove to be one of the most controversial periods of British drama, but also introduce playwrights who would be incredibly influential over the ensuing decades in not only the theater but other media as well. It was only when I returned to Florida and began to do research did I learn about the scope of this batch of young playwrights who were causing trouble across the London theater with their plays. In my reading I also noticed that there was a rush by London theater reviewers to name these upstart writers, trying to connect them all under a thematic umbrella. Attempts were made, including the bulky "The Theatre of Urban Ennui," the Frank Sinatra-referenced "BritPack," the German "Blood and Sperm Generation," and the not far off "New Brutalists,"[3] but it did not take long before Aleks Sierz, like John Russell Taylor before him with the Angry Young Writers, found the perfect moniker, "In-Yer-Face Theatre."

As a young scholar, I found these plays invigorating, exciting, and palpably so different from what I had studied throughout graduate school. I immediately shifted gears from post-World War II material and began devouring play texts, reading articles online, and tracking what was happening in London, and on return visits to London, I was able to see productions that were part of the movement, like Ben Elton's *Popcorn*, Patrick Marber's *Closer*, and Simon Bent's *Goldhawk Road*. I also inserted these new writers into my dramatic literature and playwriting courses, where the youth culture oriented content and explicitness provoked discussions about the boundaries of theater as well as testified to the exuberant power of new perspectives when it came to writing about the world.[4] Students from those classes would go onto London for semester abroad programs and seek out productions by the playwrights we studied. (One student happened to be in London during the Sarah Kane revival at the Royal Court Theatre in 2001 and attended many of the productions.)

Outside of the classroom I began doing my own scholarship, attended conferences, and published a few articles on these playwrights, introducing them to other American scholars along the way. However, what really excited me was presenting at a conference dedicated to In-Yer-Face Theatre to be held at the University of the West of England in Bristol in 2002, and co-sponsored by the Sarah Kane scholar Graham Saunders and Rebecca D'Monté, with numerous other luminaries present, including Sierz, Dan Rebellato, Elaine Aston, David Greig, Steve Waters, Ken Urban, and Kate Ashfield, who was in the original cast of *Shopping and Fucking*. Unfortunately, what I learned in Bristol from Sierz's plenary was that the In-Yer-Face movement was officially over. In looking back, if I am honest, his pronouncement was incredibly deflating. I felt as if I had finally been allowed into this incredible party only to find myself in a cavernous space, featuring half-eaten Kimberley biscuits as appetizers and a DJ playing Simply Red's B-sides. What especially stung was that I had only had a few opportunities to experience a movement that was essentially kaput. I had missed it. I had missed one of the British theaters most invigorating, energetic, and surprising eras since the Angry Young Writers.

Or had I?

While the era may have ended, a few of the writers associated with the movement, like Anthony Neilson and Philip Ridley, have kept the faith by continuing to be the headline-generating, theatrical provocateurs they were during In-Yer-Face's heyday. Neilson especially has retained the moniker associated with the movement, having had his 2002 play *Stitching* banned in Malta in 2009, and his 2011 version of *Marat/Sade* for the Royal Shakespeare Company provoked, on average, thirty audience members to walk out per night. On one especially busy night the tally climbed to eighty.[5] These protests were covered gleefully by the press, much to Neilson's consternation: "What galls me about this storm in a boudoir is that the media have devoted much more time and space to regurgitating the original, sensationalist local report ... and commenting on the resultant scandal than to the play and production itself, which was discussed in depressingly simplistic terms."[6] Similarly, Katie Mitchell's revival of Kane's *Cleansed* for the National Theatre in 2016 prompted the same heavy breathing from the London newspapers, as they too reported on the number of walkouts during previews in addition to the numerous incidences of audience members fainting. Citing the scene where Tinker cuts out Carl's tongue after professing his love for Rod, Laura Barton of *The Guardian* wrote: "It was not long after this scene that an audience member attending a preview performance of Katie Mitchell's production at the National Theatre this week collapsed. The house lights went up. Ushers hurried in to escort him out. But he was not alone: by the end of the first week's run, the production had accumulated a grand total of five faints and 40 walk-outs."[7] These examples show that even though the days of In-Yer-Face are long gone, the press still longs for the same provocative headlines that were generated during its heyday, and revivals and the occasional new production are still provoking the same type of responses from theater-going audiences and the media.

I was lucky enough to see Mitchell's production of *Cleansed* (no one walked out of the performance I attended), and afterward, I started thinking about productions by In-Yer-Face writers since Sierz's nail-in-the-coffin pronouncement in Bristol. I quickly came to realize that while I may have missed the main event, I (and other theater goers) have had great seats in seeing the continuingly impressive theatrical output of writers that came to the dramatic forefront during that era. While I was lucky enough to see *The Beauty Queen of Leenane*, I did not see the rest of the Leenane Trilogy or *The Cripple of Inishmaan*. And yet, I did find myself in the audience for the original productions of McDonagh's *The Pillowman*, *Hangmen*, and *A Very Very Very Dark Matter*. I may have missed *Some Voices* and *Love and Understanding*, both by Joe Penhall, but I did see *Blue/Orange* on the West End, *Haunted Child* at the Royal Court, and the original West End cast of *Sunny Afternoon*. I did not attend Jez Butterworth's *Mojo* as well as a more recent revival, but I saw the Royal Court production of *The Winterling* as well as the West End productions of *Jerusalem* and *The Ferryman*. While I did see *Shopping and Fucking*, I missed Ravenhill's follow-ups *Some Explicit Polaroids* and *Handbag*. However, I did see the controversial *Mother Clapp's Molly House* and his adaptation of Terry Pratchett's *Nation* (both at the National Theatre) as well as *The Cane*, Ravenhill's return to the Royal Court.[8]

In looking over these productions I have attended since Sierz's announcement, I came to realize that the disappointment I felt back in Bristol almost twenty years ago was perhaps a bit too premature in its self-pitying nature. True, a movement may have ended, but it was not the end of these writers' theatrical voices. While many of the forty-plus playwrights who were associated with the In-Yer-Face era are no longer producing new theatrical work or have significantly reduced their output, such as Judy Upton, Che Walker, Simon Block, Patrick Marber, and stage adaptations of Irvine Welsh's novels, some of the core writers, like McDonagh, Ravenhill, Butterworth, Penhall as well as Ridley, Neilson, and Roy Williams (who Sierz has remarked after the fact should have been included in his book),[9] continue to produce material for the stage as well as other mediums, like children's plays, television, movies, librettos, dance programs, and subscription services, such as Netflix. In fact, if we look at three of the most recognized writers from that period, it becomes clear that these pugilistic, explosive, and challenging writers have now actually become essential contributors to and important voices in mainstream culture, transferring their smudgy theater fingerprints onto other cultural hallmarks over the last fifteen years. Quickly, I want to use Jez Butterworth, Martin McDonagh, and Joe Penhall as examples of previous members of a young, hip, provocative group of writers becoming influencers in and of mainstream culture.

Jez Butterworth

Butterworth, who was seen as a wunderkind with *Mojo*, being the first time since John Osborne's *Look Back in Anger* that a new playwright had a play produced on the Main Stage at the Royal Court, is one of the most successful writers to emerge from the In-Yer-Face movement. Butterworth's plays have traveled successfully between the West End and Broadway. Three recent examples prove the point. His grand state-of-the-nation play *Jerusalem* transferred from the Royal Court to the West End, winning a number of Oliviers, including Best Actor for lead Mark Rylance, and moved to Broadway, where it netted numerous Tony nominations. His follow-up *The River*, after playing at the Royal Court Theatre Upstairs, transferred to Broadway, where it was a financial success, due in part to his ability to attract A-lister Hugh Jackman to star in the production. More recently, his play *The Ferryman*, which was based on a true story told to him by Laura Donnelly, Butterworth's partner, about an uncle of hers who went missing during the Troubles, featured a now unheard of cast of over twenty actors, including Donnelly, multiple kids, a baby, plus a goose and a bunny. The play started at the Royal Court, ran on the West End, netted Olivier awards, including one for Butterworth, and then transferred to Broadway, where Butterworth earned a Tony Award for Best Play.

In terms of his influence outside of the theater, he has been active in the movie industry, beginning shortly after the success of *Mojo*, when he informed his agent that he wanted to direct the film version of the play. After writing a screenplay that refused to be like *Trainspotting*, deliberately thumbing his nose at producers who wanted his film to emulate the success of the movie adaptation of Irvine Welsh's novel, Butterworth still managed to convinced the studio to let him direct. Shortly thereafter, he persuaded Harold Pinter to play the crime boss Sam Ross, who was originally an off-stage character in the play. Pinter makes a small role memorably "ticklish" and highlights through his performance how much of an influence Pinter was on Butterworth's early writing.[10] He followed *Mojo* with *Birthday Girl*, co-written with his brother, and starring another A-lister Nicole Kidman as a mail-order Russian bride. Those small, independent projects as screenwriter and director allowed Butterworth an introduction to the film business, which he found to be an exciting addition to his career. He admitted: "Movies are the most fun, and I feel like I've just started. Even though I've been doing it for 20 years. I get so excited about it. It's like Pokémon. It's like, let's play this game, how does this work? How does that work? It's a completely different way of using one's narrative technique."[11] While he has worked on the scripts for films about the American criminal Whitey Bulger and singer James Brown, his most significant contribution to mainstream culture can be found in two recent Hollywood vehicles, as the screenwriter for *Edge of Tomorrow*, a Tom Cruise starring, Doug Liman directed, science-fiction, action vehicle, and, more significantly, *Spectre*, which is currently the second-highest-grossing Bond film. Combined, these two films alone made 1.25 billion dollars, an amount none of the other In-Yer-Face writers have come close to matching through their own theater, film, and television work. No doubt, if one writes films for Tom Cruise and Britain's most famous spy, then the movement from a theatrical wunderkind to an influencer of the mainstream zeitgeist is complete.

Martin McDonagh

McDonagh, similar to Butterworth, has also successfully navigated the world of theater and cinema, as a screenwriter and director, quite successfully. His plays, like Butterworth, have found success in London as well as on Broadway. *The Beauty Queen of Leenane*, which won three acting Tony awards, announced to New York audiences that he was a playwright to watch. Since its meteoric success, almost all of McDonagh's plays have transferred to New York and Broadway. In addition, McDonagh has won two Olivier awards for Best Play, first for *The Pillowman* and then *Hangmen*, which transferred to Broadway for a limited run. Similar to Butterworth, McDonagh's work attracts some of the leading actors in Britain and the United States, including David Tennant, David Morrissey, Johnny Flynn, Christopher Walken, and Jim Broadbent, who has appeared in two plays by McDonagh. More recently, he has connected with Nicholas Hytner at his new theatrical venue The Bridge, where *A Very Very Very Dark Matter*, a dark comedy combining the storytelling of Hans Christian Anderson with the oppression of the Belgian Congo, premiered.

Like Butterworth, McDonagh also has his own connection to James Bond, but not in relation to the film franchise. Instead, McDonagh had a 1996 dust-up with Sean Connery at an awards ceremony, when he told the former and best James Bond to "fuck off," after the Scot chastised him to "Shut up, sonny, and mind your language."[12] In part, because of that exchange, McDonagh was seen as the "bad boy" of the In-Yer-Face writers. Through his film work he has continued to cultivate that pugnacious spirit, but he has allowed his characters with their racist and inflammatory comments to court controversy instead of his own behavior.[13] In fact, McDonagh has made it clear that he prefers working in film to the theater:[14] "I would be unhappy if I wrote 90 good plays and didn't make a good film. But if I made one good film. If I made one brilliant film, one really, really good film, I'd be happy. One would be enough."[15] While McDonagh's films have not been the financial juggernauts befitting Hollywood's obsession with tentpole releases, they have received critical acclaim, with three of his films receiving Oscar nominations and awards, including an Oscar for Best Action Short for *Six Shooter*, a best screenplay nomination for both *In Bruges* and *Three Billboards Outside Ebbing, Missouri*, and a Best Actress for Frances McDormand for *Three Billboards*. Ever since he swept to the forefront with the oft-awarded *The Beauty Queen of Leenane*, McDonagh has continued to solidify his position as one of England's most creative and exported playwrights and one of Hollywood's most challenging screenwriters and directors.

Joe Penhall

While the number of In-Yer-Face plays that emerged in the mid-to-late 1990s was, for some critics, an overwhelming amount of work to see and review, only one playwright could break through the crowded collection of annually produced plays and achieve recognition for writing the best play of the year at the Olivier Awards. Penhall managed to stand out from his peers and became the first playwright associated with the movement to win the Best Play Award for *Blue/Orange*. (As of this writing, only McDonagh and Butterworth have joined Penhall in this distinction.) Like his peers above, Penhall has also remained connected to the theater, having written five more plays since *Blue/Orange*. Three of them were produced by the Royal Court Theatre (*Dumb Show*, *Haunted Child*, and *Birthday*), one at the National Theatre (*Landscape with Weapon*), and one at the Old Vic (*Mood Music*). Diverging from Butterworth and McDonagh, Penhall broadened his theatrical output to include writing a book for the musical *Sunny Afternoon*. Working in collaboration with Ray Davies, leader of the British band The Kinks, Penhall crafted the story of the rise and success of The Kinks, with a glorious mid-second-act singalong (and confetti drop) to the title song, which became the theme song for English football team's World Cup victory in 1966. Running for two years on the West End, the musical garnered four Olivier awards, including one for Best Musical. Through this feel-good musical Penhall created a theatrical experience anathema to the In-Yer-Face "shock tactics" of taking "the audience by the scruff of the neck," while "smashing taboos."[16] Many of the intended audience members for In-Yer-Face Theatre were not even born or old enough to remember the events depicted in the musical, including Penhall who was born in 1967. And so, *Sunny Afternoon*'s success relied on older audience members' nostalgia for the music of The Kinks as well as the last time that England won the World Cup.

The success of *Blue/Orange* led Penhall to the realm of movies as well as television. He admitted: "I didn't have many massive commercial successes, they're all quite cult-y so I kind of had to try and be successful in film."[17] While a few of his plays have been adapted by him for film and television (*Some Voices*, *Blue/Orange*, and *Birthday*), he has gained recognition in Hollywood as an adapter for the screen of previously published material. He adapted both Ian McEwan's *Enduring Love* and Cormac McCarthy's *The Road* for the screen as well as Jake Arnott's *The Long Firm* for British television. He infamously wrote the screenplay to the

Oscar-winning movie about Idi Amin called *The Last King of Scotland*, but had his name removed from the credits after a squabble with the producers, who wanted a more commercial vehicle, even though he had worked on the story for over five years. Penhall's expression of his opinions also had him removed from the publicity tour for *The Road*, when he made political connections between the post-apocalyptic vision of the film and George W. Bush's leadership as president. While these projects and his cantankerous behavior have kept him just on the periphery of mainstream culture, Penhall in 2018 joined a long list of creative artists who have partnered with the omnipresent entertainment behemoth Netflix. Working with David Fincher, Penhall is the showrunner, executive producer, and primary writer for the first two seasons of *Mindhunter*, a well-reviewed series on Netflix, which is based on John Douglas and Mark Olshaker's book *Mindhunter: Inside the FBI's Elite Serial Crime Unit*. With this project Penhall moved from the adapter of eclectic art house films to worldwide exposure through the ever-expanding universe of Netflix streaming. With this project Penhall has reached the largest audience of his career, moving his craft, vision, and argumentative style of writing into binge-watching living rooms around the world.

After In-Yer-Face: Remnants of a Theatrical Revolution

The genesis for this book occurred in 2016 in Baltimore, Maryland, at the 40th Annual Comparative Drama Conference. Over an afternoon, scholars from around the world came together to contribute papers dedicated to the topic of "In-Yer-Face: Twenty Years On." Ranging from the international influences of In-Yer-Face to the pedagogy of teaching Martin McDonagh in the classroom, we discussed the lingering influences of In-Yer-Face on new writers as well as the continuing theatrical careers of those who were part of the movement. From those initial fifteen-minute papers, this book is the end project. Some of the original contributors from Baltimore are represented here, while other voices have been added to that initial conversation from over four years ago.

This book is comprised of three sections. The first of which looks back and re-assesses the era and writers, aiming to reveal new insights on that period of "Cool Britannia." While much has been noted about the connection between In-Yer-Face Theatre and contemporary German theater and playwrights, the second section considers the influence of In-Yer-Face on three other countries: Portugal, Russia, and Australia. The final section highlights various post-In-Yer-Face plays by looking at more recent works by members of the movement as well as examining the movement's influence on and overlap with contemporary British dramatists.

The first two chapters of the first section aim to dispel myths that the Royal Court Theater itself promulgated in the mid-1990s, especially as they related to the theater's relationship with and cultivation of In-Yer-Face writers and the overall movement. Nicholas Holden, in his piece "'In the Pursuit of New Writers': The Royal Court Young Peoples' Theatre and the Development of First-Time Playwrights in the 1990s," challenges the contention that the Royal Court produced and advertised its young writers, like Penhall, Kane, Nick Grosso, and Judy Upton, as fresh talent, free from any form of a developmental creative process, as its leaders aimed to distance themselves from the heavy-handed workshop method used by Max Stafford-Clark, the previous artistic director. Instead, Holden argues that the Court actually relied upon other entities, like the National Theatre, to develop the plays, allowing the Court to create the myth about the untouched nature of the plays and playwrights being produced. Graham Saunders, in his "'A Shop Window for Outrage': Harold Pinter's *Ashes to Ashes*, In-Yer-Face Theatre and the Royal Court's 1996 West End Season," dissects the propaganda surrounding the Royal Court's move to the West End during its Sloane Square refurbishment from September 1996 through February 2000. Using the dual-running productions of Pinter's *Ashes to Ashes* and Ravenhill's *Shopping and Fucking* as the basis for his contention, Saunders argues that the myth the Royal Court wanted to create about itself as this edgy, "rambunctious" entry into the West End ran afoul of Pinter's expectations for the promotion and production of his latest play. Using archival material, Saunders documents that Pinter "frustrated" the "contradictory and sometimes absurd ways" the Court aimed to position itself as a rebel within its temporary West End neighborhood.

The last two chapters in the section focus on two specific plays from the era, providing new perspectives on the texts. Rachael Newberry in "'The Last Rolo': Love, Conflict and War in Anthony Neilson's *Penetrator*" provides a close reading of Neilson's 1993 play by contextually framing it against the Gulf War as well as the numerous pop cultural references that dot the script. Her chapter questions whether *Penetrator* is tied to its time period or whether it still has resonance for future audiences of revived productions. Newberry ultimately posits that the play remains current because of its larger timeless thematic focus on love. Wrapping up the section is Anja Hartl's "Mark Ravenhill's Dialectical Emotions: In-Yer-Face as Post-Brechtian Theater," which re-examines the perception that a lack of political content exists in In-Yer-Face Theatre. Hartl argues that In-Yer-Face had an influence on post-Brechtian devices used by British writers. Noting that Mark Ravenhill has been a stalwart supporter and adapter of Brecht, she relies upon *Some Explicit Polaroids* as a guide to argue "how the play explores the challenges of dialectical drama today" and, in the process. It fosters "awareness, critique and resistance in the audience" by "employing emotions as a dialectical instrument."

The second section of the book moves away from the British stage and productions and looks at the influences/effects of In-Yer-Face on the theater of other countries, specifically Portugal, Russia, and Australia. Cátia Faísco in "Undressing Sarah Kane: A Portuguese Perspective on In-Yer-Face" traces the history of Kane's plays being introduced to Portuguese audiences by providing analysis of *Artistas Unidos*'s, a Lisbon theater company, decision to produce almost all of Kane's work. Through a discussion of these productions Faísco reveals numerous issues that surrounded the performance of these plays, ranging from translation questions related to *Crave* to the influence of the Carnation Revolution, which permitted greater freedom for theaters and theater companies to produce contemporary plays like Kane's. Finally, Faísco charts the stark contrast between Portuguese and English audiences in their reaction to Kane's work. The audiences in Lisbon and around the country did not experience the same shock and disgust as the English audiences. Instead, the author notes that the Portuguese saw Kane as "just another playwright who had an interesting oeuvre." While Faísco considers productions of In-Yer-Face writers in Portugal, Elena Dotsenko in "Russian 'In-Yer-Face Theatre' as a Problem or a Process" offers a wider take on the influence of British writers on the New Drama of Russia after the turn of the century. Specifically, she notes that the Royal Court's forays into Russia with plays and their playwrights partly inspired the new wave of Russian dramatists, some of whom share the similar characteristic of discomforting audiences through the play's subject matter. However, Dotsenko stresses that Russian theatrical conventions as well as governmental limitations on language have also hampered some of the more extreme influences of In-Yer-Face writers. The final chapter, "Surfing the Wave of In-Yer-Face Theatre on Australian Shores," by Sandra Gattenhof explores the appearance of In-Yer-Face in Australian theaters, arguing that the first appearance of such a play was *Fireface*, written by Marius von Mayenburg, a German playwright. She then traces various Australian productions of In-Yer-Face plays before discussing how the form and ideas of the movement, especially Sarah Kane's work, was internalized into the plays of Australian playwright Daniel Evans. She uses two of his plays *Oedipus Doesn't Live Here Anymore* and *The Tragedy of King Richard the Third* to argue that while the In-Yer-Face movement may be over in England, if Evans' work is to be a representative model, then its influence is still a theatrical force in Australia.

The final section of the book looks at the lingering influences of In-Yer-Face on the current British theater and its playwrights in two ways: examining the ripple effect on plays and playwrights in the new century and considering post-In-Yer-Face plays by playwrights associated with the movement. Chien-Cheng Chen in "The Hidden Dialogue Between Sarah Kane and Edward Bond: The Dramaturgy of Accident Time and Ethical Subjectivities" explores the connection between Kane's plays and Bond's later plays, while arguing that Bond's theories of theater, specifically his concept of "accident time," aid in understanding the behavior of Kane's characters when they experience moments of violence and madness. In addition, Chen explores how both playwrights explore the ethical conundrums of their characters, arguing that Kane's "unprejudiced examination of ethical aporetic moments" endows "her dramaturgy of accident time with ethical force." Ultimately, the chapter reveals a "hidden dramaturgical and ethical logic common" to both playwrights and their works. Sarah Kane is also the focus, along with Martin Crimp and Anthony Neilson, in Solange Ayache's chapter, "From 'In-Yer-Face' to 'In-Yer-Head': Staging the Mind in Martin Crimp, Sarah Kane and Anthony Neilson." Ayache argues that a more apt descriptor of recent British drama is "In-Yer-Head" rather than In-Yer-Face by suggesting that the interiority of the human mind has become the new focus for playwrights, who have turned their previously externally focused work inward in order to stage "psychological indeterminacy, uncertainty and instability by focusing on the troubled minds of disappearing female characters." Ayache posits that works like Crimp's *Attempts on Her Life* and Kane's *4.48 Psychosis* provide the shift to the "In-Yer-Head" emphasis through their "psychopoetic" look at the inner workings of the female mind. She then follows that Anthony Neilson's *The Wonderful World of Dissocia* fully embraces this concept a decade later. Ultimately, "In-Yer-Head" theater "questions the nature of objective and subjective reality to the point of renewing the possibilities of the dramatic form."

The next two chapters focus exclusively on the works of Philip Ridley, who Thomas A. Oldham contends is "Still In-Yer-Face." Oldham argues that even though the In-Yer-Face movement may be long over and many of the playwrights who defined the era have found cozier homes in the film industry, Ridley "still courts controversy with squirm-inducing sexual and violent imagery." He is "a playwright who still manages to divide critics and disturb audiences profoundly." Oldham makes his case by examining two of Ridley's more recent plays *Mercury Fur* and *Karagula* and posits that Ridley's work still highlights the main tenets of In-Yer-Face drama by being "gruesome, sensational, vitally theatrical, and absolutely necessary." Cath Badham continues the focus on the works of Ripley in "Tales from the East End: Dialogic and Confessional Storytelling as Therapy (?) in the Plays of Philip Ridley." Her focus is more specific than Oldham's, as she examines the "dialogic and confessional styles of storytelling that Ridley utilizes," offering the audience and characters "opportunities for therapy, confession and catharsis." She begins with *Vincent River*, a play written just in the final months of the In-Yer-Face movement and contrasts its use of dialogue-driven, therapeutic storytelling against two of Ridley's later plays, *Dark Vanilla Jungle* and *Tonight with Donny Stixx*, which rely on monologues directly addressed to the audience, making it the therapist for the characters' confessions.

William C. Boles' "Joe Penhall's Fatherhood Plays: Escaping the Influence of Sam Shepard and the Lad" focuses on *Haunted Child* and *Birthday*, which premiered within months of each other at the Royal Court. Using Penhall's declaration that Sam Shepard's *True West* was the inspirational driver for much of his plays, Boles discusses how *Haunted Child* proved to be the culmination of Shepard's influence on Penhall as well as Penhall's reliance on male characters who behave badly. In contrast, *Birthday*, which was inspired by his wife's difficult pregnancy, offers a completely new male main character for Penhall, a male who embraces roles that have long been associated with being a mother, including the ability to give birth. With the play Penhall upends the long-held pattern of his plays, opening up a new venue for theatrical exploration in the future. Korbinian Stöckl in "'Experiential, Not Speculative': Love in and After In-Yer-Face" compares Mark Ravenhill's *Shopping and Fucking* and Sarah Kane's *Cleansed* with Dennis Kelly's *Love and Money* by specifically looking at the "directness" of the playwrights' use of language. He posits that there is a distinct difference between the In-Yer-Face works, which "talk directly to the sensory apparatus rather than to the intellect," and Kelly's play, which "relies almost exclusively on the images created by language and on the emotional effects produced mainly by the imaginative and interpretive skills of the spectator or reader." In order to highlight the thematic and linguistic differences, he compares and contrasts how the three plays depict the concept of love. The book's final chapter, "The Echo Chamber: Theater in a Post-Truth World" authored by Shane Kinghorn, scrutinizes the rise of verbatim theater in the post-9/11 theatrical world, where it supplants In-Yer-Face as the next theatrical phase of British drama. The theater, he argues, "was challenging the ways audiences took meaning from stories." Audiences were seeking "a greater sense of certainty, of factual accuracy, or even *truth*, than could be found outside the auditorium." Citing the rise of a "post-truth" world where internet sites undermine authority and recent political movements question what truth is, Kinghorn explores if verbatim drama can "offer a meaningful intervention" for audience members struggling to engage with the "truth."

Finally, while I have titled my introduction as "Reflections on In-Yer-Face from Across the Atlantic," this book, as the summary above indicates, is not limited to one specific international focus on this important era of British drama. Instead, represented in these pages are scholars from eight different countries (Australia, France, Germany, Portugal, Russia, Taiwan, the United Kingdom, and the United States) and four different continents: Asia, Australia, Europe, and North America. The diversity of academic voices from across the globe and from varying points of academic careers (from PhD students to endowed chairs) is a testament to the continuing importance of these writers and plays, all from a relatively short period of time in the 1990s. No doubt, scholars and productions will continue to weigh in on the significance of these works, playwrights and the era as a whole, but, for now, this volume represents a snapshot from twenty-five years on of what In-Yer-Face was and what it has wrought. I look forward to seeing what the view of this era will be in another twenty-five years.

Notes

1. For more detail about these two productions, see William C. Boles, "Violence at the Royal Court: Martin McDonagh's *The Beauty Queen of Leenane* and Mark Ravenhill's *Shopping and Fucking*," *Theatre Symposium* VII (1999): 125–135.
2. Six years later I would once again see an audience again react with multiple screams of horror during McDonagh's *The Pillowman*.
3. Aleks Sierz, "Still In-Yer-Face: Towards a Critique and a Summation," *New Theatre Quarterly* 69 (2002): 17–18.
4. Other academics were also using this new material in the classroom. Mark Ravenhill recounted an experience in 1998 at the National Student Drama Festival, when he introduced himself to a group of students in a pub:

   > There was quiet. And then—oh, horror!—eyes rolled to the ceiling. "Oh, you," groaned one of the students. "We have to study you." En masse they moved swiftly away. Who wants to stand next to their reading list when they're having a pint with mates? I was shocked. I hadn't realised how quickly a play could move from the stage to the classroom. After all, it had only been two years since the play premiered in a small studio theatre. (Mark Ravenhill, "In 1998 I was suddenly very, very cool," *Guardian*, December 10, 2006, https://www.theguardian.com/stage/2006/dec/11/theatre1 [accessed March 1, 2019].)

5. Richard Alleyne, "Audience walks out from 'depraved' Royal Shakespeare Company production," *The Telegraph*, October 24, 2011, https://www.telegraph.co.uk/culture/theatre/theatre-news/8844513/Audience-walks-out-from-depraved-Royal-Shakespeare-Company-production.html (accessed July 5, 2018).
6. Anthony Neilson, "*Marat/Sade* director: 'I prefer the critics on Twitter,'" *Guardian*, October 25, 2011, https://www.theguardian.com/stage/2011/oct/25/rsc-director-attacks-print-critics (accessed July 5, 2018).
7. Laura Barton, "Why do plays about sex and violence written by women still shock?" *Guardian*, February 27, 2016, https://www.theguardian.com/stage/2016/feb/27/why-do-plays-about-sex-and-violence-written-by-women-still-shock-sarah-kane-cleansed (accessed 15 July 2018).
8. Boles compares the narrative structure of these two new works by Ravenhill and McDonagh with their attention-grabbing plays *Shopping and Fucking* and *The Beauty Queen of Leenane*. See William C. Boles, Review of Mark Ravenhill's *The Cane* and Martin McDonagh's *A Very Very Very Dark Matter*, *Miranda: Ariel's Corner* 18 (2019), https://journals.openedition.org/miranda/18344.

9. Aleks Sierz, "What Happened to In-Yer-Face Theatre?" April 1, 2006, http://www.sierz.co.uk/writings/what-ever-happened-to-in-yer-face-theatre/ (accessed 2 June 2019).
10. See Jez Butterworth, *Mojo & A Film-maker's Diary* (London: Faber & Faber, 1998): 143–176.
11. Suzy Evans, "Jez Butterworth Spills All His Secrets in 'The Ferryman,'" *Hollywood Reporter*, May 10, 2019, https://www.hollywoodreporter.com/news/playwright-jez-butterworth-spills-all-his-secrets-ferryman-1209467 (accessed July 30, 2019).
12. Rupert Christiansen, "If you're the greatest you must prove it," *The Telegraph*, January 11, 1997, http://www.telegraph.co.uk/culture/4707096/If-youre-the-greatest-you-must-prove-it.html (accessed January 26, 2016).
13. See, among many, Maeve McDermott, "The growing racial backlash against 'Three Billboards Outside Ebbing, Missouri,' explained," *USA Today*, January 3, 2018, https://www.usatoday.com/story/life/entertainthis/2018/01/03/growing-racial-backlash-against-three-billboards-explained-explaining-growing-backlash-against-oscar/977024001/ (accessed July 23, 2019); Joe Sommerlad, "Three Billboards is not a racist film," *The Independent*, January 27, 2018, https://www.independent.co.uk/voices/three-buildings-outside-ebbing-missouri-racism-row-twitter-martin-mcdonagh-oscars-frances-mcdormand-a8178861.html (accessed July 23, 2019); and Alissa Wilkinson, "How Three Billboards went from film fest darling to awards-season controversy," *Vox*, February 22, 2018, https://www.vox.com/2018/1/19/16878018/three-billboards-controversy-racist-sam-rockwell-redemption-flannery-oconnor (accessed July 23, 2019).
14. For further discussion of McDonagh's view of film versus theater, see William C. Boles, "Murder Amidst the Chocolates: Martin McDonagh's Multifaceted Uses of Death in *In Bruges*," in *Narrating Death: The Limit of Literature*, ed. Daniel Jernigan, Walter Wadiak, and W. Michelle Wang (London: Routledge Press, 2018), 176–179.
15. Fintan O'Toole, "Martin McDonagh," *BOMB*, no. 63 (Spring 1998), https://bombmagazine.org/articles/martin-mcdonagh/ (accessed April 20, 2016).
16. Aleks Sierz, *In-Yer-Face Theatre: British Drama Today* (London: Faber & Faber, 2000), 4.
17. Sarah Tejal Hamilton, "Joe Penhall—the interview Part 2," *Writerly*, April 24, 2017, https://writerlyblogblog.wordpress.com/2017/04/24/joe-penhall-the-interview-part-2/ (accessed July 5, 2018).

PART I

Re-assessing the Movement

CHAPTER 2

"In the Pursuit of New Writers": The Royal Court Young Peoples' Theatre and the Development of First-Time Playwrights in the 1990s

Nicholas Holden

A Changing Vision

By 1993 London's Royal Court Theatre was on the brink of change. The arrival of Stephen Daldry in the previous year prompted a revolution in the theater's leadership, following the fourteen-year tenure of Max Stafford-Clark as Artistic Director. Daldry's appointment was the beginning of a wider shift in the artistic structure of the theater that also saw Graham Whybrow replace Robin Hooper as Literary Manager in 1994. Whybrow's arrival brought a new perspective to the Court's programming after what had been, for Daldry, a challenging and "uneven" opening year.[1] The partnership of Daldry and Whybrow immediately prompted a "reassessment of the theatre's priorities"[2] and heralded the beginning of a playwriting epoch at the Court that placed new and, significantly, young first-time writers at the heart of the theater's vision. The story of this time

N. Holden (✉)
University of Greenwich, London, UK
e-mail: N.O.Holden@Greenwich.ac.uk

© The Author(s) 2020
W. C. Boles (ed.), *After In-Yer-Face Theatre*,
https://doi.org/10.1007/978-3-030-39427-1_2

in the Royal Court's history has subsequently evolved to become well established. The Court's success during this time with a number of seminal plays of the decade such as Sarah Kane's *Blasted* (1995), Jez Butterworths's *Mojo* (1995) and Mark Ravenhill's *Shopping and Fucking* (1996) saw the Court "regarded as the pioneering force" at the forefront of a wave of new plays that populated the British stage in the 1990s.[3] These works have since been subjected to sustained engagement by both academics and theater practitioners, which has further elevated the decade to one of the most prolific in modern British playwriting history. What has evaded academic attention, however, is the ways in which the Royal Court itself looked to its young peoples' division, the Royal Court Young Peoples' Theatre (YPT), to support its ambitions to program new plays by first-time writers. Indeed, this chapter will look to bring the work of the YPT in the 1990s into sharp focus. In doing so it will demonstrate both how and why the initiative could be viewed as a vital resource for the provision of plays that greatly enhanced the success of the Court across the decade.

The chapter builds to revisit what Jacqueline Bolton has described as the "flashpoint" 1994–1995 season of new plays by first-time writers.[4] This event saw a large number of young playwrights, whose development can be traced back to the YPT, catapulted into the center of the theater's ambitions, and firmly marked the Court's return to a theater that championed new writers.[5] As Bolton has previously attested in her 2012 essay "Capitalizing (on) New Writing: New Play Development in the 1990s," this return can be credited in part "to the previous decades' organized agitation for new writing initiatives" where "the capital's theatres and theatre companies were actively working with aspiring playwrights via a mixture of writers' groups, development workshops and support networks."[6] Augmenting Bolton's important study, this chapter isolates the work of the Young Peoples' Theatre to detail how the processes in place as part of this initiative enabled the Court to draw from a pool of young writers, who had emerged through the YPT, in order to pursue its agenda. In assessing the groups, workshops and structures in place within the YPT during this time, greater context can be provided that will demonstrate how the Court used its grassroots initiatives to expand its programming in the 1990s.

The Politics of Process

I have already mentioned some of the most recognizable work to be produced by the theater during the decade, such as that written by Kane, Ravenhill and Butterworth. The premiering of these plays in quick succession on the Royal Court stages has no doubt contributed to a narrative that has subsequently positioned the Court at the center of the playwriting boom that ensued, and as the figurehead of the so-called In-Yer-Face movement that came to dominate the decade. These plays formed part of a new and "aggressive policy of expansion" that came to characterize Daldry's era.[7] And while the incoming artistic director sought to secure the financial means through which this ambition could be realized, Graham Whybrow implemented what he termed as a "search for talent" as he looked to build a generous and sustainable model through which new playwrights could be programmed.[8] The increase in the theater's programming was subsequently realized through the production of over fifty new plays in the Court's Theatre Upstairs between 1994 and 1997.[9] This feat is made all the more pertinent when it is positioned against the relative contraction in the programming that the Court had experienced under Max Stafford-Clark in the previous decade, where an average of nine plays were produced in a year as opposed to nineteen by 1996.[10] The reason for this constriction was twofold: Stafford-Clark's introduction of a lengthy process, where workshops were used to conceive, develop and rewrite a play,[11] and a reduction in the theater's resources during the Thatcher years. Whybrow's arrival, however, caused a shift in the theater's priorities and brought a "clear conviction that [the Court] needed to respond to and identify the most exciting new playwrights and produce their work *without* a process,"[12] which allowed for the expansion of the theater's programming. But this ostensible rejection of the process-led methodologies of the Court's past is significant to the subsequent narrative that ensued. While stripping the development process away from the plays allowed for the number of plays to grow, the Court needed to ensure that this was sustainable. In an attempt to increase the number of scripts received by the theater, Whybrow implemented a new strategy that aimed to "strategically track first time writers in a very purposeful way."[13] The work of Ruth Little and Emily McLaughlin, along with Bolton, has identified some of the results of this strategic tracking, which saw several of the plays that came to define the success of the mid-1990s at the Court, originate elsewhere.[14] Their work identifies Kane's *Blasted* (1995), Ravenhill's *Shopping and*

Fucking (1996) along with Ayub Kahn-Din's *East Is East* (1996) as a few examples of work that had been "opportunistically snapped up by the theatre" from other theaters such as the Finborough as part of its new policy.[15] Moreover, as Bolton attests, these plays had already "benefitted from varying degrees of dramaturgical support" from other companies beyond the Court.[16] With this in mind, it is possible to deduce that while the Court was outwardly professing a policy of "rapid turn-over, rapid expansion"[17] of plays without a process, many of the most important plays to emerge out of the theater in the mid-1990s had undergone extensive development outside of the theater and therefore sit at odds with the anti-process narrative.

A Historical Focus on Process: The Royal Court Young Peoples' Theatre Through the Decades

The work of Little and McLaughlin as well as Bolton have traced an important developmental line through to production of some of the most recognizable plays to be produced at the Court in the mid-1990s. However, what has been omitted from previous engagements with the theater's work across this decade is how the Court looked closer to home in an attempt to provide a "constant stream of production" for the theater.[18] Writing in 1994, Daldry talks of the Court's own Young Peoples' Theatre and its "extremely successful" young writers' group, along with the Young Writers' Festival (YWF), as vital links in the theater's playwriting chain.[19] The acknowledgment of the YPT in this way by the Court's artistic director represents an important shift in the regard of a strand of the Court's work that had otherwise been held on the periphery by its parent theater for much of its history.

Beginning as a Schools Scheme in 1966 under the leadership of Jane Howell, the Scheme evolved into the Young Peoples' Theatre in the 1970s. By 1986, the YPT was housed on Portobello Road and was directed by Elyse Dodgson—a post that she retained until 1992. Dominic Tickell succeeded Dodgson and sought to build on many on the initiatives that she had introduced. One of the most significant developments in Dodgson's tenure came through the Young Writers' Festival, which had been founded by Joan Mills in 1975. In time for the 1988 Festival, Dodgson had reframed the event and amended it from an annual nationwide hunt for new plays by young writers to a regionally specific, process-based approach. In doing so, Dodgson had extended the parameters of the Festival and instilled a year-long process of development between the young writers and the YPT, which culminated in a selection of that work being produced as part of the Festival's season of plays in the Court's Theatre Upstairs.

In composing the Young Writers' Festival around a series of "phases," a more sustained engagement could be offered by the YPT to young people interested in writing for the theater. Integral to the Festival's objectives was the targeting of "specific regions and writers and directors from the Royal Court" who were "brought in to offer a full programme of workshops and follow up sessions within the chosen regions."[20] The selected plays from within those areas were then given full professional productions in the Theatre Upstairs as well as a tour across the selected regions. The viability of such a bold expansion of the YWF was undoubtedly inspired by enhanced opportunity for collaboration with regional companies brought about as a result of the proposals put forward in a 1984 Arts Council of Great Britain document titled *The Glory of the Garden*. The text revealed an intention by the Arts Council to "address the London-centredness of the arts" and identified the "need to develop better provision for the arts in the regions."[21] Indeed, Dodgson and the YPT looked to align their focus for the 1988, '91, '92 and '94 Festivals with those regions supported by Regional Arts Associations, demonstrating an increased awareness of national opportunities to optimize the reach of the YPT and its work with young playwrights.[22] Moreover, potential to look beyond London for opportunities to develop young playwrights had been made possible through regular sponsorship for the Festival, which had, since 1984, been subsidized by Rank Xerox. Newfound sponsorship for this vital strand of the YPT's work also allowed for an increase in the number of workshops and readings to be included as part of the Festival and, importantly, the publication of the plays that had been selected to receive professional productions as part of the event.[23]

The workshops for the Young Writers' Festivals were open to young people up to the age of twenty-five who resided within the selected regions. The initial workshops, on the subject of writing for the theater, were typically held in five centers across each region and the process was divided into five phases, with Phase One being the first workshop and Phase Five representing the culmination of the Festival where selected plays were chosen to receive a professional production. Phase One held the aim of inspiring those in attendance to try some writing. It was led by a writers' tutor as well as a workshop leader from the YPT and was open to participants regardless of previous experience. In the second phase this process was extended with the workshop leaders joined by a director from the Court along with actors provided by the venue, who would then work on the texts produced by the writers in Phase One. All those who submitted work for this phase received one-on-one tutorials with the accompanying writers' tutor. The third phase brought all the regions covered in the Festival cycle together and required the submission of a full script, which was then read by a panel of readers. Subsequently, a select group of young writers whose plays demonstrated the "greatest theatrical potential" were invited to the YPT's home on Portobello Road for a weekend of script workshops, again with actors and writers and directors from the Court.[24] It was following this penultimate phase that the plays would then be selected to receive professional productions in the Theatre Upstairs and produced as part of a tour of the participating regions.

The process-based approach described above had moved the Festival away from the methods of past Young Writers' Festivals, which has centered on an open call for submissions largely publicized in national newspapers, to a more considered period of engagement with young writers. By elongating the process and introducing a phased approach to the Festival's work, the YPT deliberately sought to nurture young playwrights over an eighteen-month period in preparation for production in the Theatre Upstairs.

COMING ON STRONG AND A SEASON OF UNKNOWN WRITERS IN THE THEATRE UPSTAIRS

Dodgson's pioneering work through the Young Writers' Festival informed the vision for the future of the Young Peoples' Theatre. By the beginning of the 1990s, the YPT had become exclusively concerned with putting new writing at the center of all of its projects. Dominic Tickell, who replaced Dodgson as the YPT's director in 1992, talks of how:

> Writing was at the heart of what we did at the YPT at all times while I was director. We did other things, so we did youth drama workshops and so on, but it struck me that that was not the point of the YPT. The point of the YPT was to be part of the Royal Court Theatre and therefore new writing was at the heart of everything.[25]

Tickell's vision to put new writing "at the heart" aligned the YPT's ambitions with that of the Royal Court in the 1990s and provided the YPT with an opportunity to compliment the Court's work in ways that it had struggled to achieve in the past.

The significance of how the YPT could be seen to support the Court's broader vision to produce new plays by young writers is made tangible in the 1994 Young Writers' Festival. Produced under the title of *Coming on Strong* and programmed to run alongside a wider season of new plays by first-time writers that included Joe Penhall and Sarah Kane, the season of new plays testifies to the YPT's centrality to the Royal Court's ambitions at this time. With the exception of Sarah Kane, all of the writers who featured both as part of the Festival and as part of the season itself had engaged to some degree with the playwriting initiatives offered by the YPT, illustrating the scheme's vital contribution to a "momentous era" in British theater history.[26] The season showed work from seven unknown writers in the Theatre Upstairs between September 1994 and January 1995. It opened with Joe Penhall's *Some Voices* and continued with the *Coming on Strong* Young Writers' Festival, which featured Nick Grosso's *Peaches*, Michael Wynne's *The Knocky*, Rebecca Prichard's *Essex Girls* and Kevin Coyle's *Corner Boys*, and was followed by Judy Upton's *Ashes and Sand* before concluding with Sarah Kane's *Blasted*.

Important Alliances: Securing Funds and Building Collaborations

With cuts in arts subsidies continuing throughout the 90s, Daldry's aptitude for securing funding from alternative means allowed for new sources of income to support the production of new plays. Although still dependent on the Arts Council for its core funding, during this time, a significant amount of sponsorship for the Court across this period was received from American donors. Importantly, the National Theatre (NT) Studio also provided vital opportunities and space, particularly during the rehearsal period, to support the programming of new plays at the Court. Under Sue Higginson's leadership, the NT Studio, which was housed in the Old Vic Annex, continued to develop new plays both at the National and through co-productions with other theaters. It was through a co-production with the NT Studio that the Royal Court was able to produce six of the plays by new writers programmed in the Theatre Upstairs between the autumn of 1994 and early 1995. The studio provided the rehearsal space and covered the cost of the actors, director and stage manager for the entirety of the rehearsal period, which effectively halved the cost of production for the Royal Court.[27]

In addition to the NT Studio collaboration, further financial aid was acquired through the establishment of a new scheme for emerging playwrights. In a partnership between the Jerwood Charitable Foundation and the Royal Court that continues today, Jerwood New Playwrights (JNP) was launched in 1994 to support the production of work by early-career playwrights.[28] JNP continues to contribute to the annual production of three plays produced across the Royal Court's two stages, but, in its inaugural year, the scheme supported five of the six young writers programmed as part of the 1994–1995 season of new plays. Penhall's *Some Voices*, which opened the season in September 1994, was the first play to benefit from the JNP initiative. Other JNP beneficiaries for the 1994–1995 season were Upton for *Ashes and Sand* along with Kane's debut play *Blasted*. Two of the plays to feature in the 1994 Young Writers' Festival were also awarded JNP funding, with Grosso's *Peaches* and Wynne's *The Knocky* completing the inaugural cohort of JNP recipients. The collaboration between the Royal Court, NT Studio and Jerwood Foundation during this time, therefore, can be regarded as a valuable alliance that allowed for Daldry's ambitious plans for the Court to reach fruition.

The regional attention in the eighteen-month build-up to the 1994 Young Writers' Festival had focused on young playwrights based in the London area and, for the first time, in Northern Ireland. There, playwriting workshops were conducted in Derry, Coleraine and Belfast. The decision to take the work of the Young Writers' Festival to Northern Ireland in 1993–1994, at the beginning of the Peace Process which aimed to put an end to almost twenty-five years of the Troubles, presents an underlying political motivation to the Festival's work. In a report to the English Stage Company Council, Tickell writes how he is "particularly excited about the range of young people who have attended our workshops," and that "a very wide range of ages, cultural and ethnic backgrounds and levels of experience" had been involved in the process.[29] The director further states how it was the responsibility of the Young Peoples' Theatre "to ensure that the Festival was able to accommodate and celebrate this diversity in the productions" as it prepared for performances in both the Theatre Upstairs in October and in Northern Ireland the following month.³⁰ The emphasis on diversity here is a feature that has been inherent in the YPT's work for some time: the commitment to staging work by young writers of diverse age, race, ethnicity, class and sexuality had been carefully considered by each of the YPT's directors since the scheme's inception.

The autumn of 1994 to the spring of 1995 marked a season that brought an influx of young writers to the Royal Court stage. Reflecting on the program of work produced over this period in the 1994 Young Writers' Festival's accompanying play text, Daldry notes "the huge success of the season," stating that "it pays testimony to the fact that there is a growing urgency in young people to express themselves through dramatic writing."³¹ The Artistic Director concludes his preface to the *Coming on Strong* published play text by crediting the important work of the Young Peoples' Theatre for its role in producing young playwrights, writing:

> I am delighted that the writers who have emerged through the Young Peoples' Theatre, and in particular the Young Writers' Festival, are now being published. I sincerely hope that you share our enthusiasm for these plays and, just as importantly, appreciate the process by which they have emerged.³²

There is an element of irony in the fact that Daldry has chosen to highlight his appreciation for the Young Writers' Festival's *process* in his foreword. Indeed, Rebecca Prichard has noted the benefit of having "access to the writing workshops" and how this allowed for time to "experiment with ideas and see what was working dramatically."³³ But as has been alluded to throughout this chapter, the Festival's process-led methods are at direct odds with the Daldry/Whybrow mantra of producing work "without a process."³⁴ What's more, the plays that evolved from the Festival follow a recognizable pattern of development that was also visible, during the same period, in the Court's acquisition of work by other previously identified writers such as Kane, Ravenhill and Kahn-Din. The YPT's methods of developing aspiring playwrights through the use of process, therefore, can be seen as a continuing influence on the Court's ability to successfully and consistently produce young writers during this day. However, as the notion of process became increasingly suppressed in the broader narrative of the Royal Court in the 1990s, the idea that many of their plays were staged without the need for prior dramaturgical support or without sustained engagement with the writers has evolved to become one of many falsehoods that has perpetuated the mythology that surrounded the Court during this decade.

Before their plays were selected for production, Wynne and Prichard had been part of the London workshops, while Coyle had participated in the Festival's workshops in Derry. London-born Grosso was a member of the YPT's writers' group and his play *Peaches* had been developed under the tutelage of Andrew Alty. Prior to *Peaches*, Grosso's first piece, a monologue titled *Mam Don't*, had been produced by the Young Peoples' Theatre and performed at the Commonwealth Institute in 1993. Elaine Aston characterizes the four plays produced as part of *Coming on Strong* as being linked "by a dramatic world in which people struggle to make sense and purpose out of difficult times or empty lives."[35] Out of these works emerged the early signs of individual styles and original voices that, in the case of Prichard, Wynne and Grosso, would go on to feature on both the Royal Court and British stages in the future. Each of the plays expresses a "politics of the individual" theme, described by Daldry as a central feature of many of the plays that emerged across the decade.[36] Evidence of this can been seen through ideas of sexuality as explored through Grosso's *Peaches* and Coyle's *Corner Boys* and in the sharp comedy and dialogue of Prichard's *Essex Girls*, a portrayal of teenage girls approaching adulthood. Wynne's *The Knocky* owes a debt to Chekhovian tradition and to Daldry's production of J. B. Priestley's *An Inspector Calls* in 1992 with its vivid perception of growing up on a council estate in England. These plays were programmed alongside other plays by young, unknown writers, which focused on mental illness, violence and the effects of war. Both Jacqueline Bolton and Aleks Sierz have previously suggested links between the 1950s and the 1990s Royal Court,[37] and echoes of the 1950s Royal Court plays ring within these works too, as "sceptical, frustrated and disempowered" voices once again occupied the theater's stages.[38]

Joe Penhall had also come through the writers' group at the Young Peoples' Theatre in the late 1980s. His short play *Wild Turkey* was produced at the Old Red Lion as part of the 1993 London New Play Festival while he was still a member of the YPT, after which he wrote *Some Voices*:

> I wrote a long play, which was *Some Voices*. I offered it to the Bush, and they didn't want it, and I offered it to the National Theatre and they didn't want it, and I offered it to Hampstead and they didn't want it, and I offered it to the Royal Court and Stephen Daldry rang me up at work and said: "come in and talk to me."[39]

During his involvement with the YPT, Penhall's writing potential had first been spotted by the writers' group's tutor April De Angelis, who, in turn, forwarded a sample of his work to the literary department at the Royal Court: "I said, 'look I just think this person has really got something.'"[40] Although the Court had initially overlooked Penhall's talent—as De Angelis recalls "we just got a no back"—the writer's potential was recognized again by Daldry, who, after an initial reading of the play at Battersea Arts Centre in 1993, selected *Some Voices* to open the new season at the Royal Court.[41] As a young writer, Penhall's experience within the YPT and his reception at the Royal Court by two artistic directors is illustrative of wider change within the structures of the theater. According to Whybrow, the Royal Court prior to Daldry's appointment had been regarded by emerging writers as a "fortress" impenetrable to new writers.[42] Penhall's initial rejection was transmuted within a matter of months to full production—an indication of the shift in attitudes taking place at the theater. Where Penhall had emerged through the YPT writers' group, Judy Upton had been "encouraged to write for the stage" during her participation in the workshop phases of the Young Writers' Festival held in Sussex in 1990.[43] Like Penhall, Upton's first play, *Everlasting Rose*, premiered at the Old Red Lion in 1992, also as part of the London New Play Festival for that year. Through their involvement in the initiatives offered by the Young Peoples' Theatre, both Penhall and Upton are likely to have been known by the Royal Court. Indeed, that their plays were produced as part of the London New Play Festival in the two years prior to their programming by the Royal Court is further evidence of the "strategic tracking" of new writers carried out by Daldry and Whybrow in the early 1990s.[44]

In the aftermath of *Coming on Strong*, three writers, Prichard, Grosso and Wynne, were commissioned to write a second full-length play for the Royal Court. For Grosso, this commission materialized as *Sweetheart* (1996), but neither Wynne's nor Prichard's second plays were produced on a Royal Court stage. Wynne did not return to the Royal Court until 2002, when his play *The People Are Friendly* was produced in the Theatre Downstairs.[45] Prichard's return was more prompt, as *Fair Game*, her third play, opened at the Duke of York's, where the Court's Theatre Upstairs had been relocated as part of an ongoing reconstruction project of the theater on Sloane Square, in October 1997. The play was deemed particularly contentious as it featured the gang rape of a thirteen-year-old girl and the Court's decision to cast the play using actors all under the age of seventeen fueled outrage from some audience members.[46] Carl Miller, who had succeeded Dominic Tickell as the YPT director, states that in order "to deal with the flack of putting this on with young performers [it was] produced by the Young Peoples' Theatre."[47] Although it was a professional production in which the actors were paid, *Fair Game* is regarded by Ola Animashawun, the then current YPT's youth drama worker, as the "last public act of the youth theatre."[48] Within a year, the YPT had been reconceived to offer a complete focus on playwriting, and the Young Writers' Programme was born.

Coming on Strong represents a significant turning point in the history of the Young Peoples' Theatre, which demonstrates its own substantial contribution to a defining moment in British theater. It is important to note here that another YPT alumni Jonathan Harvey and his third play for the Royal Court, *Babies*, occupied the Theatre Downstairs at the same time that Penhall's *Some Voices* opened in the Theatre Upstairs, illustrating, for the first time, two Young Peoples' Theatre playwrights on both stages of the Royal Court.[49] What emerged at the end of 1994, therefore, was a consistent contribution by the Young Peoples' Theatre, as a result of their work with young writers, to seasons of work at the Royal Court. This outcome confirms that the process-led Young Writers' Festival, which aimed to allow for the extended support of young writers across the country, along with the YPT writers' group offered a significant contribution toward the production of a new generation of playwrights in the mid-1990s and proved to be an invaluable platform in the provision of young writers to the Court at this time.

Conclusion

In her introduction to *The Royal Court Theatre Inside Out*, Ruth Little speaks of a mythology that is inherent to the Court's past, where details of its history are often sloughed off in order to create "a coherent narrative of purpose, resistance and resilience."[50] Indeed, the 1990s at the Royal Court is an important example of the ways in which a theater's contribution to a vital decade in British theater can rapidly accrue mythological status. This chapter has provided a counter-reading of events that surrounded the Court in the 1990s. In doing so, it has positioned the YPT at the center of the narrative and demonstrated how this initiative's important work in the end of the 1980s and into the 1990s created the foundations that allowed the Court to pursue an aggressive policy of expansion during the decade. It has illustrated how young writers who were developed through the structures in place at the YPT came to have a significant impact on the Court's programming, which aided the theater in achieving its vision for the decade.

Notes

1. Graham Whybrow quoted in Jacqueline Bolton, *Demarcating Dramaturgy: Mapping Theory onto Practice*, unpublished doctoral thesis (University of Leeds, 2011), 66.
2. Jacquelin Bolton, "Capitalizing (on) New Writing: New Play Development in the 1990s," *Studies in Theatre and Performance* 32, no. 2 (2012): 209–225.
3. James Reynolds and Andy W. Smith (eds.), *Howard Barker's Theatre: Wrestling with Catastrophe* (London: Methuen, 2015), 117.
4. Bolton, "Capitalizing," Abstract.
5. Bolton, "Capitalizing," 217.
6. Ibid.
7. Graham Whybrow quoted in Ruth Little and Emily McLaughlin, *The Royal Court Theatre Inside Out* (London: Oberon, 2007), 284.
8. Little and McLaughlin, 294.
9. Ibid.
10. Bolton, "Capitalizing," 214.
11. Little and McLaughlin, 292.
12. Ibid., 294. Author's emphasis.
13. Bolton, *Demarcating Dramaturgy*, 55.
14. Little and McLaughlin, 286, and Bolton, "Capitalizing (on) New Writing," 217.
15. Little and McLaughlin, 357, 352, 286. The authors state how *East Is East* had originally been written in 1982 and was later developed in conjunction with Tamasha Theatre, and *Shopping and Fucking* had undergone a lengthy development period with Max Stafford-Clark's Out of Joint Theatre Company at the Finborough Theatre. *Blasted* had been developed during Kane's time on the MA Playwriting course at Birmingham University.
16. Bolton, "Capitalizing," 217.
17. Little and McLaughlin, 294.
18. Ibid., 286.
19. Ibid.
20. Elyse Dodgson, "The Royal Court Young Peoples' Theatre: An Outline of Strategies and Aims for 1991–2," 1990. THM/273/4/20/13.
21. Anthony Jackson, "From 'Rep' to 'Regional'—Some Reflections on the State of Regional Theatre in the 1980s," in *The Glory of the Garden: English*

Regional Theatre and the Arts Council 1984–2009, ed. Kate Dorney and Ros Merkin (Cambridge: Cambridge Scholars Publishing, 2010): 23; and Ian Brown, "'Guarding Against the Guardians': Cultural Democracy and ACGB/RAA Relations in The Glory Years," in *The Glory of the Garden: English Regional Theatre and the Arts Council 1984–2009*, ed. Kate Dorney and Ros Merkin (Cambridge: Cambridge Scholars Publishing, 2010), 29.
22. Regional Arts Associations were housed across all of England except for Buckinghamshire.
23. Nicholas Holden, *Building the Engine Room: A Study of the Royal Court Young Peoples' Theatre and its Development into the Young Writers' Programme*, unpublished doctoral thesis (University of Lincoln, 2018), 141.
24. Dodgson, "Strategies and Aims."
25. Nicholas Holden, Interview with Dominic Tickell, 2016.
26. Aleks Sierz, *In-Yer-Face Theatre: British Drama Today* (London: Faber and Faber, 2001), 210.
27. Nicholas Holden, Interview with Graham Whybrow, 2016.
28. To qualify as part of the scheme a playwright must be within the first ten years of their career. Jerwood New Playwrights. Jerwood Charitable Foundation. http://www.jerwoodcharitablefoundation.org/projects/the-royal-court-theatre-jerwood-new-playwrights/ (accessed July 10, 2016).
29. Dominic Tickell, Report from the Royal Court Young Peoples' Theatre to the English Stage Company Council, 1994. THM/273/4/20/16.
30. Ibid.
31. Stephen Daldry, Preface. In *Coming on Strong: New Writing from the Royal Court Theatre* (London: Faber and Faber, 1995), vii.
32. Ibid., viii.
33. Rebecca Prichard quoted in *Coming on Strong*, 246.
34. Little and McLaughlin, 294.
35. Elaine Aston, *Feminist Views on the English Stage: Women Playwrights, 1990–2000* (Cambridge: Cambridge University Press, 2010), 61. In her chapter titled "Girl Power, the New Feminism," Aston critically engages with the work of some of the most significant new women playwrights on the stage in the 1990s, including the plays of Judy Upton and Rebecca Prichard.
36. Stephen Daldry, 1004, Fax to Fiona McCall. THM/273/4/20/16.
37. Bolton, "Capitalizing," 214; and Sierz, *In-Yer-Face*, xi and 15.
38. Little and McLaughlin, 295.
39. Harriet Devine, *Looking Back: Playwrights at the Royal Court: 1956–2006* (London: Faber and Faber, 2006), 242–243. Dominic Dromgoole was artistic director at the Bush Theatre from 1990 to 1996. He recalls how

the Bush liked *Some Voices* "but not enough to produce it" and the Court "snapped it up." (Dominic Dromgoole, *The Full Room: An A–Z of Contemporary Playwriting* [London: Methuen, 2000], 221.)
40. Nicholas Holden, Interview with April De Angelis, 2016.
41. Ibid.
42. Graham Whybrow quoted in Bolton, "Capitalizing," 215.
43. Sierz, *In-Yer-Face,* 215.
44. Little and McLaughlin, 286; and Bolton, "Capitalizing," 217.
45. Michael Wynne returned to the Court again in 2009 with *The Priory* and in 2015 with *Who Cares*.
46. Little and McLaughlin, 264.
47. Nicholas Holden, Interview with Carl Miller, 2015. In the summer of 1997, Stephen Daldry announced his resignation and Ian Rickson became the theater's new artistic director in August of that year. At the same point, Dominic Tickell resigned from the YPT and was replaced by Carl Miller. Miller had been an assistant director at the Royal Court, as part of the Regional Theatre Young Directors Scheme, since the early 1990s and, as a result, much of his time prior to his appointment as the YPT's final director, had been spent working on YPT endeavors.
48. Little and McLaughlin, 366.
49. Harvey had developed his first play for the Royal Court, *Mohair*, during the Young Writers' Festival's work in Hull in the build-up to the 1988 Festival. He returned to the Court again in 1992 when his second play, *Wildfire*, was produced in the Theatre Upstairs.
50. Little and McLaughlin, 9.

CHAPTER 3

"A Shop Window for Outrage": Harold Pinter's *Ashes to Ashes*, In-Yer Face Theatre and the Royal Court's 1996 West End Season

Graham Saunders

INTRODUCTION

On September 21, 1995, the English Stage Company (ESC) at the Royal Court hit the jackpot. In less than a year since its inception, the National Lottery had awarded the theater a grant of £15 million via the Arts Council, as one of the Lottery's designated "good causes." The money was to be spent on a major refurbishment to a building that was not only showing signs of its age, but its physical architecture was increasingly imposing constraints on both the outputs and the kinds of work that the theater wanted to do. With such an extensive renovation, a decision was taken to temporarily relocate premises to the West End: leases were taken out on two theaters, the Ambassadors and the Duke of York's. Both were renamed: somewhat confusingly, the former became the Theatre Upstairs, with the latter becoming The Duke of York's Theatre Downstairs. The

G. Saunders (✉)
University of Birmingham, Birmingham, UK
e-mail: g.j.saunders@bham.ac.uk

© The Author(s) 2020
W. C. Boles (ed.), *After In-Yer-Face Theatre*,
https://doi.org/10.1007/978-3-030-39427-1_3

ESC remained in the West End from September 1996 until February 2000. During this time, it produced some of its most memorable work: this included Conor McPherson's *The Weir* (1997), Ayub Khan-Din's *East Is East* (1997) and Martin Crimp's *Attempts on Her Life* (1997). This was a gilded period in the ESC's history, not only for the work it produced, but also for the opportunity it afforded for the theater to become a bold presence within the heart of the British theater establishment. This was certainly the perception that Stephen Daldry, the ESC's Artistic Director, encouraged—marketing materials proclaimed, "There Goes the Neighbourhood"; one play program showed the image of a hand holding a brick[1] and the Young Writer's Festival that year launched under the collective title "Storming." This impression of rambunctious occupation was further consolidated by knowledge that from 1952 until 1974, the Ambassadors had been the long-term home for Agatha Christie's *The Mousetrap* and roughly coinciding in 1955 with George Devine founding the ESC as an opposing force to the West End values that Christie's play represented.

Despite the hype, there was some justification associated with the ESC's provocative residency. Since the controversy over Sarah Kane's *Blasted* in January 1995, Stephen Daldry had continued to promote a succession of young dramatists who subsequently became associated through their inclusion in Aleks Sierz's influential book *In-Yer Face Theatre: British Theatre Today* (2001). The first phase of this spearhead came in the next Royal Court season that followed *Blasted* the following year. This included Jez Butterworth's *Mojo*, Joe Penhall's *Pale Horse*, Nick Grosso's *Sweetheart* and Martin McDonagh's *The Beauty Queen of Leenane*. However, what really heightened and subsequently established the reputation of these dramatists came from their associations with the ESC, which was in the fortunate position of having two West End theaters at its disposal. Daldry capitalized on this by swiftly reviving *Mojo*, which had been a notable success from the Royal Court's 1995 season, and restaging it at the Duke of York's Theatre. Later in 1998 it would become the venue for Sarah Kane's new play *Cleansed*. The Duke of York's also staged a season described as "Royal Court Classics" that included revivals of Ron Hutchinson's *Rat in the Skull* (1984), Terry Johnson's *Hysteria* (1993) and David Storey's *The Changing Room* (1965). In this way Daldry was able to simultaneously bring the ESC's past and present together through successive seasons of work during their time in the heart of London's commercial theater.

Besides Harold Pinter, whose play *Ashes to Ashes* launched the West End move, other works by his near-contemporaries, including Edward Bond's *Coffee* (1997) and Caryl Churchill's *This Is a Chair* (1997), were also staged during this period. It should also be remembered that while the ESC's time in the West End can indeed be associated with In-Yer-Face Theatre, other works that it produced, such as Phyllis Nagy's *Neverland* (1998) and Richard Bean's *Toast* (1999), seemed far removed from the brash sensibilities of *Mojo* or *Shopping and Fucking*.

Associations with the ESC's West End occupation as a form of assault could also be detected through the titles given to some of these new plays—Mark Ravenhill's *Shopping and Fucking* (1996) and Stuart Swarbrick's *Drink, Smoking and Toking* (1996), and even Jim Cartwright, a Royal Court veteran, associated with earlier plays such as *Road* (1986), gained a foothold through his provocatively titled play *I Licked a Slag's Deodorant* (1996).

While this historical account might at first appear antithetical within a volume that seeks to assess the legacy of In-Yer Face Theatre, this chapter puts forward the contention that the bedrock of this legacy was largely created and consolidated during the ESC's West End residency. Whereas the end of the In-Yer-Face period has been variously identified with the death of Sarah Kane in February 1999, or earlier in 1997 with the success of Conor McPherson's more subdued and reflective *The Weir*,[2] this shift in mood can also be found with the ESC returning to its former home in Sloane Square in 2000, when it appeared to have brought back some of the West End values it had been exposed to during its occupancy.[3] This in turn changed the nature of the work it subsequently produced. Yet this part of the ESC's history is also a highly complicated and contradictory one. Using Harold Pinter's *Ashes to Ashes* (1996) for comparative purposes this chapter both supports the significance this period holds for the ESC within its own history and reputation, and, at the same time, will draw attention to some of the contradictory and sometimes absurd ways that the theater drew attention to itself as a disruptive interloper in the West End. Ultimately, these attempts were compromised and frustrated by the West End represented through the figure of Harold Pinter, who flouted the ESC's long-observed traditions and conduct.

The 1996 Royal Court West End Season: A Clash of Values

At first it seemed as though Harold Pinter's new play *Ashes to Ashes* would fully subscribe to the values of the Royal Court. Its two principal actors, Stephen Rea and Lindsay Duncan, were each paid £206.86 per week, the same sum as any actor employed to appear in a Theatre Upstairs production, although this fee would be negotiable if the production transferred to another West End venue.[4] Harold Pinter was also paid the standard ESC director's rate of £2440.[5]

However, early on in pre-production the ESC found its values being directly challenged by Pinter. In a memo sent out to Stephen Daldry, General Manager Vikki Heywood and other senior staff, the company's Technical Manager Paul Handley succinctly described this clash in terms of the physical resources Pinter was demanding. In the memo Handley points out that "for five times the normal upstairs budget we have produced a relatively basic production—the point I'm making is that these are real costs and when the director demands professional back up from top to bottom then this is what mit (sic) costs."[6] Handley goes on to say that while the sound and lighting designers working on the production have voiced their concerns, Pinter's "response has been, apparently money isn't an issue." Handley concludes that the designers have not been extravagant and places the blame on a completely different sensibility operating from what the Royal Court was used to: "they're using professional people and professional equipment which isn't the usual ethic in The Theatre Upstairs. When the director and designers aren't committed to this way of working from a very early stage in their project then the financial constraints become intolerable."[7]

The difference in respective theater cultures was also clear to see in the choice of programming. *Ashes to Ashes* played in the newly converted Theatre Upstairs—an intimate 140-seat space, described by Michael Billington as "a miniaturised Epidaurus,"[8] that had been created out of the Ambassadors' circle area by adding a false floor. The larger downstairs space saw what would become another important inaugural premiere, Mark Ravenhill's *Shopping and Fucking*. Both productions intersected with *Ashes to Ashes* running from 12 September to 26 October and *Shopping and Fucking* from 26 September to 19 October. While this was imaginative scheduling—a new play by one of the world's most distinguished dramatists and a provocatively titled debut by a young newcomer—

conflicting values between the ESC and the West End again led to serious tensions. These arose over the seemingly minor issue of start times. In a memo, Jess Cleverly, the ESC's Head of Marketing, records an exchange in the form of a scripted dialogue between himself and Harold Pinter:

Harold: In all my conversations with Stephen [Daldry], the start time has always been 8 pm. 7.30 is far too early for Ashes to Ashes
Jess: (TACTFULLY) This was always going to be the challenge of the Ambassadors—to juggle the needs of each play to make sure that they all get the time that is right for them.
Harold: (WITH GRUFF GOOD HUMOUR) I don't feel like being juggled with—could you pass that on for me...?
Jess: Certainly, absolutely, no problem.[9]

Pinter's insistence on an 8 p.m. start time for *Ashes to Ashes* meant that *Shopping and Fucking*, playing in the Theatre Downstairs space, had to open later between 9 p.m. and 9.30 p.m.[10] This decision provoked the ire of the Royal Court's previous Artistic Director Max Stafford-Clark, who was directing *Shopping and Fucking*. In a fax to Stephen Daldry, Stafford-Clark expressed his feelings in no uncertain terms:

> This fax is as much for Harold's consumption as yours but the truth is your *Shopping and Fucking* company feel Well Fucked about. Not only do we have a bizarre starting time which does the play no service at all, but the agenda for the Front of House display appears to have been set by Harold. All your staff know this is unfair and I am sure you too believe that is the case. Please sort this one out and show the leadership one has a right to expect from the Artistic Director of the Royal Court.[11]

Stafford-Clark followed this up ten days later and interestingly justifies the perceived disparity in status afforded to Ravenhill's play by reminding Daldry about the traditions of the Royal Court and blaming the situation partly on the pernicious influences that the West End has wrought since the move:

> It's become clear that some sort of parity between Ashes to Ashes and Shopping and Fucking is not about to happen.... I'm told that Harold has forbidden it. Frankly I can't believe that you have presented the facts to him. I decline to believe that with his innate sense of justice or humanity Harold would wish to be party to marginalizing colleagues in this matter. Nobody

can imagine that a play by a first time writer is an event of the same magnitude and moment as a new play by the greatest living English playwright. But it is the Royal Court's duty to imagine the unimaginable.... At the moment Shopping and Fucking feels like a marginalized and shabby second thought on the part of the Royal Court's management. You often cite the values of George Devine, but if the Royal Court's move to the West End involves the adoption of West End policy towards its productions, prioritizing those that are more important, then this shameful abandonment of cherished principles should be widely known.[12]

Stephen Daldry responded by letter three days later, and while admitting that the matter could have been handled better as well as acknowledging that older audiences might not like the change from the traditional curtain-up at 7.30 p.m., "the new audience bred on varying cinema times will not give a toss." Daldry rejected the accusation that "I have just agreed to all of Harold's demands and sacrificed the Stage space," calling this "a cruel and untruthful version of events" and adding that "[d]ealing with Harold is difficult at times—just as dealing with you is difficult at times."[13]

Yet archival correspondence suggests that Daldry unquestioningly acceded to Pinter's demands at every turn. One of these concerned the publicity slogan, "There Goes the Neighbourhood," used to herald the ESC's move to the West End. In one fax Pinter asks Daldry not to attend a rehearsal, partly due to "conditions in the rehearsal room [being] by no means perfect," before going on to say, "I detest 'there goes the neighbourhood' in *The Guardian* today and would be grateful if the Royal Court would not associate *Ashes to Ashes* with that assertion in future advertising."[14] Daldry responded by fax the same day, confirming not only the removal of the offending slogan for *Ashes to Ashes*, but its cancellation for the entire season. Daldry also expresses concern over Pinter's comment about unsatisfactory conditions in the rehearsal room.[15] Later correspondence also records Pinter's displeasure about unreserved seating for *Ashes to Ashes*, which he regards "as outdated and redundant" and while acknowledging that this is Royal Court policy, to which "[it] can of course be whatever it likes ... it cannot be assumed that I will accept it for the presentation of *Ashes to Ashes*."[16]

Harold Pinter's objection to publicity materials likening the ESC and its clamorous group of young playwrights as an occupying force in the West End is ironic considering how several accounts of this period situate Pinter as a significant influence for a number of these dramatists.[17]

Confirmation that this was mutual appeared to come when Pinter appeared in the 1997 film version of Jez Butterworth's *Mojo* following its restaging at the Ambassadors after *Shopping and Fucking* had completed its run. However, the Daldry/Stafford-Clark exchanges challenge these: moreover, despite having had early work produced at the Royal Court (a double bill of *The Room* and *The Dumb Waiter* in 1960), directing David Mamet's play *Oleanna* there in 1993 and a regular workshop participant since 1991 at the theater's International Summer School, during his time directing *Ashes for Ashes*, Pinter seemed to show little regard for established Royal Court traditions, especially when they impinged on his own working practices or beliefs. In one of their exchanges Daldry reminds Stafford-Clark that Pinter's status "as an outsider … is always challenging," and that in his capacity as an Associate Director, "I would expect [you] to understand these pressures."[18] Little reciprocation seemed to come from Pinter's direction.

Archival evidence also suggests that Pinter's decision to give *Ashes to Ashes* to the Royal Court came about less from any desire to be associated with the theater itself, and more to do with the ESC's temporary acquisition of the Ambassadors theatre. Evidence from Antonia Fraser's diaries, from which she published extracts in her memoir *Must You Go?*, reveal that Pinter was already thinking about the newly renovated upstairs space at the Ambassadors in February 1996 as a suitable venue.[19] However, in April that year, Pinter wrote to the theater impresario George Biggs apologizing for reneging on a promise for *Ashes to Ashes* to be staged at one of his West End venues. Pinter cites practical reasons such as its short running time and it being an intimate chamber piece, making it an unsuitable proposition in a commercial 600- to 700-seat theater. At the same time the letter shows that Pinter is still tempted by the lure of the *legitimate* West End (as opposed to the ESC's temporary residency), adding in a postscript that given the star casting of Lindsay Duncan and Stephen Rea, a future transfer might be a distinct possibility.[20]

Shopping and Fucking: Ducking and Diving

Mark Ravenhill's *Shopping and Fucking* would also later enjoy its own West End run at the Gielgud Theatre as well as a successful regional tour. However, reports about backstage tensions while it was running in repertoire with *Ashes to Ashes* made their way into the press. *Time Out* illustrated this as a clash between old and new sensibilities by reporting on a new audience constituency that had been observed around the makeshift bar that had been created at the back of the stalls: "Divans are apparently scattered around for trolling and drinking before 'Shopping and Fucking.'"[21] While this account should perhaps be treated with some degree of skepticism, it is partly verified by the ESC's Paul Handley, who had responsibility for managing the building during the ESC's tenancy. He recalls the conversion of the Theatre Upstairs area at the Ambassadors as "this weird space with the bar underneath [which] became a place where people hung out and stayed for all these strange lock-ins with people drinking for hours and talking about plays."[22] The *Time Out* piece also reported that the revels had been causing "worries that the sound will seep into the Circle," where *Ashes to Ashes* was playing. The article also referred to Pinter's purported intolerance of extraneous noise in the theater, citing a past apocryphal tale of the playwright trying "to force a building site to pause during rehearsals."[23]

Activities at the bar aside, *Shopping and Fucking* can claim ample credit for being an example of where the ESC's "There Goes the Neighbourhood" tag held some justification. Much of its controversy, not surprisingly, sprang from its title, which contravened the Indecent Advertisements Act of 1889—originally passed into law by the necessity to prevent innocent members of the Victorian public inadvertently reading cards in shop-front windows advertising the services of prostitutes. While ready to court controversy, privately the ESC was wary about facing prosecution not only from the 1889 Act, but also from a clause in the 1968 Theatres Act. While their advising solicitor Anthony Burton thought "Testing the law would be interesting," he also added that it "could be an expensive error."[24] Consequently, the ESC played it safe, steering a course with the help of their legal advisors within relatively safe margins. These included making compromises that included only displaying the title of the play as "Shopping and F******" on the neon display outside the theater and on posters and front of house boards and tickets. This coyness even extended to box office staff being instructed to refer to the title as "Shopping and Effing," but once tickets had been purchased, the full name of the play could be given verbally. This also applied to displaying or mentioning the cast sheet and theater program. This last edict was especially ironic, given concerns that it might provoke outage from patrons attending *Ashes to Ashes*, a play that opens with the phrase "Kiss my fist."[25]

However, compromises over the title of Ravenhill's play also call into question just how far the ESC was willing to disrupt its new West End neighborhood. Less a full-on assault, this incident illustrates how the ESC's residency fell short of what Michael Thornton in *Punch* called "a shop window for outrage" and more a series of tentative skirmishes.[26] This attitude of risk averseness can also be demonstrated in another incident relating to *Shopping and Fucking*. With memories perhaps still lingering over the attempted prosecution of Howard Brenton's *The Romans in Britain* in 1980 over its representation of male rape between a Celt and a centurion, the ESC sent its lawyer Anthony Burton to see *Shopping and Fucking* in rehearsal to determine what he gnomically referred to as its "offence capability." Vikki Heywood, in a fax to Stephen Daldry, gave Burton's verdict that "Explicit visual image combined with strong language could cause us problems and put us at risk depending on the presentational style, particularly the last scene. The act at the end is of a criminal nature."[27] The "act" in question was the sodomy of Gary, a fourteen-year-old rent boy by two of the other characters.[28] In order to minimize the risk of prosecution Burton advised removing any references in the play to Gary's age,[29] and it is interesting to note that the first edition of the play that was published to coincide with the production gives his age as fourteen.[30] This was excised in all subsequent editions, as was a reference to Diana, the Princess of Wales. This expurgation is significant, as the play's original title was to have been *Fucking Diana*. In the first published edition the character of Mark recounts a supposed encounter with the soon-to-be Princess Diana in a nightclub toilet: "I'm fucking Diana, it's pumpity-pump against the cistern,"[31] before they are joined in the cubicle by Sarah Ferguson (the future Duchess of York), who enthusiastically fellates him.[32] However, following the death of the Princess of Wales in August 1997, when *Shopping and Fucking* was on a regional tour, Ravenhill hastily rewrote the scene, excising Mark's account of having sex with Diana, but retaining the incident with Sarah Ferguson. The rewritten scene continues with Mark's story: "door opens and there's another woman. Another policewoman … with blonde hair."[33] Robbie abruptly silences Mark before he can go any further: "SHUT UP. SHUT THE FUCK UP."[34] These textual changes, together with compromises over the title, provide important indications that the ESC's willingness to court outrage was tempered with an equal caution that at times bordered on timidity. While its West End residency gave the ESC new purpose and vigor, it also took pains to keep its acts of provocation within the law and what it gauged to be acceptable boundaries of public taste and mood.

While this account maintains that the admiration between Harold Pinter and the In-Yer-Face dramatists was more of a one-sided affair than existing accounts might suggest, evidence suggests this perception was both encouraged and contrived at the time. In what now seems more than coincidental, in September 1996, a newspaper article in the *Evening Standard* by the theater critic Nick Curtis titled "How Pinter Lit the Way for Today's Firebrands" positioned this new generation of young writers as Pinter's legitimate offspring.[35] However, the article's publication, just two days before the premiere of *Ashes to Ashes*, together with its focus on Jez Butterworth, whose play *Mojo* was about to be given a major revival at the Duke of York's Theatre the following month, suggests at least the strong possibility that the marketing department of the ESC and London theater's critical establishment had joined forces to concoct the story for their own mutual benefit.

However, not everyone was fooled by such contrivances. The actor James Fox, who had starred in Pinter's film adaptation of *The Servant* (1963), had replied in a letter earlier that year to Pinter expressing his admiration for *Ashes to Ashes* after being sent the script. He praises the play's qualities ("your brand of memory and menace and fear—that chilling, bad dream quality. It's very upsetting, disturbing."), adding that "nobody else can write in that inimitable way." As a point of comparison Fox recounts attending what he felt to be an inferior pastiche of Pinter by an In-Yer-Face upstart: "I saw what seemed a direct imitation of your style and ear in a play at the Royal Court called 'Sweetheart' [by Nick Grosso] the other day. It can't be done or even approximated. It was poor stuff."[36]

Harold Pinter and Sarah Kane

The same however cannot be said of Sarah Kane, whose work not only shared certain stylistic similarities with Pinter, but following his public support for *Blasted* after its attacks in the press, the pair established a personal friendship that lasted until Kane's death in February 1999.[37] In turn, *Ashes to Ashes* has been seen in some quarters as being profoundly influenced by *Blasted*,[38] primarily through the ways that its Leeds hotel setting inexplicably changes in Scene Two to become a warzone. Likewise, in *Ashes to Ashes*, a house in Dorset also later becomes the location where Rebecca sees a crowd of people making their way through the woods and finally into the sea ushered by "guides."[39] This reference, with its strong inference of an atrocity being witnessed together with Rebecca's accounts of visiting a factory and later railway station with her lover who would "walk down the platform and tear all the babies from the arms of their screaming mothers,"[40] both summon up imagery associated with the Holocaust. Michael Billington, writing in his biography on Pinter, sees the play simultaneously occupying a place "in the English shires and yet in Auschwitz,"[41] and when first reviewing *Ashes to Ashes*, Billington made comparisons to areas where Pinter might have drawn inspiration from *Blasted*—most notably the ways that the two plays made connections between "sexual and political fascism."[42] However, Billington contends that Pinter more successfully "colonises" these ideas, and whereas Kane had "violently juxtaposed the domestic and the political, Pinter with infinite subtly, interweaves them."[43]

Billington's originally highly skeptical view on *Blasted*—"I don't think you can simply have a bomb then translate the action from one place to another"[44]—was shared by a number of his colleagues at the time[45] and repeated (with the notable exception of Billington) later in several of reviews of *Ashes to Ashes*. This was combined with an incredulity in some quarters at Pinter combining geographical and historical displacement through Rebecca's narratives of the factory and railway visits that both evoke imagery associated with the Holocaust. In a letter to Pinter after being sent the script, fellow playwright Christopher Hampton recalled a previous conversation with Pinter about *Ashes to Ashes* being "a haunting, as you say, from the past."[46] However, Nicholas de Jongh, in his review of the play, saw the use of Nazi imagery as "gratuitous."[47] Pinter himself has spoken about the play containing images associated with Nazi Germany, but also being about much else besides,[48] including "torturers and victims."[49] Yet, the fact that Pinter felt the need to explain himself might well have been a potential danger that Sarah Kane had already foreseen and been keen to avoid when her new play *Cleansed* premiered at the Duke of York's Theatre in April 1998.

Kane had originally sent Pinter a draft of *Cleansed* in December 1996. His reply in a letter was expressed in semi-poetic form: "A prison camp of a world where Tinker rules. A savage place where love is a joke, a delusion, a trap, so fragile, a flower, born only to be destroyed."[50] Here, Pinter may be making an unconscious reference to his earlier play *Mountain Language* (1988), which is also set in a prison camp, or even further back to *The Hothouse* (1958), which takes place within an institutionalized setting in which its "patients" are abused and tortured. More likely, Pinter could be referring to the Nazi death camps that appear to haunt Rebecca's memories in *Ashes to Ashes*. During rehearsals for *Cleansed*, Kane went to some lengths to prevent the risk of such interpretations being given to her play. For example, in a fax to Jess Cleverly, Kane rewrote the copy to promote the play and explained her reasons for doing so—one issue concerned the implied meanings behind the word "camp": "I want to keep the word 'camp' out of it. It doesn't appear in the play—deliberately—and I'd rather not let anyone off the hook that easily."[51]

Fortunately, Sarah Kane's own responses to *Ashes to Ashes* are available to us through her correspondence with Pinter. This first came in brief postcard message from New York on June 19, 1996, after being sent the script:

> Dear Harold
> You were right. It's hot. I'm losing my mind. My heart's getting broken and I'd sell my soul for a beer and a cigarette. I read your play. It made me laugh and cry. Which is as good as it gets. Thank you. It was good to see you again.[52]

Later, after seeing *Ashes to Ashes* in performance, Kane provides a much more detailed critique:

> I saw Ashes to Ashes tonight. I think it's devastating. It's one of those rare and extraordinary theatrical experiences that happen once every decade and make the persistence in between times worth the effort. I hardly know what to say about it. I walked out of the theatre utterly decimated, and couldn't understand why everyone was chatting and intellectualizing when it seemed the world had just caved in. It's shot through with the most painful and appalling images, and breathes incredible life into those images of atrocity that have become almost clichéd. It contains a landscape within language without ever becoming verbose – it's so simple, clear and direct, yet weaves unbelievably complex patterns of thought and image. I just wanted to thank you for writing a play that is so wonderful, beautiful and terrible.[53]

Some years after Kane's death Pinter took the *Observer* newspaper to task about a story in circulation that Kane had been asked to review *Ashes to Ashes*, but had been tacitly encouraged to do so in negative terms.[54] Yet, Kane's response to the play is illuminating in the way it echoes Aleks Sierz's own response to the work of experiencing Kane and several of her contemporaries for the first time being a purely emotional and physical basis.[55] On being sent *Ashes to Ashes*, the playwright Arthur Miller also reacted in much the same way, commenting: "One can't be sure what the desensitized will make of it, whether they will wish to enter the door you've opened."[56]

While the critical reaction to *Ashes to Ashes* was mixed, a few, including Michael Bywater in the *New Statesman*, underwent a remarkably similar response to Kane:

> Most plays you go to the theatre and you watch them. In this case, that's just the beginning. You go to the theatre and you're bemused. Maybe you feel cross. Later, when you think about it, you feel shaky and you want to cry. Something's been planted. And its growing. And you wait.[57]

CONCLUSION: IN-YER FACE AND AFTER

In retrospect, the ESC's sojourn in the West End was pivotal in promoting work that subsequently changed the playwriting landscape of the late 1990s; this is frequently seen as synonymous with In-Yer-Face drama, its origins and later its legacy. Stephen Daldry, in originally championing the move, was more than vindicated when he set out the justification: "We need to be seen to be taking risks in the heart of the commercial sector, and originating work in the middle of town rather than just transferring work into it."[58] Through its temporary ownership of two West End theaters, not only could the ESC significantly increase its output of new work, but it also afforded the opportunity for restaging earlier examples of the In-Yer-Face genre, *Mojo* and *The Beauty Queen of Leenane*. Their presentation in the West End subsequently helped produce a greatly amplified *imprateur*. The same also applied to productions that had originally been produced at regional theaters (such as Ayub Khan-Din's *East Is East* at Birmingham Repertory Theatre) or from within the London fringe (such as Anthony Neilson's *The Censor*, originally staged by The Red Room at the Finborough). It should also be remembered that what later came to be known as Martin McDonagh's *Leenane Trilogy* was originally produced in Dublin by the Irish company Druid, while Sarah Kane's *Crave* (1998) was originally produced by the touring company Paines Plough. With two theaters at its disposal the ESC was quickly able to respond to plays that had met with success at its "Upstairs" location at the Ambassadors, such as Conor McPherson's *The Weir*, after which it was swiftly moved to the more capacious 650-seat Duke of York's Theatre. Under this strategy, that also saw revivals of past "Royal Court Classics," this period can rightly be seen to represent a golden one for the ESC.

Yet, the time the ESC spent in the West End was not without its problems. Harold Pinter's working practices during *Ashes to Ashes*, for instance, indicates that his sensibilities were more attuned to the values of the West End than of the Royal Court. Georgina Brown puts this less politely in her review of the play, commenting that "arrogant old Harold cares more about his image within the Establishment than the Royal Court's establishment of new territory within the West End."[59] Yet, it is also churlish to simply assume that Pinter cynically used the ESC simply for the convenience it provided as a venue, and it would also be to the Royal Court that Pinter would make a final return in 2008 shortly before his death, this time as an actor in Ian Rickson's production of Samuel Beckett's *Krapp's Last Tape* (1958).

While undoubtedly a watershed in the ESC's history, its residency in West End also seemed to mark the beginning of a significant change in outlook for the theater. Writing in February 1997, Jess Cleverly commented, "we cannot occupy the trendy 'bad boy' ground forever. If we try, it will wear pretty thin and we will end up looking like someone's dad trying to look cool at their kid's party. The Royal Court must be seen to grow up."[60] Although Little and McLaughlin attribute this response being influenced by the competition that the ESC faced from other new writing venues such as the Gate, the Bush, the Old Vic, the National Theatre, the Donmar Warehouse and the newly rebuilt Soho Theatre, Cleverly's warning could also have been prompted after just four months working within West End culture. Certainly, by the time the ESC returned to its refurbished home in Sloane Square, a change in mindset seemed to have taken place. Vikki Heywood describes what she calls "a very 1975 attitude" as predominant before the move toward fundraising and management structure, whereas after the return in 2000, "we'd certainly crashed through the money issue [with] the Royal Court [...] pulling in over a million pounds a year in sponsorship and donations ... [as well as] a much more sophisticated management structure."[61]

During its time in the West End the ESC had been able to play the part of rebels. Yet, it could be argued that these were faux provocations rather than genuine acts of rebellion. Nowhere was this more apparent than in the temporary conversion of the smaller Theatre Upstairs space at the Ambassadors. The ESC's stage designer William Dudley described this as a process of creative vandalism, whereby the space was "made to feel like a bunker, but a friendly one. You pull up the carpets, distress the walls, take down the chandeliers remove some of the red plush and occupy it."[62] While some, such as Georgina Brown in her review of *Ashes to Ashes*, signaled alarm—"The Royal Court has stormed the jewel-box that was the Ambassador's Theatre ... tearing down the chandeliers, painting the bar chocolate brown"[63]—the changes themselves were essentially cosmetic, with the theater simply reinstating its chandeliers and plush red carpets after the ESC left in 2000.

Once back at Sloane Square one of ESC's Associate Directors James MacDonald also spoke about its long-held stance as provocateur no longer being a viable position. Recalling that under Stephen Daldry the ESC had been seen as a "pirate ship, and that we were naughty pirates in this leaky, brown painted vessel, being naughty and challenging bigger ships and making off with prize goods and so on," following the renovation, attitudes changed: "An audience can't come in to a £27 million building and think it's a pirate ship. It's more like a slightly eccentric but expensive powerboat... It's harder to be subversive and harder to be heretical."[64]

Whether it was the refurbished Royal Court or the ESC's three-year exposure to West End values that initiated these shifts in culture, it is difficult to say, but much like the period of "Cool Britannia" itself, the image that the ESC tried to present for itself could sometimes run up against some inconvenient realities. Whereas the ESC liked to see itself as anarchic squatter in a theater that had once been the former home of Agatha Christie's *The Mousetrap*, Aleks Sierz's account of attending a performance of *Shopping and Fucking* at the venue gives this interpretation a different complexion:

> By chance, I sat just behind a black homeless man who, making the most of the 10p standing tickets, was sheltering from the cold October night. During the play, the tramp's constant bemused glances at the mainly white middle-class audience were perfectly eloquent: what are these nice people doing watching these horrors?[65]

In truth, the ESC's occupancy of the West End resembled less "a shop window on outrage" and more a series of provocative skirmishes that often resulted in some hasty retreats when challenged by the likes of Harold Pinter or statute law. Sierz's comment about the black homeless man's bemusement at the predominantly white middle-class audience's engagement with a play that included a knife attack at a twenty-four hour petrol station, a man being tortured with an electric drill and the twilight world of teenage rent boys also forms part of the legacy of both the period of In-Yer Face Theatre and the Royal Court itself.

Notes

1. Ruth Little and Emily McLaughlin, *The Royal Court Theatre: Inside Out* (London: Oberon, 2007), 347.
2. Aleks Sierz, "Still 'In-Yer-Face'?: Towards a Critique and a Summation," *New Theatre Quarterly* 19, no. 1: 23.
3. Looking at the 2000 season that marked their return to Sloane Square, this is not immediately apparent. There was a mix of debut work (such as Holly Baxter-Baine's *Good Bye Roy*), the return by recent dramatists who had struck up associations with the theater (David Eldridge's *Under the Blue Sky* and Martin Crimp's *The Country*) and long-established writers with a long association with the Royal Court (Jim Cartwright's *Hard Fruit* and Caryl Churchill's *Far Away*) as well as international work (Marius von Mayenburg's *Fireface*, David Gieselmann's *Mr Kolpert* and Christopher Shinn's *Other People*). However, the unexpected appearance of David Hare's new play *My Zinc Bed*, a playwright whose work in the 1990s was often produced with the National Theatre before transferring to the West End, is a possible indicator of a change in culture.
4. Royal Court Archive, V&A Performance Collection, Letter from Lisa Malkin to Jeanette Chambers, April 25, 1996. GB71 THM/273/4/2/25.
5. Royal Court Archive, V&A Performance Collection, *Ashes to Ashes* budget, August 16, 1996. GB71 THM/273/4/2/254.
6. Royal Court Archive, V&A Performance Collection, Memo from Paul Handley, "T.U Budgets," September 4, 1996. GB71 THM/273/4/2/254.
7. Ibid.
8. Michael Billington, *The Life and Work of Harold Pinter* (London: Faber & Faber, 1996), 383.
9. Royal Court Archive, V&A Performance Collection, Memo from Jess Cleverly, "Ashes to Ashes," July 11, 1996. GB71 THM/273/4/2/254.
10. Mark Ravenhill recollects a start time between 9 p.m. and 9:15 p.m. (Mark Ravenhill to Graham Saunders via Facebook Messenger, February 9, 2019). Aleks Sierz, in his account of seeing the production, also reports it starting at 9:15 p.m. (Aleks Sierz, *In-Yer-Face Theatre: British Drama Today* [London: Faber, 2001], 127).
11. Royal Court Archive, V&A Performance Collection, Fax from Max Stafford-Clark to Stephen Daldry, September 7, 1996. GB71 THM/273/4/2/254.

12. Royal Court Archive, V&A Performance Collection, Fax from Max Stafford-Clark to Stephen Daldry, September 27, 1996. GB71 THM/273/4/2/254.
13. Royal Court Archive, V&A Performance Collection, Letter from Stephen Daldry to Max Stafford-Clark, September 30, 1996. GB71 THM/273/4/2/254.
14. Royal Court Archive, V&A Performance Collection, Fax from Harold Pinter to Stephen Daldry, September 4, 1996. GB71 THM/273/4/2/254.
15. Royal Court Archive, V&A Performance Collection, Fax from Stephen Daldry to Harold Pinter, September 4, 1996. GB71 THM/273/4/2/254.
16. Royal Court Archive, V&A Performance Collection, Fax from Harold Pinter to Stephen Daldry, September 5, 1996. GB71 THM/273/4/2/254.
17. See Billington, *Harold Pinter*, 114; Amelia Howe Kritzer, *Political Theatre in Post-Thatcher Britain: New Writing: 1995–2005* (Basingstoke: Palgrave 2008), 58–59; Graham Saunders, *About Kane: The Playwright & the Work* (London: Faber, 2009), 38, 98; Mark E. Shaw, "Unpacking the Pinteresque in *The Dumb Waiter* and Beyond," *Harold Pinter's The Dumb Waiter*, ed. Mary. F. Brewer (Amsterdam: Rodopi, 2009), 221; Andrew Wyllie, "The Politics of Violence After In-Yer-Face: Harold Pinter and Philip Ridley," in *Pinter* Et Cetera, ed. Craig N. Owens (Cambridge: Cambridge Scholars Press, 2009), 63–78.
18. Royal Court Archive, V&A Performance Collection, Letter from Stephen Daldry to Max Stafford-Clark, September 30, 1996. GB71 THM/273/4/2/254.
19. Antonia Fraser, *Must You Go? My Life with Harold Pinter* (London: Weidenfield & Nicolson, 2010), 215.
20. In the end the production did not transfer to the West End, although it did tour to Italy immediately following the production at the Ambassadors. See Harold Pinter Archive, Letter from Harold Pinter to George Biggs, April 25, 1996. ADD MS 88880/6/15.
21. Anon, "Whither the Royal Court?" *Time Out*, September 18, 1996.
22. Little and McLaughlin, 348.
23. Anon, "Whither."
24. Royal Court Archive, V&A Performance Collection, Letter from Anthony Burton to Vikki Heywood, April 25, 1996. GB71 THM/273/4/2/254.
25. Harold Pinter, *Ashes to Ashes*, in *Plays 4* (London: Faber, 2005), 395.
26. Michael Thornton, "A Shop Window on Outrage," *Punch*, September 21–27, 1996: 70.
27. Royal Court Archive, V&A Performance Collection, Fax from Vikki Heywood to Stephen Daldry, June 17, 1996. THM/273/4/16.
28. Mark Ravenhill, *Shopping and Fucking*, in *Plays 1* (London: Methuen, 2001), 82–84.

29. Royal Court Archive, Memo from Jess Cleverly, May 24, 1996. GB THM/273/4/16.
30. Mark Ravenhill, *Shopping and Fucking* (London: Methuen, 1996), 55.
31. Ibid., 73.
32. Ibid., 74.
33. Ibid., 77.
34. Ibid.
35. Nick Curtis, "How Pinter Lit the Way for Today's Firebrands," *Evening Standard*, 17 September 1996.
36. Harold Pinter Archive, Letter from James Fox to Harold Pinter, February 26, 1996. ADD MS 88880/6/15.
37. William Baker's *A Harold Pinter Chronology* records three meetings between the pair between June 1996 and December 1997. See William Baker, *A Harold Pinter Chronology* (London: Palgrave, 2013), 228, 230, 240.
38. Mark Batty, "What Remains? *Ashes to Ashes* & Atrocity," in *Pinter Et Cetera*, ed. Craig N. Owens (Cambridge: Cambridge Scholars Press, 2009), 101.
39. Pinter, *Plays 4*, 416.
40. Ibid., 419.
41. Billington, *Harold Pinter*, 382.
42. Michael Billington, "The Triumph: Poet of Darkness," *Guardian*, September 21, 1996. Reprinted in *Theatre Record*, Vol. XVI, issue 19, October 14, 1996: 1187.
43. Ibid.
44. Graham Saunders *"Love Me or Kill Me": Sarah Kane and the Theatre of Extremes* (Manchester: Manchester University Press, 2002), 40.
45. These included Robert Gore-Langton, *Daily Express*; Paul Taylor, *Independent*; and Charles Spencer, *Daily Telegraph*. See *Theatre Record*, Vol. XVI, issue 19, 1996: 1183–1185.
46. Harold Pinter Archive, Letter from Christopher Hampton to Harold Pinter, October 9, 1996. ADD MS 88880/6/15.
47. *Theatre Record*, 1996, 1184.
48. Harold Pinter, *Various Voices: Prose, Poetry, Politics 1948–2000*, rev. ed. (London: Faber, 2005), 226–227.
49. Lois Gordon, ed., *Pinter at 70: A Casebook* (London: Routledge, 2001): lxi.
50. Harold Pinter Archive, Letter from Harold Pinter to Sarah Kane, December 18, 1996. ADD MS 88880/6/15.
51. Royal Court Archive, V&A Performance Collection, Fax from Sarah Kane to Jess Cleverley, February 5, 1998. THM/273/4/1/287.

52. Harold Pinter Archive, Postcard from Sarah Kane to Harold Pinter, June 19, 1996. Add MS 88880/6/15.
53. Harold Pinter Archive, Letter from Sarah Kane to Harold Pinter, September 17, 1996. Add MS 88880/6/15.
54. In her response to Pinter, the *Observer*'s Arts Editor Jane Ferguson wrote: "I never spoke to Sarah Kane. I would never ask a playwright to review another's work and I cannot think that anyone else at the *Observer* would be asking people to review theatre… It is irritating that Aleks Sierz has committed this 'story' to print" (Harold Pinter Archive, Letter from Jane Ferguson to Harold Pinter, March 19, 2001. ADD MS 88880/6/50). In his reply Pinter acknowledges that the origins of the story are a mystery, and that unfortunately Sarah Kane is no longer alive to provide collaboration (Harold Pinter Archive, Letter from Harold Pinter to Jane Ferguson, March 23, 2001. ADD MS 88880/6/50). In fact, the story originated from Sarah Kane herself in an interview that she gave to students at Royal Holloway on November 3, 1998 (see Dan Rebellato, Sarah Kane Interview. www.danrebellato.co.uk/sarah-kane-interview [Accessed November 19, 2018]; Graham Saunders, *About Kane: The Playwright and the Work*, London: Faber, 86–87). The interview was recorded by Rebellato and recounted in Sierz's book *In-Yer-Face Drama: British Drama Today* (120–121). The story in many ways reflects Kane's own hostility toward journalism and journalists, and is distilled into its most extreme form through the character of Ian in *Blasted*.
55. Sierz, *In-Yer-Face*, 4
56. Little and McLaughlin, 356.
57. Michael Bywater, "The Question: What's It All About Harold? The Answer. You Don't Need to Know. Business as Usual Then," *New Statesman*, September 27, 1996: 52.
58. Stephen Daldry, "Royal Court Moves," *Plays International*, October 1996.
59. Georgina Brown, Review of *Ashes to Ashes*, reprinted in *Theatre Record*, Vol. XVI, issue 19, October 14, 1996: 1185.
60. Little and McLaughlin, 367.
61. Ibid., 366.
62. Ibid., 348.
63. Brown, 1185.
64. Little and McLaughlin, 394.
65. Sierz, *In-Yer-Face*, 127.

CHAPTER 4

"The Last Rolo": Love, Conflict and War in Anthony Neilson's *Penetrator*

Rachael Newberry

The 2010s have been a prolific decade for Anthony Neilson, with plays such as *Unreachable* (2016) and *The Prudes* (2018) at the Royal Court, and, perhaps more surprisingly, an adaptation of Shirley Jackson's novel *The Haunting of Hill House* (2015) and a Christmas production of Lewis Carroll's *Alice in Wonderland* (2016). Surprising because Neilson is perhaps best known as a writer of the In-Yer-Face, "Cool Britannia" genre that made its name in the 1990s, a movement that has generally been regarded, at least in critical terms, as superficially brutal and violent. Neilson's earlier plays adhere to Aleks Sierz's description of the genre in the way that it takes "the audience by the scruff of the neck and shakes it until it gets the message."[1] However, despite Neilson's own description of himself as a "purveyor of filth," his relationship with the term "In Yer Face" is problematic. He states, perhaps somewhat disingenuously: "In-Yer-Face was all about being horrid and writing about shit and buggery. I thought I was writing love stories."[2] Neilson, who both directed and acted the part of Max in the original 1993 production of *Penetrator*, describes the genre as "experimental theatre," rather than In-Yer-Face,

R. Newberry (✉)
Goldsmiths College, University of London, London, UK
e-mail: r.newberry@gold.ac.uk

© The Author(s) 2020
W. C. Boles (ed.), *After In-Yer-Face Theatre*,
https://doi.org/10.1007/978-3-030-39427-1_4

refuting the label attributed by Sierz.[3] In keeping with Neilson's assertion that he was writing love stories, this chapter considers the themes of love, erotic desire and, as a counter-narrative, the overarching menace of war and male violence in *Penetrator*, which first played at the Traverse Theatre in Edinburgh. It also, in line with the general focus of this collection and what the "remnants" of this contentious movement may offer, considers what the play might have to say to contemporary audiences, whose cultural frames of reference will be very different than those offered by Neilson. I write from the position of a white British woman who grew up around the time of which Neilson is concerned and would have been a similar age to the protagonists of the play when it was set. I thus recognize and appreciate the specific cultural references that he uses to ground the story in its historical era.

The opening scenes of *Penetrator* center upon the intimate relationship between Max and his flat mate, Alan. Conversation between the men revolves around the laundry, cups of Happy Shopper tea and icons of 1980s British and American popular culture. The cultural frames of reference are numerous—Bruce Forsyth and *The Generation Game*, Laurel and Hardy, and Nestle's Rolos are just some of the signifiers that Neilson uses to ground his writing in a past to which the protagonists escape when the present becomes too dangerous for them to confront. The play looks inwards, being set entirely within a cheaply furnished living room, a domestic space in which we learn that "the credibly masculine fights with a softer influence."[4] (In fact, Neilson's plays generally tend towards the domestic, as seen in the titles *Hoover Bag*, *Stitching* and *The Year of the Family*.) The two men, in their relationship with one another and the space that they occupy, navigate gendered representations of intimacy that dictate a normative set of learnt behaviors, Max adopting the position of "credibly masculine," whilst Alan is a far more sensitive character, or what Trish Reid, quoting John Beynon, calls "the post-feminist 'anti-sexist, caring, sharing' version of masculinity that had 'gained credibility and strength throughout the 1980s.'"[5] Alan and Max play cards, smoke weed, verbally abuse one another and behave like partners in a long-term marriage—bickering, but also caring deeply for one another. Into this space arrives Tadge (so called because of an erection he had in the showers when he was in primary school), a childhood friend of Max's, who turns up unannounced midway through the play. From his unreliable and erratic dialogue, and physically threatening behavior, we can deduce that Tadge has been discharged from the army, almost certainly suffering from post-traumatic stress disorder after serving as a "squaddie" in the 1991 Gulf War.

War, and associated male violence, is a central theme of the play, and Max and Alan's confinement within the privacy of the flat offers them a mediated experience of war as a spectacle that is broadcast live from their television screen. As Max says, "If they'd just start bombing again we could have some *decent* telly."[6] Despite Alan's initial objection to this tasteless comment, he is quickly seduced into the possibilities that mediated war imagery has to offer, preferring this to the alternative programming of a French film. We can theorize this conflation between the reality of war and a televised, contrived version through the work of Jean Baudrillard, particularly his writing on the simulacra and hyperreality. "Simulation threatens the difference between the 'true' and the 'false,' the 'real' and the 'imaginary.'"[7] For Baudrillard, the popular media has created and shaped war, so that war is no longer a real event, but instead becomes a simulacrum of reality itself. As Baudrillard asserts: "It is no longer a question of imitation, nor duplication, nor even parody. It is a question of substituting the signs of the real for the real."[8] Baudrillard's essay "The Gulf War Will Not Take Place" argues that, specifically, the Gulf War that Neilson references was a "virtual" war, or event, which had been carefully scripted by the media. Baudrillard states: "We are all hostages of media intoxication, induced to believe in the war [...] and confined to the simulacrum of war as though confined to quarters. We are all already strategic hostages in situ; our site is the screen on which we are virtually bombarded day by day."[9] Baudrillard uses the language of war—hostages, confinement, quarters, bombardment—to position the viewer as both a spectator and a casualty of war in a virtual sense. Real human suffering, or "collateral damage," as the loss of civilian life has disingenuously been termed, is transformed into a series of selected images that render the event, at best, benign. Indeed, the claustrophobic setting of the play is one of confinement and (when Tadge arrives) hostage-taking, and the television screen becomes central to the dynamics of this exchange. Neilson himself reinforces both the ubiquity and the anonymity of war, stating in his *Notes*: "This play was written not long after the Gulf War [...] You could choose to keep it as it is and treat the play as period, or you could substitute another item of topical news, preferably a similar conflict."[10] These instructions, and further notes in relation to cultural icons and events within the play, are remarkably fluid given the playwright tends to direct and act in many of his own works and states: "I have always kept a fairly tight authorial grip on work."[11] Furthermore, the suggestion here that all wars are synonymous or interchangeable reinforces Baudrillard's theory of hyperreality whilst at the same time revealing the nature of reported war as a constructed and circulating set of images within the marketplace, devoid of defining characteristics. Baudrillard again: "war is not measured by being waged, but by its speculative unfolding in an abstract, electronic and informational space, the same space in which capital moves."[12] In its associations with capital, war is commodified, fetishized and trivialized to the point where the lived experiences of warfare (most particularly the loss of human life) become erased, and manipulated television images are substituted for coverage of real events, which themselves are regarded as either fictionalized or, in the extreme, non-existent.

The intertextual, mediated links between war and popular culture are further cemented in the play by Max, who, following a discussion with Alan about Tadge's erratic behavior, sings a line from "The War Song," a well-known pop song by the band Culture Club: "War is *stoo*-pid and *pee*-puhl are *stooped*."[13] It is interesting to see a reference here to Boy George, the androgynous front man for Culture Club, who displayed and performed a highly ambiguous sexual identity, experimenting with make-up, clothing and the myriad possibilities of gender performance. By introducing Boy George, if only obliquely, into the range of cultural signifiers that the play offers, Max's reference opens up a discourse surrounding gender difference, inviting the audience to imagine alternative possibilities and hinting at aspects of the play itself as a dialectical negotiation about the fluidity of gender performance. Furthermore, the music video that accompanied "The War Song" opens with androgynous models in military clothing dancing along a catwalk that has been constructed and immersed within the debris of bombed-out streets and buildings. Military style fashion and popular music are intercut with the iconic image of the Hiroshima mushroom cloud of 1945, drawing attention to the uncomfortable relationship between war, the media and the world of fashion. The "speculative unfolding" of war to which Baudrillard refers, and its relation to capital, is exposed in "The War Song," which, even if we argue is an *anti*-war song, responds particularly well to Baudrillard's argument: "The media promote the war, the war promotes the media [...] it allows us to turn the world, and the violence of the world into a consumable substance."[14]

Whilst Max and Alan's exposure to war is shaped through music videos and television highlights, it is Tadge and his traumatic first-hand understanding of warfare and its sustained long-term effects that inject a more threatening atmosphere into the play, generating much of the conflict between the three men. Alan gestures towards the cause of Tadge's behavior by stating: "He's been totally *brainwashed*! He's been out there learning to *kill* people."[15] Indeed, it is not until Tadge's arrival, introducing an aspect of life outside the confines of the domestic space, or "quarters," that raw emotion truly surfaces. Tadge is the only "real" victim, or hostage, of war in this play, believing himself to be pursued by "penetrators," who threaten to "stab him up the arse" with a hunting knife. He constructs an alternative identity than that displayed by his childhood friends in his attempts to make sense of the world and justify his own part in the war. As well as being preoccupied by the penetrators, he rejects his own biological father, believing himself to be the son of Norman Schwarzkopf, the American military general who led coalition forces in Operation Desert Storm in 1991. By identifying himself as the son of "Stormin' Norman," as he was popularly known, Tadge both rewrites his own personal history and problematizes the construction of family that the play as a whole attempts to critique. Indeed, *Penetrator* can be read more generally as a socio-cultural response to a political climate that celebrated the cult of the individual and the rise of neoliberalism under the leadership of Margaret Thatcher. As Ken Urban argues, In-Yer-Face playwrights "are Thatcher's children [...] There is a shared hatred for the Tories dismantling of the socialist state."[16] Specifically, Tadge's personal dismantling and reconstruction of his own family structures presents a challenge to Thatcher's definition and endorsement of the nuclear, stable, married, heterosexual family espoused by her call for the return of "traditional family values."

Although Tadge's conflation of real experiences with fabricated events echoes the illusions of warfare that Max and Alan are exposed to through media representations, of the three protagonists, it is Tadge, in his violent destruction of Alan's teddy bear (holding a knife to its throat and eventually, reluctantly, tearing it to shreds), who comes closest to confronting the truth about his past head on. The disembowelment of the teddy bear is a physical and symbolic enactment of the destruction of his past, of innocence and childhood, of family and of a place that can never be revisited, despite Max and Alan's yearning to recreate their own nostalgic memories of childhood. The three men navigate their gendered roles, negotiating and adapting their own position within the triangulated group dynamics as they vie for recognition and affection. We might imagine these complex relationships between the three men in terms of Eve Kosofsky Sedgwick's reworking of Rene Girard's formulation of the erotic triangle, which considers the relationship between two male rivals for a female.[17] Sedgwick argues that it is not simply the heterosexual coupling that is under threat in this scenario, but relations of male homosocial desire that operate by, and through, the exchange and transfer of the female. In other words, the male subject is constituted in relation to other men by way of women. Sedgwick states: "the bond that links the two rivals is as intense and potent as the bond that links either of the rivals to the beloved: that the bonds of 'rivalry' and 'love,' differently as they are experienced, are equally powerful and in many senses equivalent."[18] In this play, however, the male/male "homosocial" bond that Sedgwick identifies is constantly challenged, disturbed and reinforced, not only through the exchange of the female, but through the bonds of love, same-sex desire and rivalry between the three *male* characters. Tadge's arrival (or penetration) into the internal space poses a threat to the domestic world created by Max and Alan and challenges the notion of what Michel Foucault and, later, Adrienne Rich label "compulsory heterosexuality."[19] The violent form of patriarchal and, at the same time, misogynistic power that dominates early scenes of the play and reasserts itself through Tadge is ultimately destabilized through the interactions that the men have with one another. This is most obviously played out by Alan, the "softer influence" that threatens to pierce the masculine veneer, challenging hetero-normative patterns of gender and sexual identity. But it is also seen in Tadge, who, as Max pleads with him, holds a knife to Alan's throat, forcing Max to erase Alan from his own history:

Max: Alan's your friend. He's *our* friend [...] We used to trip together, the three of us, remember? The three wasters, remember? [...]
Tadge: But what about us?! It was *better* before! You were the brains, I was the brawn! We were friends, we were *real* friends, tell me about *that*, tell me what you remember about *that*![20]

Yet despite the tacit homosexual connotations of Tadge's plea for Max to remember (and his assertion that it was better when it was just the two of them), he ultimately reinforces a heterosexual code of violent masculinity as he brandishes the knife that he has already used to slash Alan's childhood teddy to shreds. That the teddy happens to be Alan's is an example of the power of the homosocial bond that is reinforced through the (usually heterosexual) erotic triangle. Echoing Foucault and Rich, Sedgwick labels this performative masculinity "obligatory heterosexuality" and considers it necessary to the maintenance of the status quo and a patriarchal system. Her notion of "obligatory heterosexuality" and theatrical masculinity is evoked in this play through pornographic imagery, masturbation and misogynistic comments about voiceless, unseen women. It is "built into male-dominated kinship systems [and] homophobia is a *necessary* consequence of such patriarchal institutions."[21] Reid renders this link still more palpable in her analysis of *Penetrator*: "As the play's title provocatively suggests male homosexuality functions as a kind of indictment in the world depicted, and while this indictment is certainly embellished with the arrival of Tadge, casual homophobia is standard fare in the first part of the play."[22] Although a violent form of patriarchal power dominates early scenes, underscoring an implicit homophobic element, the play avoids such binary distinctions through the complexities of characterization. As we come to learn, Tadge's frequent violent references to anal sex reveal a preoccupation with homosexual penetration that is at once terrifying yet also shamefully pleasurable. Tadge fears the imagined "Penetrators," one of whom "put his arm up my arse, right up to *here*. *He indicates his elbow*."[23] However, later, holding Alan hostage, he recalls a pleasurable sexual encounter he shared with Max when they were children:

Tadge: And I touched you.
Max: (*nods*) Yes.
Tadge: Where did I touch you?
Max: You touched my balls. You asked me to cough. You turned me over and spread my arse.
Tadge: Do you remember the smell of me?
Max: (*nods*) Yes.
Tadge: I remember the smell of you.[24]

This coaxing language, in which Tadge begs Max to remember, affirm and validate his own story, operates on a number of levels. Homosexual desire is not only made explicit in this scene, but is reinforced through childhood memories that are framed through innocence. Furthermore, as Tadge's hostage, Alan is maintained in the position of threat or rival in the dynamics of the erotic triangle to which Sedgwick refers.

Indeed, we may explore Sedgwick's thesis still further in her engagement with Gayle Rubin's argument that "[t]he suppression of the homosexual component of human sexuality, and by corollary, the oppression of homosexuals is [...] a product of the same system whose rules and relations oppress women."[25] The representation of women in this play cannot go without comment. Their physical absence from the stage is not matched by their very symbolic presence throughout. The play opens with Max masturbating into a pornographic magazine. This follows an anonymous voice-over describing an explicit scene in which a girl "hitched up her tiny skirt to reveal her gash, spreading the lips of her fuck-hole like some filthy tart, a flood of cunt juice cascading down her long legs."[26] As this description graphically illustrates, women are not embodied characters, but instead operate as commodities, their use-value being measured either sexually or domestically, thus functioning primarily as signs of the male characters' fragile masculinity. The faceless "girl," defined through her sexualized body parts, is one of only a few women who are briefly referred to within the play, the others being Alan's mother, who does Alan and Max's weekly laundry; a "fanny-basher [and] professional *feminist*" Max argues with at the pub; Mrs. Taylor, who helped Tadge learn to read as a child; and Max's ex-girlfriend, Laura, who is referred to by Max as a "slut." It is the absent Laura who moves from use- to exchange-value towards the end of the play, and it is ostensibly Laura who fractures the friendship between Max and Alan with the revelation that she has recently (and perhaps implausibly given the ways in which the audience is guided towards understanding his character) slept with Alan. Thus, Laura reinforces the dynamics of the traditional hetero-normative erotic triangle, although in this instance, the homosocial bond is both destroyed (Alan finally banished from the play altogether) and further cemented in the final scenes that see Max and Tadge share a packet of Rolos.

Penetrator ends as follows:

Tadge gets up. He wanders into the kitchen. Pause. He comes out with two packs of Rolos. He kneels down beside Max, handing him some Rolos. Max looks at them. Pause. He opens a packet. They sit there eating them.[27]

There are at least two ways of reading this final scene. The telling absence of dialogue is perhaps best explained by looking at Roland Barthes' treatise on the dilemma of language in representing the experience of love. Pre-empting Baudrillard's work on the simulacra, he writes: "To try to write love is to confront the muck of language; that region of hysteria where language is both too much and too little, excessive (by the limitless expansion of the ego, by emotive submersion) and impoverished (by the codes on which love diminishes and levels it)."[28] Language—and its very absence in this scene—is exposed as a postmodern device, never really telling the truth, or being able to tell the truth, finally and definitively deferred. Furthermore, if we consider the connections between love and confectionary through this postmodern perspective, the reference to a brand name that sells the promise of love as a commodity (in a similar way in which war is also commodified) blatantly reveals itself as the very simulacrum of love that it hopes to eschew. It is only in the intimacy of the relationships between these men that we can escape the cult of the commodity and move some way towards an understanding of the value of intimate friendship. Whilst this scene is made the more poignant by its relation to the cultural framework from which it emerges, only British audiences of a certain generation will understand the cultural signification of the Rolos. Indeed, the tube of Rolos, which Max initially shares with Alan, is a highly significant popular cultural reference. The very successful UK television advertising campaign that began in the 1980s, with the tagline "Do you love someone enough to give them your last Rolo?" is silently played out in this final scene.[29] Yet although modern audiences may well be unfamiliar with the Rolo advertising campaign, this poignant, almost homoerotic take on a classic heterosexual love story is as pertinent today as when the play was written. Kneeling beside Max, Tadge becomes the wooer, taking the place once occupied by Alan and enacting the scene of a conventional marriage proposal. Reid asserts: "the plays closing image of unlikely domestic harmony between Tadge and Max opens up a place of possibility that at least potentially destabilizes the wider social order."[30]

The wider social order is, of course, the heterosexual norm, and Reid's analysis allows us to imagine not just the homoerotic connotations of this final scene, but the way in which the play as a whole potentially destabilizes a social order that is nurtured and reinforced by the politics of Thatcherism. Written at the end of ten years of Thatcher's administration, the reconstruction of familial structures (e.g. as shown in Tadge's perceived familial connection to Stormin' Norman) is a recurring theme in much of Neilson's work and, as argued earlier, challenges Margaret Thatcher's ideology that the traditional nuclear family is paramount to a civilized society. In a speech at the Conservative Party conference in 1981, Thatcher declared: "the family is the basic unit of our society. It is within the family that the generation is nurtured."[31] It is noteworthy that Thatcher refers to the family as a "basic unit," a term of currency closely associated with capital and exchange. Neilson's own work persistently challenges assumptions about the family as the primary site of nurturing. In his play *Year of the Family*, the character Sid asks: "Why do you think they call it a nuclear family? Because they're burning alive."[32] Similarly, in *Penetrator* Max subverts the idea of the family as a place of nurturing and trust with the comment, "[f]amilies are *built* on fucking. Fucking and secrets."[33] He recounts the story of his friend, Pete, who "is selling his *jism* for fifty quid a shot [...] he sells some *here* and then gets the cheap bus over to Glasgow and sells some *there*. So that's a hundred undeclared quid a week for *two* hand shandies."[34] Like the faceless woman in the early pornographic scenes of the play, the body is displayed as a site of capital and commodification, but in this case, it is a virile male body. Pete's entrepreneurial skills are dependent upon his body as both use- and exchange-value. Although the families that Pete creates are not actually built on fucking (through the medicalization of fertilization and pregnancy), they may well be built on secrets. Again, through the erasure of the biological father, the concept of the nuclear family is challenged, becoming fragmented and dispersed and opening the possibility of alternative definitions of family than that espoused by the ideology of Thatcherism.

The men in the play create their own idea of family, built on their nostalgic memories of childhood. True to form, Alan is probably the most sensitive of the three in his nostalgic romanticizing of the past as a place of comfort and familiarity. Childhood is the place to which all the protagonists alternately return, their memories often unreliable and fractured. Tadge's rejection of his biological father rewrites his own experiences of childhood, whilst Alan and Max turn to popular culture to strengthen their memories of the past. Alan is emphatic in his wistful recollections, telling Max: "I *refuse* to believe that *Starsky and Hutch* was shite."[35] (Starsky and Hutch, Laurel and Hardy, iconic male/male partnerships that were built on homoerotic foundations.) However, Max is far more critical and dismissive of these shared childhood memories, challenging Alan's memory and reducing the past to a series of low-quality television shows. Yelling theatrically from the off-stage kitchen, Max argues:

> *Rrrriiinnngg*!! This Is Your Wake Up Call. It was shite *then* and it's shite *now*. It was all shite. *The Persuaders, The Protectors, The Invaders, The Avengers, The* fucking *Waltons, Thunder*-fucking-*birds, The Man from Bollocks, The Hair-Bear Fucks, Mary, Mungo and* fucking *Midge, all* of it—*shite*.[36]

Perhaps anticipating Tadge's later obsession with "the Penetrators," Max's response questions the reliability of memory and how it rewrites the past in our own desire to create a recognizable identity. His blanket assertion that "it was all shite" devalues and undermines all of Alan's nostalgic recollections, which are more nuanced and thoughtful. Max's conflation of the names of television shows that actually aired with those he has fabricated blurs the boundaries between fantasy and reality, between truth and fiction in the same way that "highlights" of the Gulf War complicate our perceptions of reality. The fictionalized nature of television informs many of Alan and Max's verbal exchanges, anchoring their relationship to an unreliable past and complicating the boundaries between a simulation of truth and the truth itself. The television, as a focal point of their claustrophobic lives, enables them to fortify their own memories of their past, and their inner reality is constructed and reduced to a fictionalized narrative. And although they regard themselves in an altogether alternative psychological category than Tadge, Alan and Max's differing accounts of childhood television are constructions that they have built in order to make sense of themselves in the same way that Tadge's rejection of his biological father is a strategy that he uses to rewrite his own past.

I move now, in this final section, to address the subtitle of this collection, *Remnants of a Theatrical Revolution*. What are the remnants of such a revolution? What do In-Yer-Face plays have to say to us today? Are they products of a particular socio-political period that cannot translate for today's social-media-savvy audiences? Given the culturally and historically specific signifiers that pepper much of Neilson's work, how might *Penetrator* translate for a new generation of theater goers who may feel alienated not just from graphic sexual language, but also an unfamiliar socio-political landscape that has no recognizable frames of reference? What does this play have to offer audiences of today and how can references to characters such as Hambel from *Play School*, or the firemen Cuthbert, Dibble and Grubb from *Camberwick Green*, or Nestle's Rolos speak to a twenty-first-century audience? These questions address this notion of remnants, responding directly to the subtitle of this collection. As I have argued, audiences today will be unlikely to recognize the weight of specific signifiers from popular culture, nostalgic reminders of childhood in the 1970s. Neilson himself is generous in his recognition for the need of adaptation. He comments in the *Notes* at the end of the play: "change them as you see fit [...] adapt to suit [....] you might find that all references can be lost [...] bear in mind that disillusionment with childhood is a theme of the play [...] You might want to leave this open so as to react to topical events."[37] Neilson's recognition of the need to adapt the play to suit, however, may not be as straightforward as he suggests. For example, as I have argued, the tube of Rolos that is first shared by Alan and Max, and then, in the final scene, shared between Max and Tadge, is a highly significant popular cultural reference. The cultural signifier of the Rolos does, indeed, add a historiographical layer to the meaning of the play. Yet although this anchoring to a specific cultural framework may enhance audience experience, without this knowledge, audiences are still able to understand the tenderness inherent in the scene. The Rolos were initially shared by Max and Alan, and this exchange continues throughout the play despite a change in partners. The enduring signifier in each case is the Rolos; it is the Rolos that cement the bonds of love.[38]

Thus, given the quantity of cultural signifiers in this play, the question of whether *Penetrator* can successfully translate for a contemporary audience is complex. The play is seldom performed, last being staged in 2015 at the Hope Theatre, a fifty-seat venue in London. Popular cultural signifiers from the original are substituted with contemporary references to ISIS (Islamic State of Iraq and Syria), nerf guns and internet porn. In her online review of the production, Verity Healey asks:

> one questions whether the update can have the same social significance as it did in the Royal Court's 1994 production. Other than the exploration of crude male fantasies and repressed homosexual feelings that show difference only in the way in which they find expression and outlet, is there anything else this play can give?[39]

Although Healey provides no answers to this question, she does end her review by asserting that this play is about love. I would agree with this and look back at Neilson's quotation, cited earlier, which asserts that he thought he was writing love stories. Finally, despite the extreme sexually explicit opening scene, and physical violence and misogyny throughout, *Penetrator* is a play about loyalty and love, enduring topics that have as much resonance today as they did in the 1990s. There is a nostalgic yearning for a seemingly innocent return to childhood, a past that was, at least in the minds of the protagonists, untainted by war, debates about sexual identity and the proliferation and celebration of materialism and individualism. The play asks us to consider our own childhoods, both as a nostalgic yearning for something past and as an unreliable and potentially threatening place that ultimately disappoints. As Neilson himself argues: "We all believe ourselves to be the directors of our own lives. We are all trying to batter the chaos of our lives into some kind of shape and the other people in that are actors in a sense of our drama."[40] Dominic Dromgoole echoes this in his analysis of Neilson's work: "You can hear behind his work the wish that the world was all roses, blue skies and the missionary position, but it isn't and it grieves him that it isn't. As well as the violence, the fragility and the anarchy, there's an overwhelming feeling of sorrow."[41] Neilson's work is at once shocking, violent, tender and lonely, yet is, at heart, an exploration of the vulnerability of human existence and an often-futile search for meaningful human connection. These themes are just as sensitive and pertinent today as they were when Neilson was writing *Penetrator* twenty-five years ago.

Notes

1. Aleks Sierz, *In-Yer-Face Theatre: British Drama Today* (London: Faber and Faber, 2001), 4.
2. Anthony Neilson, "Don't be so boring," *Guardian*, March 21, 2007, https://www.theguardian.com/theguardian/2007/mar/21/features11.g2.
3. Sarah Kane also rejects the label, describing her own understanding of the genre as "experiential" in a letter to Aleks Sierz, January 4, 1999.
4. Anthony Neilson, *Penetrator*, in *Plays: 1* (London: Bloomsbury Methuen Drama, 1998), 62.
5. Trish Reid, *The Theatre of Anthony Neilson* (London: Methuen, 2017), 23.
6. Neilson, *Penetrator*, 67.
7. Jean Baudrillard, *Simulacra and Simulation*, trans. Sheila Faria Glaser (Ann Arbor: University of Michigan Press, 1994), 3.
8. Ibid., 2.
9. Jean Baudrillard, *The Gulf War Will Not Take Place*, trans. Paul Patton (Bloomington and Indianapolis: Indiana University Press, 1995), 25.
10. Neilson, *Penetrator*, 118.
11. David Lane, *Contemporary British Drama* (Edinburgh: Edinburgh University Press, 2010), 89.
12. Baudrillard, *The Gulf War*, 56.
13. Neilson, *Penetrator*, 81.
14. Baudrillard, *The Gulf War*, 31.
15. Neilson, *Penetrator*, 81.
16. Ken Urban, "An Ethics of Catastrophe: The Theatre of Sarah Kane," *PAJ: A Journal of Performance and Art*, 23, no. 3 (2001): 39.

17. Rene Girard, *Deceit, Desire and the Novel. Self and Other in Literary Structure* (London: John Hopkins University Press, 1965).
18. Girard's erotic triangle theory is cited by Eve Kosofsky Sedgwick in *Between Men. English Literature and Male Homosocial Desire* (Columbia University Press, 1985), 21.
19. Adrienne Rich, "Compulsory Heterosexuality and Lesbian Existence," *Signs* [e-journal] 5.4 (1980): 631–660.
20. Neilson, *Penetrator*, 108.
21. Sedgwick, 698.
22. Reid, 21.
23. Neilson, *Penetrator*, 99.
24. Ibid., 112.
25. Gayle Rubin, "The Traffic in Women: Notes on the Political Economy of Sex," in *Toward an Anthropology of Women*, ed. Rayna Reiter (New York: Monthly Review Press, 1975), 180.
26. Neilson, *Penetrator*, 61.
27. Ibid., 116.
28. Roland Barthes, *A Lover's Discourse: Fragments* (London: Vintage Classics, 2002), 99.
29. https://www.youtube.com/watch?v=5x8z9I3mu0o (Accessed December 4, 2019).
30. Reid, 26.
31. Margaret Thatcher, Speech at Conservative Party Conference, 1981 (plus address to overflow meeting), https://www.margaretthatcher.org/document/104717 (accessed May 20, 2018).
32. Anthony Neilson, *Year of the Family*, in *Plays 1* (London: Bloomsbury Methuen Drama, 1998), 145.
33. Neilson, *Penetrator*, 74.
34. Ibid., 68.
35. Ibid., 66.
36. Ibid.
37. Ibid., 118.
38. It is worth noting that many In-Yer-Face plays end with the exchange or theme of food and feeding, for example, Mark Ravenhill's *Shopping and Fucking* (1996), Sarah Kane's *Blasted* (1995) and Joe Penhall's *Some Voices* (1994).
39. Verity Healey, Review of *Penetrator*, http://exeuntmagazine.com/reviews/penetrator/ (accessed July 22, 2018).
40. Anthony Neilson, www.unreachabletheplay.com (accessed July 22, 2018).
41. Tim Auld, "Career suicide, or the role of a lifetime?" *The Telegraph*, July 3, 2016, https://www.telegraph.co.uk/theatre/what-to-see/career-suicide-or-the-role-of-a-lifetime-matt-smith-on-why-his-n/ (accessed July 22, 2018).

CHAPTER 5

Mark Ravenhill's Dialectical Emotions: In-Yer-Face as Post-Brechtian Theater

Anja Hartl

In-Yer-Face theater, a term coined by Aleks Sierz to describe a visceral theatrical style based on the use of shock aesthetics and provocation through explicit representations of violence and sex designed to "[take] the audience by the scruff of the neck and [shake] it until it gets the message,"[1] has represented a highly contested category ever since plays by Mark Ravenhill, Sarah Kane and Anthony Neilson set out to radically transform the British stage in the mid-1990s. What has particularly sparked controversy among critics is the question of In-Yer-Face drama's status as political theater. Thus, scholars have stressed that these plays "never [potentialize] change"[2] and have claimed that their "voyeuristic glamorization of violence" as well as their potential entanglement with "the very aspects of globalization and consumer capitalism that they set out to critique" may run counter to any progressive thrust commonly attributed to (leftist) political drama.[3] While In-Yer-Face theater has gradually "been reassessed as acutely responsive to the political climate of its time" over the past years,[4] the precise nature of the plays' politics has remained largely

A. Hartl (✉)
University of Konstanz, Konstanz, Germany
e-mail: anja.hartl@uni-konstanz.de

© The Author(s) 2020
W. C. Boles (ed.), *After In-Yer-Face Theatre*,
https://doi.org/10.1007/978-3-030-39427-1_5

unexplored. As Sierz perspicaciously asks in the light of these discussions: "But if the term really is political, what do its politics imply?"[5]

Taking up this question as its point of departure, this chapter aims to introduce a fresh perspective on 1990s In-Yer-Face drama by defining the political value of these plays in terms of their (post-)Brechtian qualities. As I argue, the In-Yer-Face sensibility has not only helped reinvigorate British drama at the turn of the millennium, but, more importantly, has also stimulated a reinitiation of Brechtian epic theater in a period of "disengagement and dismantlement from recognizable forms of political engagement."[6] In this respect, far from representing a closed chapter in theater history, the In-Yer-Face plays are indicative of a new approach to Bertolt Brecht's enduring legacy, which has continued to influence British playwriting and theater practice into the twenty-first century, for example in the work of David Greig, debbie tucker green, Tim Crouch and Caryl Churchill. Hence, critically examining the relationship between the provocative and the political in In-Yer-Face theater, my analysis will look at the techniques typically identified as characteristic of the In-Yer-Face wave through a post-Brechtian lens, suggesting that they are instrumental in initiating a new direction for Brechtian-inspired drama. For this purpose, my reading of Brecht will foreground the importance of dialectical criticism, which is based on an understanding of reality as shaped by dynamic contradictions and thus as changeable, for Brecht's theater practice, which is more aptly described as dialectical rather than epic.[7] To illustrate my argument, I will draw on the work of Mark Ravenhill, whose 1990s plays are widely considered prime examples of In-Yer-Face theater and whose dramatic oeuvre continues to engage with and intersect both In-Yer-Face and Brechtian-inspired aesthetics in the new millennium. Focusing on *Some Explicit Polaroids* (1999), I will investigate how the play explores the challenges of dialectical drama today in an effort to revive dialectics as a progressive aesthetic and epistemological method for fostering awareness, critique and resistance in the audience.

RAVENHILL AND THE BRECHTIAN DIALECTICAL TRADITION

"Don't bash Brecht"—Ravenhill's passionate defense of Brecht in an article published in *The Guardian* in 2008 attests to the central role the German playwright's legacy has played for Ravenhill's own theatrical projects.[8] For example, the British theater-maker has translated several of Brecht's plays, including *A Life of Galileo* (2013) for the Royal Shakespeare Company, and his plays feature many intertextual references to Brecht's works. Most importantly, Ravenhill's oeuvre reflects a profound commitment to dialectical theater in the Brechtian tradition, and it is on this political, theoretical and aesthetic level that the extent to which Brecht has represented an important point of reference, departure and contestation for Ravenhill's work is most evident. Thus, the plays are preoccupied with the question of the nature and value of dialectical criticism and dialectical aesthetics today. This is above all reflected in Ravenhill's concerns about the state of political theater, which he considers threatened by recent social and political developments, because they have challenged the role of the theater as a progressive force in an environment deemed increasingly hostile to cultural expression and sincere political engagement. Responding to these issues, Ravenhill calls for "[n]ot a theatre of relativism and consensus but a *genuinely dialectical theatre* where opposing ideas, forces, energies can be fully experienced, embodied and examined and the most difficult even insoluble problems can be witnessed and confronted."[9]

Emphasizing the significance of a dialectical approach to theater, Ravenhill's quote echoes fundamental concerns at the core of Brecht's theater theory and practice: What has shaped Brecht's understanding of society and, subsequently, his conceptualization of theater is dialectics. Foregrounding the fact that reality is characterized by contradictions, Brecht's dialectical worldview posits a dynamic understanding of reality in which everything is transitory and subject to change rather than predetermined and fixed, which implies that it is possible for everyone to intervene, influence and shape society and politics.[10] What is key is precisely not the question of how to resolve and synthesize the contradictions, but the productive force evolving from the underlying tensions themselves: It is here that the "revolutionary impact" of dialectical thought emerges, and that it takes on its "role as the best possible gravedigger for bourgeois ideas and institutions."[11] Aiming to empower his spectators, Brecht employs these dialectical mechanisms as a dramaturgical method in order to stage a dialectical perspective on the plays' action and characters, innovating theater practice to challenge the audience's understanding of what they take for granted as reality, to present the social and political conditions as changeable and thus to spur skepticism and dialectical thinking as a prerequisite for intervention. Hence, in dialectical spirit, Brecht's plays foreground contradictions in order "to expose rather than to hide change and to understand its dynamics and its consequences,"[12] thereby creating a theater that is fundamentally "in disunity with itself."[13]

However, while Ravenhill's statement above reflects Brecht's ongoing relevance for the contemporary, ostensibly anti-dialectical moment, dialectical criticism has come under immense pressure over the past decades. The end of "grand narratives," the demise of communism and the subsequent triumph of neoliberal globalization have created major obstacles to dialectical thinking by problematizing notions of difference and opposition, immobilizing conventional dialectical dynamics and rendering thinking in contradictions ineffective.[14] Engaging with this fundamental paradox, Ravenhill's plays critically examine the role of dialectics both as a means of understanding reality and as a progressive aesthetic method in their search for a new form of dialectical theater which may resist the challenges of the contemporary moment. As I argue, it is through their In-Yer-Face sensibility that the plays reinitiate dialectical conflict in the relationship between stage and auditorium by providing a more emotional and individual, rather than rational and collective, experience. As I will show with reference to *Some Explicit Polaroids*, Ravenhill employs a (post-)Brechtian framework to stage the crisis of conventional dialectical theater and to explore the possibility of reinvigorating dialectical thought by employing emotions as a dialectical instrument—both on the part of the characters and, crucially, in the relationship with the audience, who is attributed a central role for unlocking the play's resistant potential.

STAGING THE CRISIS OF DIALECTICAL THEATER IN *SOME EXPLICIT POLAROIDS*

Written on the cusp between two millennia, *Some Explicit Polaroids* (1999) represents a *fin-de-siècle* play which is particularly well suited to explore the challenges of political theater on the threshold to the twenty-first century. At the heart of the play, a series of confrontations—between different historical contexts, generations, worldviews, forms of political commitment and personal motivations—drive the plot. These dynamics are triggered by Nick's sudden reappearance, which marks a distinct interruption and a moment of (unpleasant) surprise for Helen, his former girlfriend:

HELEN: Nick. Fucking hell. Nick.
NICK: Hello Helen.
HELEN: Fucking hell.[15]

Nick has just been released from prison, where, since 1984, he has served a sentence for assaulting his nemesis, the capitalist entrepreneur Jonathan. He now returns to a world which has been fundamentally transformed to the extent that it is unrecognizable. Notably, Nick's socialist ideals have become obsolete in the globalized world, as the conflict-laden encounters with the other characters make him realize that there is seemingly no alternative to neoliberalism. In this respect, Nick represents "a human framing device" which invites us to critically examine these social and political developments. Constructed as "both anachronistic and deliberately theatrical,"[16] Nick thereby serves as a catalyst not only for the play's investigations into politics, but also, as I suggest, for its metatheatrical explorations of the role of political theater today, uncomfortably diagnosing the inadequacy of traditional forms to respond to the challenges of the contemporary context. For this purpose, the play employs a conventional, Brechtian-inspired dialectical strategy, which first and foremost manifests itself in a preference for binary structures on the level of content and form, notably with regard to the play's character constellations as well as its temporal framework. Rather than facilitating, in Brechtian spirit, analysis and critique, though, these dialectical aesthetics exacerbate the sense of crisis at the heart of the play, reflecting the extent to which these techniques have become dysfunctional and ineffective at the turn of the millennium.

In this vein, the play stages dialectical encounters between Nick and the other characters to reveal a fundamental disconnection: They try, but eventually fail to negotiate and overcome their conflicts as well as their different ideals, motivations and intentions. Renowned as a radical socialist, Nick undergoes a profoundly disorientating experience when he realizes that the categories he used to base his political convictions and indeed his whole identity on have become meaningless. In the light of the demise of Marxism and the increasing spread of neoliberal globalization, clear-cut distinctions between left- and right-wing political agendas have been replaced by a form of politics which presents "global capitalism" as "a permanent and irremovable fact of life, not an inhuman and ultimately self-destructive system: correspondingly, politics is the art of living with it, not a vocation to overcome it."[17] This conceptualization of politics as mere management of the status quo, as it is most explicitly embodied by Helen in the play, radically clashes with Nick's belief in protest and resistance. Thus, Nick accuses Helen, who used to fight alongside Nick "for the big targets,"[18] but who has exchanged her ideals for a career in party politics, of "[j]ust rearranging the same old shit backwards and forwards [...]. And you call it politics."[19] Trying to adapt to and profit from the profoundly transformed social and political conditions, Helen's compromises reveal that their former socialist struggles have become insignificant: "What did we ever do? Sure talk, talk, talk, march, march, protest. Ban this, overthrow that, but what did we ever do?"[20] Nick's gradual realization that his political beliefs have become "largely useless" is coupled with a strong sense of disorientation.[21] Toward his enemy Jonathan, he acknowledges that "[i]t was much easier. Before. When I hated you. I knew where I stood," and that he feels "[l]ost" in his new environment.[22] According to Sierz, this undermining of conventional (dialectical) categories represents a key concern in In-Yer-Face drama, which "challenges the distinctions we use to define who we are [...]. These binary oppositions are central to our worldview; questioning them can be unsettling."[23]

This impression of disconnection is reinforced by Nick's disturbing encounters with Nadia, Tom and Victor, who have been growing up in the anti-ideological and neoliberal era of post-Thatcher Britain and thus under completely different circumstances from the protagonist. Hence, the younger generation's values are diametrically opposed to Nick's, which they unequivocally reject: Nick's ideals of progress through opposition have, to them, turned out to be a "[b]ig fucking lie."[24] Instead, the youths have retreated from the political into the private sphere, where they aim for pleasure and happiness alone, asserting that "we're content with what we've got," that "we take responsibility for ourselves" and that "we're not letting the world get to us."[25] Their understanding of "happiness," though, is synonymous with "a numb and inert state of existence that is bolstered by chemicals such as Ecstasy" and based on purely materialist and neoliberal concepts of ownership and consumption.[26] It thus runs counter to any genuine expression of feelings, eschews any binding, sincere form of either personal or political commitment, and instead implies a retreat into a purely individualistic, self-centered life. This attitude is symptomatic not only of "the Thatcherite mantra that insists that there is no such thing as society,"[27] but also of New Labour's appropriation of the "Cool Britannia" movement—ideologies which have both heavily transformed the public sphere in the 1990s. Associated with a "libertarian attitude of 'Whatever'" as well as a deeply rooted individualism,[28] New Labour's promotion of "surface appearance and presentation" has complicated,[29] indeed rendered "uncool," any genuine form of political engagement. Crucially, while a clear binary between Old and New Labour as well as between Labour and Tory politics has discursively been maintained, the difference between these seemingly rigid categories has in truth collapsed.[30] What results from these developments is a disorientating political field which paralyzes efforts of engagement, as both Nick's struggles and the younger characters' attitudes illustrate: None of their attitudes to politics is viable and they are unable to establish meaningful connections with each other. On a metatheatrical level, the play's use of conventional dialectical aesthetics through the bifurcating constellations established between Nick and the other characters exacerbates this diagnosis, suggesting the inadequacy of traditional theatrical forms to respond to the radically transformed contemporary context. Manipulated by political rhetoric, dialectical contradictions have become a distorting tool which, as the play illustrates, spurs indeterminacy, stifles critique and can thus, in its traditional design, no longer fuel a progressive form of political theater.

This sense of disconnection is reinforced by the characters' historical consciousness and, crucially, the play's use of history as an aesthetic medium. In dialectical thought, a historical perspective is vital for identifying historically specific and thus unique contexts and factors which have brought about events and decisions in the past and which have an impact on the present.[31] Instead of "treat[ing] the past as if it were the same as the present," dialectics encourage us to understand that "actions and behaviours are relative rather than absolute."[32] With the intention of "expos[ing] what we *perceive* to be natural and show[ing] how it has been constructed,"[33] Brecht turned history into a central device of dialectical theater. This form of Brechtian historicization has, however, become fundamentally compromised by the end of the twentieth century: With no fixed political (or other) stances left as an anchor, Ravenhill describes his generation of playwrights as "disconnected from history" and as "locat[ing] everything in the now."[34] Referring to his 1990s plays, he explains that "it was almost impossible to make the present talk to the past [...]. We seemed to be inmates that are trapped in an eternal present, only existing in the now without a contact."[35] Regarding *Some Explicit Polaroids*, Ravenhill's diagnosis is reflected both in the characters' incapacity to engage meaningfully with their own past, present and future, and in the inadequacy of the play's own conventional dialectical framework to establish perspective.

Thus, the characters' struggles with the past illustrate this lack of meaningful engagement as well as its paralyzing impact on political agency, which the play presents as symptomatic of the turn of the millennium. While Nick is at once stuck in his obsolete political ideals and incapable of "fac[ing] up to [his] past" by coming to terms with his crime,[36] the past represents a source of pain for Jonathan, who is intent on finding closure by taking revenge on Nick.[37] When they finally meet, however, they indulge in a nostalgic yearning for the past rather than attempting to reconcile their dissonant experiences of past and present. By contrast, Helen has opted for denial, pretending that her former socialist self "was another person."[38] While the older generation reflects a certain degree of commitment to history—unproductive because shaped by denial or sentimentalism though it may be—Nadia, Tim and Victor are completely deprived of any sense of the past. All that counts for them is the present: "We see each day as a new day" and as unrelated to either yesterday or tomorrow.[39] Regarding these corrupted forms of historical awareness, none of the characters manages to engage fruitfully and sincerely with the past and its complex challenges for the present. Consequently, the characters are incapable of adopting an analytical perspective on historical developments which would facilitate critique and change. Instead, they are powerless, and the status quo remains unchallenged at the end of the play.

Employing history as a medium for its political and metatheatrical investigations by overlaying and contrasting two radically different temporalities—the early 1980s and the late 1990s—in a seemingly conventional dialectical way, the play decidedly goes beyond Brecht's use of historicization: In *Some Explicit Polaroids*, history does not serve to critically examine the contemporary moment, but rather to dramatize and exacerbate the play's diagnosis of a fundamental disconnection of present from past. While the characters are forced to confront the past through Nick's appearance, they are incapable of engaging in this dialogue and of adopting a different point of view. History, just as the contradictory, antithetical character constellations described above, is thus employed *ex negativo* in *Some Explicit Polaroids* to stage this crisis of conventional dialectical theater. Instead of facilitating distance and analysis, the play holds up an uncomfortable mirror to the audience which encourages the spectators—as opposed to the characters—to adopt a historical perspective, to take into account the wider context and, hence, to find a way of bringing past and present into a productive dialogue again.

Dialectical Emotions: Post-Brechtian Dialectical Aesthetics in *Some Explicit Polaroids*

Rather than rejecting dialectics as a potentially progressive and empowering aesthetic and epistemological framework, however, *Some Explicit Polaroids* searches for a new form of Brechtian-inspired dialectical theater which may respond to the fundamentally transformed context and its ambivalent political terrain. In a post-Brechtian vein, this reinvigoration of dialectical aesthetics and thought can be connected, as I suggest, to the play's commitment to emotions as a means of spurring political engagement—regarding both the characters and the audience. Yet, at the turn of the millennium, the form of authentic emotional expression the play seeks has become increasingly problematic: "Action assumes a connection between the emotions and intellect, and that connection has been severed" in what Meštrović refers to as "postemotional societies."[40] Thus, feelings have become manipulated under the impact of neoliberalism's experience economy and have been turned into "bite-size, pre-packaged, rationally manufactured emotions [...] that are consumed by the masses."[41] Responding to the challenge of reconnecting with genuine emotions as a prerequisite for enabling political engagement, Ravenhill describes his plays as distinguished by "a dialectics, not necessarily a dialectical argument, but a *dialectic* [sic] *emotion or mood*, dialectic in the sense of contradiction."[42] It is this focus on "dialectical emotions" which I consider characteristic of the In-Yer-Face sensibility and which initiates a new approach to Brechtian theater based on a deeply emotional, unsettling experience both for the characters and for the spectators.

On stage, it is again Nick whose appearance not only drives the play's diagnosis of dialectical crisis by underscoring the disconnection between the characters and their environment, but whose intervention also spurs a new approach to dialectical criticism by inciting the characters to interrogate their emotional investments. Through his rebellious, angry nature, his emotional attachments and his care for others, Nick introduces "an emotional thaw" into the play.[43] He "serves as the return of the repressed: not socialism, or activism, or even a politicized sensibility, but emotions."[44] Thus, while they categorically reject his attitudes, Tim, Nadia and Victor's encounters with Nick nevertheless seem to enable them to adopt a different perspective on their own lives and to acknowledge their profound unhappiness. Trying to deny feelings, which they perceive as a weakness, the omnipresence of violence in their lives symbolizes "a perverse attempt at connection."[45] The destructive quality of their relationships reflects how "[t]he political anger once voiced explicitly [...] through protest and immediate social action is now displaced through acts of physical and psychological violence."[46] In this respect, Tim's death represents a turning point for Victor and Nadia, who are confronted with their genuine feelings in the face of loss.[47]

In a similar vein, Helen and Nick are both forced to revisit their past and present emotions in the course of the play. Thus, Nick's anger is incomprehensible to Tim: "I think you must have spent so much time being angry that it's left you all hard and bitter, and now there's no way for you to deal with today."[48] Nick's embracing of the "happiness" dogma, however, comes too late and is vehemently rejected by the grieving Victor: "Fuck this Happy World okay? Big fucking lie."[49] Likewise, Helen's tactical and calculating spirit is challenged by her confrontation with Nick, but the conflict between reason and emotion they embody remains unreconciled. Far from an authentic expression of love,[50] the renewal of their relationship in the last scene is based on Helen's need for Nick's anger as an antidote to her rationality: "I want you to be angry. [...] I want to make you into what you used to be"—an attempt which is, however, doomed to fail, as Nick makes clear: "I can't be your memory."[51] Hence, while "Nick's return [...] provokes those around him out of their stasis,"[52] the ending is characterized by a radical openness in which the characters' conflicts remain unresolved: Rather than proposing "a fully formed narrative that creates a tentative paradigm for political action,"[53] the play's fundamental contradiction between "an acknowledgement of the appropriateness of the end of history (in the revolutionary sense)," on the one hand, and "an observation of the problems inherited by those who follow this demise" of socialism, on the other, persists.[54] What the play emphasizes in dialectical spirit through its ambiguity regarding Nick and Helen's relationship is the significance of opposition, conflict and debate over harmony and closure. It is, as I suggest, in the play's recognition of these fundamental dialectical values rather than in a sentimentalist vision of love that an alternative path opens up, implicitly handing over the responsibility of articulating a new politics to the audience.

Indeed, it is this diagnosis of open-endedness and ambivalence which underscores the crucial role of the audience for an interpretation of the play and which thereby paves the way for a new understanding of dialectical theater and critique in the post-Brechtian vein. Confronted with the play's unanswered questions and left without clear orientation, the spectators are, just as the characters, forced out of their stasis to respond to the unresolved paradoxes. In this respect, *Some Explicit Polaroid*'s dramaturgy illustrates a post-Brechtian approach to dialectical theater in David Barnett's understanding of the term to the extent that it "offer[s] contradiction to an audience without interpreting it on stage and instead pass[es] the work over to the audience."[55] As a result, "the audience is involved in a more sensuous experience of dialectical theatre. Because interpretation takes place in the auditorium rather than on the stage, the audience is not so busy decoding information; instead it *experiences* it."[56] As Ravenhill's play illustrates, it is in the relationship with the spectators rather than on the stage itself that conflict, interpretation and critique are reinitiated. Crucially, this experiential mode of reception may facilitate a new form of dialectical engagement with the indeterminacy of the play and of the wider contemporary context. Importantly, the experiential is realized in *Some Explicit Polaroids* not first and foremost on the level of language or stage imagery, as conventional readings of In-Yer-Face theater suggest, but, as I propose, on the level of form. What I consider most provocative about the play is its diagnosis that conventional patterns of thought and knowledge have become dysfunctional, as the play's staging of the crisis of dialectics underscores. In this respect, In-Yer-Face drama may in fact "be understood as an aesthetic discussion, as in some ways very meta-theatrical pieces."[57] This idea is reinforced by Elizabeth Kuti, who argues that Ravenhill's plays self-reflexively suggest that "the crucial stages in the development of western drama (and indeed civilization)—from Greek tragedy, to Enlightenment rationalism, to Brechtian socialism"— can no longer be considered "available modes for the playwright of the late twentieth century."[58] To the extent that *Some Explicit Polaroids* challenges dramaturgical conventions and, as a result, the spectators' processes of interpretation, it may cause an "aesthetic shock."[59] As Spencer Hazel writes, ventriloquizing Sierz's definition quoted at the beginning of this chapter, the In-Yer-Face playwrights "took the staid post-1980s conventions by the scruff of the neck and shook them until they got the message: that they were no longer fit for purpose."[60] Paradoxically, it is thus the profoundly experiential potential emerging from the play's complex engagement with dialectics on the level of content and form and its diagnosis of a devaluation of dialectical thought which may, in post-Brechtian spirit, reinvigorate analysis, reflection and critique in the relationship between stage and auditorium by fostering a decidedly more individual, emotional and associative form of dialectical interpretation in the light of the play's ambivalence.

In-Yer-Face as Post-Brechtian Drama: Toward Twenty-First-Century Political Theater

As part of the core of the In-Yer-Face sensibility, *Some Explicit Polaroids* stands out among other works of its time because of its profound metatheatrical engagement with questions of commitment and political theater at the turn of the millennium. Its emphasis on notions of contradiction, change and intervention establishes, as the previous analysis has shown, an important connection to dialectical theater in the Brechtian tradition, foregrounding, but also critically examining the value, forms and functions of dialectics as a progressive epistemological and aesthetic tool for responding to the challenges of the contemporary context. At the heart of the play's investigations, a fundamental paradox emerges: Employing a rigid dialectical framework, *Some Explicit Polaroids* reflects the dysfunctionality of conventional dialectical categories and strategies. Rather than a sign of nihilistic resignation, however, this diagnosis serves as a provocation to reimagine dialectical theater and criticism for the twenty-first century. In confrontational spirit, this new approach to Brechtian-inspired dialectics is based on a revaluation of the emotions: Underscoring the central role of the audience for the play's political impetus, it is the experience of openness and uncertainty the play facilitates which may spur critique and reflection on a more individual, but also decidedly more tentative and ambiguous level.

Through its focus on post-Brechtian dialectical emotions, *Some Explicit Polaroids* explores the political value of the personal, "primal" and visceral quality typical of the In-Yer-Face wave and thereby reinvigorates a form of twenty-first-century political theater which is characterized, as I have argued, by a creative and critical re-engagement with the Brechtian tradition on the contemporary British stage.[61] This post-Brechtian dimension, which manifests itself in an emphasis on the use of dialectical methods combined with a focus on the spectators' individual experience of the performance, is not only evident in Ravenhill's, but also in other playwrights' twenty-first-century work.[62] This underscores the extent to which the radical renewal established by the 1990s In-Yer-Face plays has not only contributed to shaping a new understanding of Brechtian theater, but also continued to influence political playwriting beyond its immediate impact during the "Cool Britannia" era: Inspired by the innovations of the In-Yer-Face wave, contemporary drama casts the audience as protagonist and enables dialectical analysis "at the level of feeling and metaphor, rather than explicit analysis,"[63] thereby reimagining Brechtian dialectics for the new millennium and laying the ground for a new form of "genuinely dialectical theatre" based on, as Ravenhill advocates, experience, embodiment as well as examination.[64]

Notes

1. Aleks Sierz, *In-Yer-Face Theatre: British Drama Today* (London: Faber & Faber, 2001), 4.
2. Sanja Nikcevic, "British Brutalism, the 'New European Drama' and the Role of the Director," *New Theatre Quarterly* 21, no. 3 (2005): 264.
3. Graham Saunders, "Introduction," *Cool Britannia? British Political Drama in the 1990s*, ed. Rebecca D'Monté and Graham Saunders (Basingstoke: Palgrave, 2008), 7; see also Vera Gottlieb, "Theatre Today— The 'New Realism,'" *Contemporary Theatre Review* 13, no. 1 (2003): 5–14; Klaus Peter Müller, "Political Plays in England in the 1990s," in *British Drama of the 1990s*, ed. Bernhard Reitz and Mark Berninger (Heidelberg: Winter, 2002), 15–36; and Clare Wallace, "Responsibility and Postmodernity: Mark Ravenhill and 1990s British Drama," *Theory and Practice in English Studies* 4 (2005): 269–275.
4. Ariane de Waal, "Expel, Exploit, Exfoliate: Talking on Terror in Mark Ravenhill's *Shoot/Get Treasure/Repeat* (2007)," in *Finance, Terror, and Science on Stage: Current Public Concerns in 21st-Century British Drama*, ed. Kerstin Frank and Carolin Lusin (Tübingen: Narr, 2017), 64; see also Saunders, "Introduction."
5. Aleks Sierz, "'We All Need Stories': The Politics of In-Yer-Face Theatre," in *Cool Britannia? British Political Drama in the 1990s*, ed. Rebecca D'Monté and Graham Saunders (Basingstoke: Palgrave, 2008), 25.
6. Saunders, "Introduction," 3.
7. Bertolt Brecht, *Brecht on Theatre*, ed. Marc Silberman, Steve Giles, and Tom Kuhn, 3rd rev. ed. (London: Bloomsbury, 2015), 284.
8. Mark Ravenhill, "Don't Bash Brecht," *Guardian*, May 26, 2008, https://www.theguardian.com/stage/theatreblog/2008/may/26/dontbashbrecht.
9. Mark Ravenhill, "Theatre and Democracy," *Dramaturgs' Network*, 2016, https://www.dramaturgy.co.uk/copy-of-dramaturgy-papers-hanna-sla. Author emphasis.

10. David Barnett, *Brecht in Practice: Theatre, Theory and Performance* (London: Bloomsbury, 2015), 5.
11. Brecht, *Brecht on Theatre*, 51.
12. Barnett, *Brecht in Practice*, 57.
13. Brecht, *Brecht on Theatre*, 242.
14. See Bertell Ollman and Tony Smith, "Introduction," *Dialectics for the New Century*, ed. Bertell Ollman and Tony Smith (Basingstoke: Palgrave, 2008), 4; Bertell Ollman, "Why Dialectics? Why Now?," in *Dialectics for the New Century*, ed. Bertell Ollman and Tony Smith (Basingstoke: Palgrave, 2008), 11.
15. Mark Ravenhill, *Some Explicit Polaroids* (London: Bloomsbury, 1999), 1.
16. Sean Carney, *The Politics and Poetics of Contemporary English Tragedy* (Toronto: Toronto University Press, 2013), 251.
17. Leo Panitch and Colin Leys, *The End of Parliamentary Socialism: From New Left to New Labour*, 2nd ed. (London: Verso, 2001), 248.
18. Ravenhill, *Some Explicit Polaroids*, 8.
19. Ibid., 52.
20. Ibid., 8.
21. Carney, *The Politics*, 252.
22. Ravenhill, *Some Explicit Polaroids*, 81.
23. Sierz, *In-Yer-Face*, 6.
24. Ravenhill, *Some Explicit Polaroids*, 41.
25. Ibid., 43.
26. Carney, *The Politics*, 253.
27. Ibid., 252.
28. Ken Urban, "Towards a Theory of Cruel Britannia: Coolness, Cruelty, and the 'Nineties," *New Theatre Quarterly* 20, vol. 4 (2004): 358.
29. Saunders, "Introduction," 11.
30. See Urban, "Towards a Theory," 356; Dick Pountains and David Robbins, *Cool Rules: Anatomy of an Attitude* (London: Reaktion, 2000), 172.
31. See Brecht, *Brecht on Theatre*, 187–188.
32. Barnett, *Brecht in Practice*, 75.
33. Ibid., 74.
34. Mark Ravenhill, "Locating History on the Contemporary Stage," *Journal of Contemporary Drama in English* 3, no. 1 (2015): 160.
35. Ibid., 161.
36. Ravenhill, *Some Explicit Polaroids*, 51.
37. See ibid., 34.
38. Ibid., 33.
39. Ibid., 48.
40. Stjepan G. Meštrović, *Postemotional Society* (London: Sage, 1997), xi.
41. Ibid.

42. Enric Monforte, "Mark Ravenhill," in *British Theatre of the 1990s: Interviews with Directors, Playwrights, Critics and Academics*, ed. Mireia Aragay, et al. (Basingstoke: Palgrave, 2007), 103. Author emphasis.
43. Carney, *The Politics*, 254.
44. Ibid., 253.
45. Dan Rebellato, "'Because It Feels Fucking Amazing': Recent British Drama and Bodily Mutilation," in *Cool Britannia? British Political Drama in the 1990s*, ed. Rebecca D'Monté and Graham Saunders (Basingstoke: Palgrave, 2008), 204.
46. Caridad Svich, "Commerce and Morality in the Theatre of Mark Ravenhill," *Contemporary Theatre Review* 13, no. 1 (2003): 91.
47. See Carney, *The Politics*, 254–255.
48. Ravenhill, *Some Explicit Polaroids*, 41.
49. Ibid., 72.
50. See Amelia Howe Kritzer, *Political Theatre in Post-Thatcher Britain–New Writing: 1995–2005* (Basingstoke: Palgrave, 2008), 45–47; Svich, "Commerce," 92.
51. Ravenhill, *Some Explicit Polaroids*, 84.
52. Carney, *The Politics*, 256.
53. Kritzer, *Political Theatre*, 45.
54. Carney, *The Politics*, 251.
55. Barnett, *Brecht in Practice*, 216.
56. Ibid.
57. Julia Boll, *The New War Plays: From Kane to Harris* (Basingstoke: Palgrave, 2013), 46.
58. Elizabeth Kuti, "Tragic Plots from Bootle to Baghdad," *Contemporary Theatre Review* 18, no. 4 (2008): 460.
59. Boll, *The New War Plays*, 44.
60. Spencer Hazel, "In Whose Face?! (Angry Young) Theatre Makers and the Targets of Their Provocation," *Coup de théâtre* 29 (2015): 63.
61. William C. Boles, *The Argumentative Theatre of Joe Penhall* (Jefferson, NC: McFarland, 2011), 11.
62. See Anja Hartl, "Finstere Zeiten: Post-brechtsche Dialektik im Werk von Caryl Churchill," in *Bertolt Brecht – zwischen Tradition und Moderne: Studien zu seinem Werk und dessen Rezeption*, ed. Jürgen Hillesheim (Würzburg: Königshausen & Neumann, 2018), 337–357; Anja Hartl, "Recycling Brecht in Britain: David Greig's *The Events* as Post-Brechtian Lehrstück," in *Recycling Brecht*, eds. Tom Kuhn, David Barnett, and Theodore F. Rippey (Rochester, NY: Boydell & Brewer, 2018), 153–170.
63. Rebellato, "'Because It Feels,'" 202.
64. Ravenhill, "Theatre and Democracy."

PART II

A Movement's International Influences

CHAPTER 6

Undressing Sarah Kane: A Portuguese Perspective on In-Yer-Face

Cátia Faísco

In 1992, Sarah Kane saw Jeremy Weller's *Mad* in Edinburgh, a production which involved both professional and non-professional actors who had experienced mental illness. Kane was only twenty-one years old. She had just finished her drama degree in Bristol, and that experience as a spectator changed her perspective on the type of theater she wanted to make. In her own words, "I was taken to a place of extreme mental discomfort and distress (…) *Mad* took me to hell."[1] Subsequently, that night, Kane decided to shift the focus of her work to a more experiential aesthetics. Hence, what we now recognize as a strongly embodied oeuvre was the result of the influence theater can have in our lives.

Curiously enough, I too was twenty-one when I made my first acquaintance with Kane's work. It was through a performance of *Cleansed* (1998). The play had its Portuguese stage debut in 2002 and was directed by

---

This chapter was written under the financial support of the Portuguese FCT institution.

C. Faísco (✉)
CEHUM - Centre for Humanistic Studies, University of Minho, Braga, Portugal
e-mail: cfaisco@ilch.uminho.pt

© The Author(s) 2020
W. C. Boles (ed.), *After In-Yer-Face Theatre*,
https://doi.org/10.1007/978-3-030-39427-1_6

Nuno Cardoso. I saw it that same year in Coimbra, and I distinctly remember my restlessness and the impact it had on me as a spectator. For instance, the scene in which Tinker forces Robin to eat the chocolates and Robin pees himself was so powerfully disturbing that I could not stop crying. The depiction of this and other acts of cruelty along with the words and the confrontations about the nature of love marked me so profoundly that they have influenced both my subsequent artistic and academic paths. As Sarah Kane so wisely expressed, "If theatre can change lives, then it also can change society. Theatre is not an external force acting on society, but a part of it. It's a reflection of the way people within that society view the world."[2] To me, Kane's work was remarkable and it shaped not only the work of fellow playwrights but also critics and academics. Therefore, as it happens with all great artists, I was not alone in my opinion.

In the early 2000s, Portuguese artists were being encouraged to engage with other artists of the European Community by Portugal's first-ever Ministry of Culture. Founded by Manuel Maria Carrilho in 1995, this new political mechanism which institutionalized art also expressed the Portuguese government's awareness of the need to support theater companies. Nonetheless, this behavior has to be considered and contextualized within the country's history, as it had only been twenty years since the Carnation Revolution.[3] The absence of censorship and the recently acquired freedom, in all its dimensions, transformed the will of the Portuguese artists and consequently the Portuguese theater landscape. There were many young theater companies taking their first steps, and most of them, in an effort to match the European dynamic, were choosing to perform plays that had already influenced theater and audiences in other countries. According to Eugénia Vasques,

> Two types of groups, therefore, compose the Portuguese theater landscape of the 1990s and the corresponding (although necessarily heterogeneous) new generation: 1) the group of new projects which rely on continuity, on a more or less stable collective, on a differentiated artistic direction, and that fight for the right to be recognized and quickly institutionalized; 2) and the other "projects"—sort of collective, occasional or recent—usually based in Greater Lisbon, Greater Oporto or Coimbra, which are either radically antisystem (although not anti-subsidy) or whose identity fluctuates between the mainstream and the territory of the shy and ambiguous Portuguese fringe.[4]

The truth is that only after the Carnation Revolution were theater companies able to work without the restraints they had been under for forty years. As Mickaël de Oliveira describes in his thesis, the end of *Estado*

Novo, of the colonial war and of censorship, along with the return of state subsidies and a new socio-economic reality, gave birth to independent theater companies.[5] The Portuguese generation of the 1990s was, thus, freer to create and be heard.

In the late 1990s, the Portuguese director Jorge Silva Melo and several actors founded the theater company *Artistas Unidos*, which was based in Lisbon. One of their main objectives was to promote contemporary drama. In 1999, the government assigned the troupe a building called *A Capital*, a former newspaper headquarters, and quickly they started to revitalize the space through their programming. For example, a cycle dedicated to the complete works of Sarah Kane.[6] Jorge Silva Melo had recently come across Kane's plays when her work was being performed at the Royal Court Theatre. He noted:

> The first play I read was *Blasted*. I didn't yet know who she was and as I read the play at night, I was instantly captivated. Why? Because of the beauty of the play and its muteness. What I mean is that the play begins in a certain way and, as it moves forward, it starts to change its scope, its structure. That's one of the things I love about her work: she strolls around her writing, around being incoherent and not trying to control the same world with the language.[7]

The aesthetic intensity of Kane's work did not go unnoticed by Silva Melo. In her dramatic voice, he recognized something that deserved to be shared with the Portuguese audience. To explore all the works of an artist in a single cycle was very unusual, as most theater companies tended to work solely on one or two plays by the same playwright and rarely at the same time. The enterprise took place at *A Capital*, located in Bairro Alto, one of the most traditional neighborhoods of Lisbon. It began in 2000 with staged readings, which not only explored Kane's strong use of language, but, in some way, also functioned as an opportunity to gauge how the audience would react to her work. Francisco Frazão, artistic director of *Teatro do Bairro*, a theater venue in Lisbon, was one of the members of the audience during those first try-outs:

> The first thing I saw, and I had not yet read anything, was the *Blasted* reading, which was amazing, much stronger than the performance they presented after. [...] It was a Wednesday afternoon and the room was full. We are talking about around 50 people. Nowadays, there is no such audience for readings. At the time, I think there was a need in Lisbon for people to get to know more, because there was little work around writing for contemporary theater, so there was a lot of desire to know what was going on.[8]

After these staged readings, the company began to work on the performances of all her plays. The first work to be presented was *Ruínas* (*Blasted*) in 2000. Directed by Jorge Silva Melo and Paulo Claro, *Ruínas* was performed at *Teatro Paulo Claro*, a theater venue lodged in the *A Capital* building. Carla Bolito, the actress chosen to portray the innocent and disturbed Cate, recalls her first impression of the play: "I was absolutely shocked. [...] The play has a mixture of disgust and entertainment that sometimes made me interrupt the reading. But Cate seduced me right away."[9] *Blasted* had premiered in 1995 at the Royal Court Theatre and provoked a media frenzy due to the visceral reactions of the newspaper critics; the majority of the reviewers, though, would only truly understand *Blasted* many years later. In Portugal, the buzz was not so evident. Most critics found the performance fascinating and understood the essence of the play without questioning Kane's intent to depict the world as she saw it: cruel and violent.

When *Ruínas* was performed, critic João Carneiro highlighted that the production directed by Jorge Silva Melo and Paulo Claro admirably recreated the oppressive atmosphere suggested by the play. Furthermore, he also implied that what they did was perhaps even more radical, since it worked as a trigger, leading to the explosion of violence re-created in everything and everyone as the play moved forward.[10] Vanessa Rato, who at the time was a critic for the daily newspaper *Público*, pointed out that *Ruínas* was "a raw performance in which sex, masturbation, rape, defecation, anthropophagy and the schizophrenic balance of a mankind in ruins rise up and collapse with cinematic impact."[11] In both appraisals, there were no hypercritical values, just an analysis of the uniqueness of the performance, which gave the audience a sense of the authenticity of the play. Given all the years of censorship and the recently acquired freedom, it is clear why Portuguese critics and audience members found Kane's discourse so distinctive and reacted so positively to it. David Ian Rabey's understanding of the play helps to elucidate their reactions:

> The play is disturbing not just for *what* happens, but *how* it happens. *Blasted* also suggests people's capacities for resil[i]ence and adaptability in persistence with some form of life, however grueling and removed from the form of life they might have wished for; even here, as elsewhere in Kane's work, the surprising eruptions of black humor should not be avoided.[12]

The work of Sarah Kane was especially well received in Portugal. However, unlike what happened in England, there was not a need to correlate her with the In-Yer-Face movement or any of the playwrights associated with it.[13] She was just another playwright who had an interesting oeuvre.

A year later, in 2001, Jorge Silva Melo directed *Falta* (*Crave*), which he considered to be one of Kane's most original plays. In Silva Melo's opinion, this was one of the least well received of their productions, as "the audience was greatly disturbed by the fact that there wasn't a clear narrative line."[14] The story appeared to be missing. *Crave* allows the audience to engage in a simultaneously collective and individual poetic discourse, which may cause discomfort since there is a tendency to associate theater with narrative. When Sarah Kane wrote the play, she only defined one of the characters as clearly being a woman; all the other characters could be interpreted as being either male or female. In English, it is possible to keep the characters just like Kane wrote them, but the Portuguese language does not allow for them to be genderless. Acknowledging and, in a way, submitting to the powerful mechanisms of a language can force the director and the translator to choose the gender of a character, which may affect the audience's perception of and response to the play. While translating the play, Pedro Marques transformed the genderless characters into two men and two women. Sarah Kane was once asked about how she would like her play to be staged; she did provide an answer. Her structuring of the play allows a freedom that Silva Melo embraced in order to create his site-specific production.

On 18 January 2001, *Artistas Unidos* premiered *Crave* at the *A Capital* building, a decayed five-story edifice with an endless number of small rooms. To maximize the usage of the space, and without labeling it, they transformed the play into a site-specific performance. When Silva Melo was asked about the concept behind the production, he explained that:

> The idea of *Crave* was not to see everything, but only a part, and I think that was quite well achieved. I did it on a very realistic basis: the audience was in [a] V [shape], and there were four doors and four rooms through those doors. Sometimes the actors were on the front stage (if we can call it that), sometimes they were in the rooms. And it was funny to see that beautiful declaration of love at the edge of a door, to feel that one of the girls was present, but not evidently on display.[15]

The audience was confined by the performance as if they were intruding in someone else's home, witnessing the anger and the love expressed between doors and rooms in a kind of hide-and-seek game. However, even though the scenic space had all of these characteristics and tried to convey a sense of closeness, the reaction of the audience was unexpected. Even the critics seemed to be more critical than they had been with any of the other performances or readings in the cycle. Nevertheless, critic João Carneiro congratulated the actors and emphasized their ability to establish a performative common ground within a dramatic discourse that created real differences. In addition, he also pointed out that this work demanded "great attention from the viewer, even if we sometimes wish for a greater intensification of the rhythmic and discursive contrasts."[16] Much of the reception of the play was shown not only by how critics reviewed it, but also by the lack of reviews—*Crave* received less critical attention than the other plays performed by the troupe.

Apart from the aforementioned cycle, in 2002, the Oporto director Nuno Cardoso directed the Portuguese stage debut of *Purificados* (*Cleansed*). For Cardoso, the English playwright Sarah Kane and some of the other In-Yer-Face playwrights gave voice to his generation.[17] There was a whole new wave of directors, actors and playwrights, among other artists, who were the first to confront the freedom provided by the Carnation Revolution.[18] Cardoso and many others had not yet found a way to externalize all the angst that had been accumulating. Cardoso relayed:

> In Portugal, the first generation after the 25 April 1974 carried a rage that had been restrained between the memory narrated by the liberators and the fact that they didn't feel worthy enough to fully enjoy that freedom. Suddenly, that generation, and I speak from the perspective of someone who had almost the same age as Kane, is absolutely seduced by those texts. One of the In-Yer-Face premises is that it is a kind of theater that takes place in the present moment and allows you to give an opinion. That's what I found in Sarah Kane.[19]

The first play Nuno Cardoso was passionate about was *Phaedra's Love*, but since Silva Melo owned its production rights, Cardoso was left with *Cleansed*, a play he had not previously considered directing. Interestingly enough, his version of *Cleansed* would be acknowledged as one of his greatest productions. Cardoso explained that there was something personally striking in Kane's words. Moreover, according to him, "the worst thing you could do to someone of the In-Yer-Face generation was to sting them."²⁰ And Sarah Kane's plays did just that to him. When Cardoso began his career, in the 1990s, he could not have imagined that he would encounter such a theatrical opportunity like the one offered by Sarah Kane's works. Contrary to the previous generation and pursuant to Jorge Louraço Figueira, Cardoso began his career at "the height of neoliberalism, with the press diminished, actors paid by the day, and only a dozen performances per play in a space that is dependent upon a producer."²¹

When Sarah Kane wrote *Cleansed*, she based its structure on Georg Büchner's *Woyzeck*, because while reading it for the first time, even though she did not understand it, she realized that a play did not have to be coherent in order to be comprehended. Hence, instead of fixating on the violence (which was also used as a metaphor), Kane wanted the audience to see *Cleansed* as a story of extreme love and all the things the characters had to do in order to survive.

When Cardoso's production of *Cleansed* premiered in Portugal, in 2002, it did not have the same impact as in England. Rather than focusing on the playwright or the play, the press focused on the director, with some saying that Cardoso's work was becoming increasingly violent, and that his version of *Cleansed* brought out an aggressiveness that was latent in the play. The columnist Eduardo Prado Coelho was so strongly impressed that, in his review, he quoted from the production's program: "Abandon yourselves to the play. Submit. Lose your money, throw it out the window. Enter the play as if it were a convent. Just like in a religious order, when one paradoxically takes the vow of obedience, the only vow that really rips one to shreds."²² Most reviews written at the time also praised the actors' work. Nuno M. Cardoso, the actor who played Graham, had previously worked with Cardoso and was therefore familiar with his directing methodologies: the very hard physical improvisations made during the rehearsals became less violent once they were converted into stage directions. M. Cardoso also recalls how he enjoyed playing his character alongside Cátia Pinheiro, the actress who played Grace, and how in "this work, there was a very strong confrontation with the body, since in Sarah Kane's play there is the destruction, erosion and reconstruction of the body. Also, the title itself: *Cleansed*. What kind of cleansing is this which is proposed by love and destroys it or constructs it or purifies it?"²³

The questions raised by the actor seem to translate some of Sarah Kane's thoughts while writing *Cleansed*. Considered the most disturbing and darkest of her works, *Cleansed* was crafted so it could only be staged and not transformed into a movie or any other artistic object. The director Nuno Cardoso likes to test limits and his staged performance of *Cleansed* depicts the way he challenges his actors. For instance, Ana Pais wrote that Cardoso's *Cleansed* "lived from its energy on stage, from the powerful physical component of the bodies that are not there to serve the word, but for the word to use them."[24] Nuno Cardoso's *Cleansed* was the only performance that reached a broader audience, since it toured through multiple cities, such as Oporto, Viseu, Coimbra and Lisbon. (It was this tour that introduced me to Kane's work when I was 21.) All the previous work developed by *Artistas Unidos* around the oeuvre of Kane had been confined to Lisbon, thus limiting the opportunities for the interior population of the country to be exposed to Kane.

In *The Pleasure of the Text*, Roland Barthes explains the concept of "*text of bliss*" as the "text that imposes a state of loss, the text that discomforts (perhaps to the point of a certain boredom), unsettles the reader's historical, cultural, psychological assumptions, the consistency of his tastes, values, memories, brings to a crisis his relation with language."[25] When reading Sarah Kane's plays, it is impossible not to incorporate this notion into the world she crafts for the reader. *4.48 Psychosis* can be conceptualized as the play that is closer to bringing the disruption of the self and the aforementioned unsettledness. Although it clearly serves as an imaginary portrait of a suicide, many tend to read it as an autobiographical last note written by Kane before she committed suicide. In Portugal, *4.48 Psychosis* was one of Kane's most publicized plays with six theater productions (performances or adaptations) between 2001 and 2012. In 2002, Jorge Silva Melo invited the Portuguese choreographer João Fiadeiro to direct Sarah Kane's last play. Prior to this performance, Silva Melo had previously directed a staged reading with the same actors. As for the choices Fiadeiro made to direct this play, Melo wondered if the audience had the opportunity to fully understand the world of the play since he relied more on choreography rather than directorial blocking to present the piece.[26] João Carneiro addressed the choreographed nature of the production, noting:

> The tone of the movement is precise and subtle, the verbal and discursive tone is always on a strange threshold between the certainty of who is going to die—our knowledge of the fate of the author of the text raises, once

again, complex questions about the autobiographical discourse and fictional work—and the sometimes fleeting nature of her arguments or the difficulty of saying them, as if the play and the world were thrown into a tone between the verifiable case (the "fait-divers") and the more metaphysical of the tragedies.[27]

4.48 Psychosis, which revolves around the struggle of the self, psychoactive drugs, therapy and the everlasting return to the hour of darkness, catches glimpses of a tragedy about to happen. For the journalist and columnist Alexandra Lucas Coelho, Gracinda Nave, one of the actresses chosen to portray the voice that wants to die, became the only performer who could embody those last words of Sarah Kane because, even though she had never heard of the playwright prior to her casting, the performance gave her a sense of profound closeness to Kane.[28] Using a fragmented discourse and distorted reality, *4.48 Psychosis* relies upon introspective monologues and dialogues, and has been acknowledged as a natural extension of *Crave*'s structure.

After all these performances and staged readings, in February and March 2004, *Artistas Unidos* and *Centro Cultural de Belém* (CCB) organized a cycle that assembled the previous productions of Sarah Kane. CCB, being one of the most respected art centers in Lisbon and in the country, attracted a much wider and assorted audience than the previous productions. In this cycle, Silva Melo not only revisited the plays which he had already directed, but also premiered *Amor de Fedra* (*Phaedra's Love*), the only play by Kane that had yet to be staged. *Phaedra's Love* maintains the central theme of the original Seneca's tragedy, in which the queen falls in love with her stepson; however, Phaedra is no longer the main character, Hippolytus is. Yet, Kane locks him inside the castle, inside his own mind and desires. In this play, Kane continues the experience of disembodiment of naturalism, while submitting the characters to a life of self-destruction. During this cycle at CCB there was also a photography exhibition by Jorge Gonçalves called *Até aos olhos*, which was dedicated to the performances of Kane's plays. Jorge Gonçalves photographed the work of *Artistas Unidos* at *A Capital* as well. In addition, from a more theoretical perspective, the cycle also included *Um mundo em Ruínas* (A World in Ruins), a colloquium on the work of the playwright, held on 13 March, 2004, with the participation of Jorge Silva Melo, Francisco Frazão, and Pedro Marques.

To conclude this chapter, it is important to note that the cycle devoted to the work of Sarah Kane—comprised of presentations, staged readings at *A Capital* and the cycle at CCB—was only completed four years after it had begun. It was and still is considered unique in its form, as it explored the oeuvre of such a young playwright in an extraordinarily consistent way. Besides the staged readings and performances, *Artistas Unidos* and the publishing company Campo das Letras compiled the translations of the plays into one volume called *Teatro Completo* (*Complete Theater*). Other playwrights of the In-Yer-Face generation, like Mark Ravenhill, did not gather the same attention, and very few translations were ever published. When questioned about this volume and the repercussion of the plays, Silva Melo stated that what struck him the most was realizing that

> her writing didn't influence anyone, even with the book being revised and having a second edition, which is very rare for a theater author. While in England it is evident that Pinter influenced Sarah Kane and that she influenced Ravenhill and a number of young people who came afterwards, here the plays were staged and they died. I see no one interested in developing that writing. It's closed. That is, everyone saw the performances and that was it.[29]

In Portugal, the presence of Sarah Kane's work did not have the impact it did in the playwright's home country. Although, as Nuno Cardoso argues, it served as a vehicle for the angst of a generation, there was not a specific repercussion in the works of either playwrights or directors.

In a lecture titled "Blasted and After: New Writing in British Theatre Today" held at the Victoria and Albert Museum in 2010, Aleks Sierz reflected upon the aftermaths of In-Yer-Face and its relation to New Writing. His point of view seems to differ from Silva Melo and Cardoso's perspective, allowing us to question whether or not, implicitly or expressly, the contemporary generation of artists still lives under the influence of what was written and performed almost 20 years ago:

> My final point about the new writing scene in the 1990s is that although it was not confined to In-Yer-Face theatre, In-Yer-face theatre did represent its cutting edge. This style of theatre was an avant-garde, and it was exported to theatres all over Europe. [...] The repercussions of the success of this avant-garde of In-Yer-Face new writers is clear. Although this particular new wave crested in about 1999, at least a decade ago, we still live in its backflow.[30]

It is interesting to realize that while in England Sarah Kane's plays were presented mainly in the Royal Court Theatre, one of England's most important theater venues, in Portugal that was not the case. Apart from

Cleansed, which toured through *Teatro Helena Sá e Costa* (Oporto), *Teatro Viriato* (Viseu), *Teatro Académico Gil Vicente* (Coimbra) and *Teatro D. Maria II* (Lisbon), the plays premiered at *A Capital*, a building which was closer to a more experiential aesthetics that characterized Kane's work and the foundations of In-Yer-Face Theater. Furthermore, while in her own country her words were scrutinized and used to violently attack her, in Portugal the critics and the audience appeared to have reacted rather peacefully.

Sixteen years later, the Portuguese theater landscape is greatly changed. Nevertheless, the fight for funds and proper venues to present performances still occurs. When it comes to state cultural funds and grants, Portugal faces one of its biggest challenges. Artists from every field are protesting against government policies and demanding that one percent of the state budget be allocated to culture. Portugal has returned to an era in which actors are underpaid (or not paid at all) and economic values seemingly top every other area. Consequently, this may prove to be a great time to recuperate the angst of those who, like Sarah Kane, wanted to expose everyday horrors and atrocities. Cardoso stated:

> I think the social/emotional reality has changed drastically. At the moment, you live more in the digital world than in the real world. It's as if Sarah Kane's nightmares had somehow materialized. I have not read Sarah Kane in about four years, but during that time reality has taken a very big turn. Market, opinion and good taste are the attributes of the programmer who is a kind of postmodern *übermensch*, the little patron of the age without nobility.[31]

Bearing in mind that a generation has passed since the 2002 performance of *Cleansed* and Sarah Kane's influence on his work, Nuno Cardoso recognizes that that production brought out the violence and performed a visceral consciousness that still exists in his own work. Although he is open to the possibility of directing *Cleansed* again, he also says that "a person grows and ages, and realizes that they can also make blood with cotton."[32] Just like Cardoso, Silva Melo is, as well, open to the possibility of returning to the world of Sarah Kane, and even though he knows he would not be able to perform it in the same building, he would choose to go back to *Crave*.

If Sarah Kane were still alive today, she would have celebrated her 47th birthday. So, why not return to her plays? Why not try to make a difference by using her words? In the early 2000s, when all the plays were performed, they were presented mainly in city theaters, where the audience skewed more cosmopolitan. Considering that everyone should have access to all forms of culture, would it not make sense to show Sarah Kane's oeuvre to other Portuguese audiences? For instance, how would a play like *Cleansed* or *4.48 Psychosis* be performed in a small village theater? And how would the audience react? Even though there are other playwrights who write about global, local or personal issues, few strike so close to them with the ferocity of the words of Kane. Maybe time has given the audience more self-awareness. Maybe the disparity caused by the political engagement has led everyone to protest out on the streets. Maybe we are all learning that theater is crucial to our lives. Maybe like Greg, the character from *Sleeping Around* says, "Time doesn't care what you believe. It just goes on. And everything is temporary. All of us. All of this."[33] If everything is temporary, why not now?

NOTES

1. Ibid., 92.
2. Sarah Kane, quoted in Aleks Sierz, *In-Yer-Face Theatre: British Drama Today* (London: Faber and Faber, 2000), 93.
3. The Carnation Revolution was an event that profoundly altered Portugal by bringing down António Salazar, who had encapsulated the country in a dictatorship for more than fifty years. It took place on the morning of 25 April 1974, and it was an historical moment for every Portuguese, because it radically changed their notion of freedom and opened up their lives to new possibilities. As Stewart Lloyd-Jones explains, it "was the date that Portugal's transition to democracy began. The Armed Forces' Movement (MFA) has been credited with finally ridding Portugal of the final decaying remnants of Salazar's regime, and with setting Portugal firmly on the path to social/liberal democracy. Without 25 April, we must assume, Portugal would have remained immune to the economic and globalising realities of the past thirty years" (Stewart Lloyd-Jones, "An End or a Beginning for Portugal? Some Notes on the Legacy of 25 April 1974," 2002: 142, http://www.lusotopie.sciencespobordeaux.fr/lloyd.pdf [accessed February 10, 2018]).

4. Eugénia Vasques, *O teatro português e o 25 de Abril: uma história ainda por contar*, 1999: 9. Author translation, http://hdl.handle.net/10400.21/3378 (accessed March 28, 2019).
5. See Mickaël de Oliveira, "Para uma Cartografia da Criação Dramática Portuguesa Contemporânea (1974-2004)," *Os Autores Portugueses do Teatro Independente: Repertórios e Cânones* (2010), https://estudogeral.sib.uc.pt/ (accessed January 28, 2018).
6. This cycle was not only about the In-Yer-Face playwright; it was also about the decaying walls and rooms of *A Capital*. In an interview to the daily newspaper *Público*, Silva Melo stated the obvious, which the city council seemed to be missing: "Because it's funny to come here to see one, two shows in bad conditions, with cold and cats coming in, etc., but as the third year begins to run out, the possibilities for the scenography also diminish. Little by little, people will see the same dirty wall with the same actors at the front, and they will not return." This political statement was one of many printed in the media which made reference to the poor conditions the theater company had to face. Later on, *Artistas Unidos* would be evicted from *A Capital* and moved into *Teatro da Politécnica*, where they still are now (Jorge Silva Melo, Personal interview, March 2018. Author translation).
7. Melo, Personal interview.
8. Francisco Frazão, Personal interview, April 2011. Author translation.
9. Carla Bolito, "Movimento em crescendo, texto em pianíssimo," Interview by PauloMoura, *Pública*, December 17, 2000: 37-44. Author translation.
10. See João Carneiro, "Explosões," *Expresso – Cartaz*, November 11, 2000.
11. Vanessa Rato, "A obscenidade da vida," *Público – Artes*, October 20, 2000. Author translation.
12. David Ian Rabey, *English Drama Since 1940* (London: Longman, 2003), 206.
13. In-Yer-Face is an artistic movement that left a mark on the British and world theater of the 1990s. It was born from the ashes of the 1980s generation as well as of the followers of Andrew Lloyd Webber. It became a renewing force which opposed the previous decade's aesthetic, social and political values, while aspiring to a place where its voices could echo: "By the mid-90s, a divergent group of young writers had emerged whose plays addressed violence and sexuality in an unflinching manner, and many were produced by the Royal Court. Kane, along with Mark Ravenhill, Anthony Neilson, Martin McDonagh, Joe Penhall, Jez Butterworth, and Judy Upton, were quickly dubbed by the press the 'New British Nihilists' or 'New Brutalists'. These writers of 'smack and sodomy' plays do not represent a coherent artistic movement. Like the work of the 'Angry Young

Men' of the late 50s, their plays demonstrate too wide a range of theatrical styles and methods to have a unified project. Yet, they share many central political and aesthetic concerns" (Ken Urban, "An Ethics of Catastrophe: The Theatre of Sarah Kane," *PAJ: A Journal of Performance and Art* 23, no. 3 (2001): 37).
14. Melo, Personal interview. Author translation.
15. Ibid. Author translation.
16. João Carneiro, "Um imenso desejo," *Expresso – Cartaz*, February 2, 2001. Author translation.
17. Nuno Cardoso, Personal interview, February 2018.
18. See note 3.
19. Cardoso, Personal interview. Author translation.
20. Ibid. Author translation.
21. Jorge Louraço Figueira, "Democratic Regime and Stage Regimes: Three Directors (Nuno Cardoso, Bruno Bravo and Gonçalo Amorim)," in *Contemporary Portuguese Theatre: Experimentalism, Politics and Utopia*, edited by Rui Pina Coelho (Lisbon: TNDMII/Bicho do Mato, 2017), 43.
22. Eduardo Prado Coelho, "Sem a morte em troca," *Público*, April 10, 2002. Author translation.
23. Nuno M. Cardoso, Personal interview, March 2013. Author translation.
24. Pais also noted that "one of the highlights is the interpretations of Cátia Pinheiro (Grace), who maintains a fair deaf tension, Nuno M. Cardoso (Graham) who will have a beautiful and intense theatrical love scene with his sister/mistress, and António Fonseca (Tinker), master of contention, of meticulousness and astonishment. *Cleansed* belongs to the actors" (Ana Pais, "Palavras à flor da pele," *Público – Cultura*, April 6, 2002. Author translation).
25. Roland Barthes, *The Pleasure of the Text* (New York: Hill and Wand, 1998), 14.
26. Melo, Personal interview.
27. João Carneiro, "O fim do mundo," *Expresso – Cartaz*, October 10, 2001. Author translation.
28. See Alexandra Lucas Coelho, "4.48 Psicose," *Público – Espaço Público*, March 25, 2002.
29. Melo, Personal interview. Author translation.
30. Retrieved from http://www.theatrevoice.com/audio/new-writing-in-british-theatre-today/ (accessed January 22, 2018).
31. Nuno Cardoso, Personal interview, February 2018. Author translation.
32. Ibid. Author translation.
33. Abi Morgan, Hilary Fannin, Mark Ravenhill and Stephen Greenhorn, *Sleeping Around* (London: Bloomsbury, 1998), 55.

CHAPTER 7

Russian "In-Yer-Face Theatre" as a Problem or a Process

Elena Dotsenko

The parallels between British and Russian New Drama are rather common place for theater critics, but different aspects of these interrelations are still the subject of scrutiny. There is, first of all, a question concerning the very scope of "Russian New Drama"—in comparison with the British phenomenon of the 1990s–2000s. Another problem to explore is to what extent British In-Yer-Face Theatre could influence the Russian theatrical equivalent and to what extent comparisons can be found in some concrete theatrical phenomena—the plays and performances by Russian and British contemporary authors. This chapter will concentrate on Russian In-Yer-Face Theatre as a problem: what could be called "Russian In-Yer-Face" (in quotations because Alex Sierz's term was originally applied only to the British theater process) or "New" drama. And, is this kind of theater still in existence in the second decade of the twenty-first century? The plays by leading authors of New Drama, such as Ivan Vyrypaev, Vassily Sigarev, Asya Voloshina, and Anjelica Chetvergova, plays commissioned for performance by leading experimental theaters, such as Praktika, Teatr.doc, Gogol-center, and the Chekhov Moscow Art Theatre, and by famous directors, such as Kirill Serebrennikov, Yuri Butusov, Konstantin

E. Dotsenko (✉)
Ural State Pedagogical University, Yekaterinburg, Russia

© The Author(s) 2020
W. C. Boles (ed.), *After In-Yer-Face Theatre*,
https://doi.org/10.1007/978-3-030-39427-1_7

Bogomolov, Mikhail Ugarov, and Elena Gremina, will all be considered. Mark Ravenhill's plays, as they are known or performed in Russia, will also be discussed.

History and Geography of Russian New Drama

"New Drama" in Russian theater is a movement from the last two decades. The trend was formed in the late 1990s and became highly prolific at the start of the millennium. In the 2000s it was possible to speak of several literary schools or, more specifically, theater geographical areas of New Drama. New Dramatic associations were based around talented young authors in cities or regions of the country: city Togliatti school (Vyacheslav and Mikhail Durnenkovs, Vadim Levanov, Yurii Klavdiev); Urals school (the Presnyakov Brothers, Vassily Sigarev, Oleg Bogayev); and Yevgeni Grishkovets and Ivan Vyrypaev, who are from Siberian cities Kemerovo and Irkutsk, respectively. Most of these playwrights are now internationally recognized, as their plays have been produced in not only Moscow and St. Petersburg, but also around the world. A newly published anthology *New Russian Drama*, edited by Maksim Hanukai and Susanna Weygandt, attests to the significance of these works and playwrights, and it includes plays by Vassily Sigarev, the Presnyakov Brothers, Elena Gremina and Mikhail Ugarov, Mikhail Durnenkov, Pavel Pryazhko, Ivan Vyrypaev, Yaroslava Pulinovich, Andrey Rodionov, and Ekaterina Troepolskaya.[1]

Later, it became more popular to identify this growing dramatic movement not as different schools (as the "schools" did not manifest their specific rules or aesthetics), but as "generations" of the New Drama, for example, the generation of thirty-year-old playwrights in the 2010s, like Yaroslava Pulinovich, Yulia Tupikina, and Asya Voloshina. The questions though still remain as to whether "New Drama" is still alive at the moment and has it become more relevant recently? The New Drama movement has become a substantial research topic for many scholars and the subject of several theater conferences. Scholars have noted that the movement was initially drawn to the search for new dramatists (or "new names") for Russian theater in reaction to a theater that was oriented toward and controlled by the directors. Since 1999 numerous festivals of New Russian Drama have taken place.[2]

Some critics see a confrontation brewing between the new drama and theatrical and even political and social mainstreams in the country; thus, Maria Sizova defines "New Drama as the movement of dissent."[3] She believes that a main instigation for the new movement was the social shift of the 1990s in the territory of the former Soviet Union. She noted: "Those changes challenged the young dramatists to want to speak of what happened around them clearly and simply."[4] Maya Merkulova compares the new drama to the theater at the turn of the nineteenth and twentieth centuries, finding the "understanding of exhaustion of traditional forms—of life and art—and necessity to search for something new" as the basis of both "turns of the centuries."[5] From the scholar's point of view, the most common collision of current "new drama" is "the conflict of self-determination, self-identification of individuals in the process of communication."[6] Ilmira Bolotyan speaks of provocative and "generational" basis of New Drama, "when the experience comes not only from the older generation to the younger one, but, vice versa, youth experience is regarded as equal to the most actual, innovative…and 'of status': the youth are 'messianic people' <…> (they developed new theatre places, festivals etc.)."[7] One of the most striking features of the new dramatic aesthetics is "the orientation on 'reality', 'documentary' <…> It is supposed that New Drama is impartially interested in the surrounding reality, studies it with the help of documentary devices (interview, video record, fact gathering and so on). This kind of drama proposes a spectator or reader the very 'real things' on stage."[8]

NEW WRITING: BRITAIN AND/VERSUS RUSSIA

The book *Performing Violence* by Birgit Beumers and Mark Lipovetsky is the first and most reputable English-language study of the current boom in Russian drama and follows the history of the trend's formation and comments on its relevance to the country's cultural life.

> [T]hough it is not proportionally reflected in mainstream Russian theatre…
> New Drama has achieved two important things: first, it has proven the need for the new stage language (mastered by a few directors) and for new plays, whether they are Russian or foreign <…> Second, it has innovative forms of dramatic writing which had a wide-reaching impact on literary production in general and film scripts in particular.[9]

In contrast, in his 2009 Foreword to *Performing Violence* Kirill Serebrennikov, one of the most prominent New Drama directors, says: "New Drama for me means simply that there are new plays … Nowadays young playwrights are encouraged by competitions and awards, and new plays are largely discovered and promoted through these mechanisms."[10]

The director's point of view and the increasingly large amount of new plays over the last few decades in Russia could be correlated with the situation in British theater, as argued by Aleks Sierz:

> In British theatre today, new writing is everywhere. Everywhere, you can watch plays that are examples of new writing; everywhere, you can meet new writers; everywhere there are new writing festivals ... And the new bears the stamp of contemporary ... But what is new writing? Well, it's a very British idea—in the United States of America, very few people have heard of new writing; in Europe it's only sporadically glimpsed.[11]

If British new writing and Russian New Drama are comparable, the question about influences arises and, again, has no unity in its solution. Ilmira Bolotyan asserts that there are several impacts as far as the poetics of current New Drama in Russia is concerned:

> not only Russian 'new wave' ['post-Vampilov dramaturgy', 1970s] and 'late new wave' [Perestroika, mid 80s], but European drama, to some extent, In-Yer-Face Theatre (*sic!*—E.D.) and especially—New Writing, the whole Europe cultural movement, first of all represented by tough social theatre, criticizing the culture of consumerism (Mark Ravenhill, Sarah Kane, Marius von Mayenburg, etc.).[12]

In contrast, M. I. Sizova believes, that "current New Drama is an exclusively Russian language phenomenon, i.e., the New Drama of the turn of the 20th and 21st centuries does not have pan-European roots. Sprouted on the post-Soviet space, it has not got any connection with the European tradition."[13] But even the opponents of British and European influences on Russian New Drama recognize the effect of emissaries from the Royal Court visiting Russia at the end of the 1990s and the beginning of the new century. Sasha Dugdale, at the time a representative of the British Council in Moscow and then a translator of new Russian plays into English, related the history of "the involvement of the Royal Court in Russian New Writing" in her preface to Birgit Beumers' and Mark Lipovetsky's book. She wrote that "many week long seminars for the playwrights" were organized and that "The wave of documentary theatre was an entirely Russian response."[14] In a later interview with John Freedman for *The Theatre Times* Dugdale remarked on her surprise about how the Russian playwrights adopted and adapted documentary theater into their aesthetic.

I don't think any of us were prepared for that....The degree of engagement with verbatim and documentary theater was completely unexpected. And, of course, like anything in Russia, it took its own course completely. It had a very different life form in Russia. It didn't really obey the laws of verbatim, or it did occasionally but it didn't have to. It was very free and liberating and it became very important for a lot of people in new writing.[15]

VERBATIM AND DOCUDRAMA: A SPECIAL ACCENT

Verbatim was the technique that the Royal Court seminars presented in Russia, but it is difficult to make the famous British theater "responsible" for the widespread use and even for the meaning of "verbatim" in the Russian theater process. Verbatim has been often regarded in Russia as the synonym of the New Drama movement. While the term would not actually be familiar to the general public or "ordinary" theater goer, during the last two decades the term has become a necessary subject of study any contemporary drama course in Russian universities. The article by Bolotyan for the *Experimental Dictionary of Russian Drama of the Turn of the Centuries* concentrates on several connotations of the term.[16]

Electronic encyclopedia "Alternative culture" offers a more practical definition to the artistic meaning of "verbatim": "the technique of creating a theatrical performance, presupposed the rejection of the literary play as written in advance. The material for a performance comes from interviews with the representatives of the social group related to the theme and heroes of the planned production. Decoding of the interviews forms an outline and dialogues of Verbatim (documentary play)."[17] It is also important to consider the point of view of Mikhail Ugarov, one of the "docu" directors and a founder of Moscow Theatre.doc. Ugarov and his theater did not want to produce any popular or classical plays— neither Ibsen, nor Aristophanes, for example.[18] The director declared that a theater should not be "a relaxing experience," but instead should cause a physiological effect in the audience, drawing them to a "pain threshold." In essence, he espoused an In-Yer-Face Theatre. A performance "about the reality" for Ugarov means the dark, probably motivated by political dissent, part of the social life in this country.[19] This description shows how the New Drama emulates a tenet of In-Yer-Face Theatre, which states that an In-Yer-Face play "takes the audience by the scruff of the neck and shakes it until it gets the message."[20]

"Closed Circle" of the Theater Persons

There are two more contradictions in this comparative research. First, since the original, British In-Yer-Face Theatre is not based in verbatim drama, it appears difficult to draw the parallels between British and Russian New Drama of the turn of the centuries. But, this is not actually the case. At the very end of the 1990s and at the beginning of the 2000s, Russian readers and spectators became acquainted with the works of Mark Ravenhill, Martin McDonagh, and Sarah Kane. Ravenhill's *Shopping and Fucking* and *Some Explicit Polaroids* were translated into Russian (by Alexander Rodionov) in 1999; McDonagh's *The Lieutenant of Inishmore* in 2001, *The Pillowman* in 2003 (both translated by Pavel Rudnev); and Kane's *Blasted* in 2004 (by Roman Markholia). It is relevant that the plays by Ravenhill were produced by the same directors and at the same theaters where the first Russian New Drama pieces by Vyrypaev, Sigarev, and the Presnyakov Brothers were performed. Ugarov directed *A Number* and *Far Away* by Caryl Churchill. Olga Subbotina directed *Shopping and Fucking* by Ravenhill and the plays by the Presnyakov Brothers at the Center for Playwriting and Directing (CDR). The first production of Ravenhill's play in Russia was practically at the same time (1998–1999) with the first performance of *How I Ate a Dog* by Grishkovets (also at CDR). As Beumers and Lipovetsky observed, "the circle of both theatre companies and playwrights remains fairly closed [sic!]."[21] The authors and directors of Russian New Drama considered British In-Yer-Face Theatre, and especially Mark Ravenhill, to some extent to be part of this "closed circle." Reciprocally, Russian plays were produced at the Royal Court Theatre in London, for example, *Plasticine* (*Plastilin*, 2002), *Black Milk* (*Chernoe Moloko*, 2003), and *Ladybird* (*Bozh'i korovki vozvrashchayutsya na zemlyu*, 2013), all three by Vassily Sigarev. *Terrorism* by the Presnyakov Brothers premiered at the Chekhov Moscow Art Theatre in 2002 and was then translated by Sasha Dugdale into English and directed by Ramin Gray at the Royal Court Theatre in 2003. There were also staged readings at the Traverse Theatre of plays by Mikhail and Vyacheslav Durnenkov and Yury Klavdiev.

The second apparent contradiction concerns theater directing. The New Drama in Russia has been positioned as a playwright-oriented theater, so, it seems, the directors should not be mentioned as a principal part of the movement. But there are New Drama directors as well—new figures and some already famous, as well as several theater persons, passing from dramaturgy to directing and producing. Among the most important directors and producers of the New Drama movement are—or were—Kirill Serebrennikov, Yury Butusov, Konstantin Bogomolov, Mikhail Ugarov, and Elena Gremina.[22] It is worth noting that plays produced by famous directors are better known and get more attention from the public and critics. (The play productions in popular theaters in Moscow and St. Petersburg have a larger resonance for the audience than the award-winning plays of drama contests and festivals, even the most respected ones.) Not only dramatic texts, but real theater process also allows us to understand the dynamics and artistic evolution of the playwright and his dramaturgy.

Ivan Vyrypaev

Ivan Vyrypaev, for example, began his career as a "pure" theater person—an actor, director, and dramatist, then he became a film director and screenwriter, and for several years the art director of the Praktika Theatre in Moscow. Another Siberian born writer Yevgeni Grishkovets, even though he does not necessarily agree with every aspect of Vyrypaev's activity, considers Vyrypaev as "the greatest artist among all his contemporaries."[23] Beginning with his sensational *Oxygen* (*Kislorod*, 2002), the theater of Vyrypaev has pursued philosophical and existential aims. His heroes boldly appeal to Biblical commandments and use the word "God" probably too often,[24] "because there is, in my opinion, a certain force, call it God, energy, consciousness, which creates everything. But He does not create according to the laws that we want to see."[25] At the same time, Vyrypaev's plays are openly naturalistic, but the author combines naturalism of the scenes and blatant language with the high level of artistic convention. Depicting the grotesque is among his favorite devices.

The play *The Drunks* (*P'yanye*, 2012) was chosen for performances by two leading theaters of both Russian capitals: Chekhov Moscow Art Theatre (MAT) and Tovstonogov Bolshoi Drama Theatre (BDT). The performances were directed by Victor Ryzhakov, artistic director of the Meyerhold Theater Center, and Andrey Moguchiy, the artistic director of BDT, respectively. The directors and "qualified" spectators of the performances believe that the play is not actually "about drunks." Practically, all personages of the play are inebriated and desperately swear. Their "Russian disease" is not fully correlated with the European names of the heroes:

Mark, Karl, Laura, Gustave, Linda, Matthias; however, the drunks are searching for God "in their soul" or looking for "the main thing" in their lives, and they succeed, even if in a drunk condition. At one point, Mark says: "God is like a cosmic mob boss we stole money from. He'll only let us out when we give him everything back. <...> We're here until we give it all up, until we give it all up, we're not gonna be let go, you know. So you have to return everything, return everything to the end, and then you're let go, then go, you're free."[26]

The indisputably strong sides of Vyrypaev's dramatic talent are his sense of comedy and the controlled construction of his plays. *The Drunks* consists of several episodes and uses the possibilities of comedy of situations. Several heroes or groups of heroes are not supposed to be acquainted with each other, but, being drunk for different "reasons," they meet each other one night (which produces a comic effect, indeed) and find some truth: *in vino veritas*. The rhythmical patterns of the parts are described by the playwright in the stage directions and found an adequate (though, of course, different by their means) realization in both performances: the drunks cannot actually stand on their feet, are unable to come and go, and farcically "lose their balance and fall into a dirty puddle."[27] Formulated for his earlier play *Oxygen*, the definition of his plays' structure as a "contemporary nonclassical music harmony" can be applied to Vyrypaev's *The Drunks*.[28] But if *Oxygen* was then successfully turned into a film script and then film by the same author, *The Drunks* seems to stay—due to the famous performances—a highly theatrical play. One final quote characterizes Vyrypaev reception and estimation of British drama: "There is just one playwright, who I envy. Yes. McDonagh. I think he writes great pieces. Especially *Three Billboards*. But this is not envy, of course. It is rather a happiness that such a phenomenon exists."[29]

Vassily Sigarev

If Vyrypaev (to some extent) could be compared with McDonagh, Sigarev more often resembles Ravenhill.[30] Kirill Serebrennikov, who directed *Plasticine* by Vassily Sigarev in 2001 and *Some Explicit Polaroids* by Mark Ravenhill in 2002, says the following about Russian New Drama authors:

> Sigarev and Vyrypaev are quite unique: they can extract from their selves or from the environment characters who are terrifyingly human while embodying typological features that echo an entirely independent and different

world. Sigarev's heroes all experience violence, in one way or another; they live in a world of violence, which is condensed. He uses more dark colours than he needs to, and his characters acquire depth thanks to the environment and the secondary characters.[31]

Vassily Sigarev's career is multi-layered too: he is known as a playwright, screenwriter, and film director. The tragicomedy *The Land of Oz* (*Strana OZ*, 2015; Sigarev is the director and one of the screenwriters; another screenwriter is Andrei Ilyenkov) is interesting because of its connection to the American literature classic *The Wonderful Wizard of Oz* by L. Frank Baum. The plot of Baum's tale is not fully recognizable in Sigarev's script, as the new story takes place at the New Year. *The Land of Oz* aims to overcome the traditional happy "New Year film" by providing a contrasting cultural code for Russia, which exists without a real memory about its past. "Instead of focusing on the wizard," Olga Mukhortova writes in her review of the film, "The plot clearly accentuates Lena [the protagonist] and the Ural city [Yekaterinburg] in the magical land, which in Russian can be read in two ways: as 'Oz' and as the number 'zero three' to call for an emergency ambulance."[32] The situations, in which the heroine happens to get involved, are not from a fairy tale at all. There are many examples of life absurdities and in the festiveness of the New Year celebrations during the long (and—again—drunk) holidays in Russia. But the protagonist almost accidentally remains unharmed in the most dangerous encounters with bandits and drug addicts, and her New Year morning in a hospital after an accident looks—tragicomically—almost like a happy ending.

One of the markers of British and Russian New Drama has been the obscene lexis of the plays. A significant challenge to the texts of the New Drama is the Russian law against obscene language, which strictly bans its use during public performances. The law was issued in 2014, and it was therefore not applicable to previous works by Sigarev or many other New Drama playwrights. *The Land of Oz* has been mounted in two versions—with and without the obscenities. Although the experiment of New Drama is connected with the rejection of the "norm" of speech from the beginning, it is probably time (not because of censorship, but due to it as well) to find the new forms to play with language. The New Drama texts have already been overwhelmed with the aggressive lexis. After 2014, the plays by Sigarev and Vyrypaev reveal their artistic potential, as they creatively search for comic neologisms or onomatopoeia to replace Russian profanity on stage—in such a "fairy land" of 03 (Oz).

Political Drama

As far as the protest function of any art is concerned, political drama should be mentioned as a trend or achievement of Russian New Drama of the new century. The theater of cruelty in Russia was first connected with an innovative aesthetic and was regarded by critics and drama scholars as a post-Soviet breakthrough to freedom, if it has any social meaning at all. The political situation in the country has gradually changed, and New Drama theaters, which earlier positioned themselves as politically "neutral" or unengaged, have obtained an ideological position. They are concerned, first of all, with documentary (docu) drama, and Moscow Theatre. doc. is in the vanguard of such a tendency. Theatre.doc. was founded in 2002 by Elena Gremina and Mikhail Ugarov, the key figures for the development of New Drama in Russia. The first interest of the theater was connected with verbatim and other innovative theater techniques. The conscious turn to political theater occurred in 2010 when Ugarov, as a director, and Gremina, as a playwright, created a new performance piece in response to the scandalous and famous "Magnitsky case." The play was called *An Hour and Eighteen*: one hour and eighteen minutes was the duration of Sergei Magnitsky dying in prison without medical help in 2009. Theatre.doc. presented their drama as an investigation of human rights violations in Russia.[33]

More recent politically significant production (and one of the last one for the playwright and director Elena Gremina) was *War is Coming* (*Voina blizko*, 2016). It is composed of three one-act plays: *The Diary from Lugansk* by a non-professional writer, an "ordinary" witness of the war on the South-East Ukraine; *Engagement*, E. Gremina's documentary play, dealing with the materials of Oleg Sentsov case—once again about the violations of the human rights; and a new "text" by Mark Ravenhill about the civilian victims of war in Syria, and, what seems typical for the author of *Product* and *Shoot/Get Treasure/Repeat*, mass media manipulation of the facts.

Mark Ravenhill in Russia

The topic of this chapter may be concerned with the influences of British In-Yer-Face Theatre authors in Russia; however, Mark Ravenhill is rightfully perceived as the leader of British New Drama, but it is rather curious that in Russia he has a reputation associated with political theater. The political theater in Britain has a long and proud tradition, and the In-Yer-Face iteration of Mark Ravenhill had practically nothing in common with this genre of theater. He remarked: "In the 90s, my generation had pretty much given up on politics. They tried to be cool and ironic and detached. Certainly, I feel much more passionate and more engaged now."[34] Due to the Russian performances of Ravenhill's *Shopping and Fucking* and *Some Explicit Polaroids*, Ravenhill acquired a reputation of one of the most famous contemporary playwrights in the Russian cultural space, but the aftershocks of those two first productions were different. *Shopping and Fucking*, directed by Olga Subbotina, was perceived by Russian critics as highly provocative. The translators did not change the original title of the play, but just transliterated the first word "Shopping" into Cyrillic: *Шоппинг & Fucking*. This name has become common for numerous productions of Ravenhill's most influential play in Russia. *Some Explicit Polaroids*—perhaps with the help of Serebrennikov' directing at the Pushkin theater—produced rather specific associations with Russian social and political life of the 1980s–2000s: the wars in Afghanistan and Chechnya, new economic relations on post-Soviet space, the rise of former criminal elements, and the high level of violence in society. So, the playwright could find himself "a socially responsible person," "writing from this socially engaged, responsible viewpoint."[35] The play was perceived as realistic and performed in several theaters around Russia. It seems remarkable that a decade later Russian theaters are less interested in the political plays of Ravenhill or other British playwrights dealing with twenty-first century conflicts and questions about the war on terror. Recent or relatively recent Ravenhill's play are known for their productions at "small" theaters with a proud reputation as an opposition theater, as *Product* at the theater Praktika (director Alexander Vartanov, 2007), *Shoot/Get Treasure/Repeat* at the theater Post in St. Petersburg (directors Dmitrii Volkostrelov and Semen Aleksandrovskii, 2012), and the play for Theatre.doc, mentioned above.

The most recent major plays by Ravenhill have not yet been performed in Russian theaters, though there is "explicit" political potential in *Candide* (2013), *When the terror has ended the victims will dance* (2015), and *The Cane* (2018). In his play, "inspired by Voltaire," Ravenhill presents an interpretation of the classic *Candide* story, as well as an original story of the modern heroine Sophie, killing her own family to save the planet from environmental disaster: "The Earth is not our garden to own and tend."[36] In addition, the playwright criticizes the concept of optimism which is,

Ravenhill believes, particularly relevant nowadays. One can add that this slogan and its critical analysis would be appropriate for Russian spectators of New Drama as well, since there is a new version of *Candide* performed in Moscow. *Candide* in Russian New Drama is written by Andrey Rodionov and Ekaterina Troepolskaya and music by Andrey Besonogov and is "a multimedia musical based on <…> the story of Voltaire, designed by graduates of the British Higher School of Art and Design" and has been released by the Studio of Dmitry Brusnikin under the auspices of the theater Praktika in 2016.[37] The same troupe and the same authors are responsible for the successful *Project SWAN* (2013)—a poetic anti-utopia about migration policy.

Classical adaptations, or secondary texts, are also quite typical for New Drama in order "to problematize the exemplary status of the classics and of literature as a whole."[38] Olga Bagdasaryan believes that "Even imperfect (in the artistic sense) literary remakes can show what kind of recycling strategies are used by modern playwrights and, also, what kind of concepts of history and cultural memory are revealed by the 'remake.'"[39] *Candide* has been dramatically remade many times, especially memorable are musical versions of the piece (e.g., *Candide* by Leonard Bernstein; play by Lillian Hellman).[40] Both new *Candides*—British and Russian—are quite "perfect" (in the artistic sense), but musical adaptations raise a question about the proportion of audience pleasing material versus shocking theatrical conceits, especially as far as In-Yer-Face Theatre nowadays is concerned. The theatrical version by Ravenhill, to some extent, becomes Brechtian, as the songs in *Candide* remind us about epic theater technique. As for Rodionov's poetic dramas, the very shock of those plays is milder than of "real" In-Yer-Face.

SECOND GENERATION OF NEW DRAMA:
FEMALE PLAYWRIGHTS

Antigone: Reduction (Antigona: Reduktsia, 2013) is by Asya Voloshina, a playwright of the second generation of New Drama. More recently, women's writing appears to be where support for the authentic aesthetics of Russian In-Yer-Face Theatre is occurring. This time Sophocles' tragedy is "reduced" to a "Black allegory," according to the author. There is no choir on stage, but instead two personages, called Young Demos and Mature Demos, play the parts of the choir and anti-choir. The play has a quite clear political dimension, as tyranny is in no way new in politics.

> TIRESIAS. Looks like despotism is in fashion…
> International experts are seriously concerned about the readiness of Thebes to accept the new regime. During the time of tyranny there have not been fixed any attempt of rebellion, no protester action or picket, or at least a performance with political overtones.[41]

What is new in this reduced *Antigone* is the structure of the whole history: after her rebellion, aiming to bury her brother, Antigone has vanished, and nobody knows where she is or whether she existed at all.

Asya Voloshina has become a rather popular author nowadays. Another play—this one with an allusion to E.T.A. Hoffmann called *The Man of Fish* (Chelovek iz ryby, 2017)—was produced at Moscow Art Theatre and directed by Yury Butusov. The author has defined the piece as "a Play with no walls." The walls have a real sense of dimension for the play which is set in a communal apartment, and where some characters (non-relatives) share the rooms. But Voloshina's play is a "philological" piece, rather than a social one. Practically, all personages are philologists, though few of them work as teachers at the moment. Their dialogues and monologues pretend to be intellectual, whether they speak of metaphysics or ecology. The parallels between *The Man of Fish* and Hoffmann's *Der Sandmann*, as well as some other appeals to different arts objects, are more or less understood by the characters themselves, including an off-stage heroine—an eight-year old girl—and it makes the play's meaning deeper, and the moments of reception for a spectator—more interesting to decode.

Two other plays by women writers cover economic and psychological problems of lower level social class, but this is not the reason to underestimate the plays as New Drama representative pieces. Plays by Yulia Tupikina, *Shame and Mold* (*Styd and plesen'*, 2014), and Anjelica Chetvergova, *Purple Clouds* (*Fioletovye oblaka*, 2014), are of different "schools" and styles. But they were released in the same year and were devoted (besides other problems of non-successful social life) to motherdaughter relations. Chetvergova's *Purple Clouds* is set in Yekaterinburg and was performed in 2015 at the Center of Contemporary Playwriting in Yekaterinburg, directed by Alexander Vakhov. The heroines of the play belong not only to different generations, but to different social strata, and could any one of them be on the right moral side in their inadaptability to "real" life remains an open question.

It seems remarkable that in both 2014 plays, the main romantic ideal of heroes is associated with the novel *Headless Horseman* by Mayne Reid. But there are no more places for mustangs in our life, or there were no places for them at all, at least in Russia, and thus, the romantic dream is discredited in both plays. Yulia Tupikina's heroine in *Shame and Mold* is a fifty-year old alcohol addicted woman Valya, dreaming of Morris the Mustanger, but the author's sympathy to the protagonist is revealed, more than in Chetvergova's *Purple Clouds*, due to the use of a monologue. M. Merkulova writes:

> Monologue, based on the dialogical nature of the character's self-reflection, dominates in the structure of the dramatic action of current drama. The accentuated disputability of New drama of the previous turn of the century shifts in recent dramaturgy to the area of subconscious of the characters.[42]

To conclude, it is possible to acknowledge that New Drama remains a highly prolific and flourishing trend. Since its start, the movement has been increasingly modifying and has moved from the protest potential of In-Yer-Face Theatre. But new playwrights continue to associate with the New Drama movement in Russia, as in Britain, and there is clearly no reason to believe that this phenomenon will cease any time soon.

Notes

1. *New Russian Drama: An Anthology*, ed. Maksim Hanukai and Susanna Weygandt (New York: Columbia University Press, 2019).
2. The New Drama movement, its origin and background are the subject of several recently issued books: B. Beumers and M. Lipovetsky, *Performing Violence: Literary and Theatrical Experiments of New Russian Drama* (Chicago: Intellect, 2009); A. V. Vislova, *Russkij teatr na slome ehpoh. Rubezh XX–XXI vekov.* [*Russian theatre at the turn of epochs. The turn of XX–XXI centuries*] (M.: Universitetskaya kniga, 2009); and P. Rudnev, *Drama pamyati. Ocherki istorii rossijskoj dramaturgii. 1950–2010-e.* [*Memory drama. Essays on the history of Russian drama. 1950–2010s.*] (M.: Novoe literaturnoe obozrenie, 2018). The festival and competition components of the movement are described in detail in each research.
3. M. I. Sizova, "'Novaya drama': istoriya i geografiya" ["'New drama': history and geography"], in *Novejshaya drama rubezha XX–XXI vv.:*

predvaritel'nye itogi [*The Newest Drama of the Turn of XX–XXI Centuries: Preliminary Results*], ed. T.V. Zhurcheva (Samara: Izd-vo Samarskogo universiteta, 2016), 7.
4. Ibid., 6.
5. M. G. Merkulova, "Novaya drama" ["New drama"], in *Eksperimental'nyi slovar' novejshej dramaturgii [Experimental Dictionary of New Drama]*, ed. S. Lavlinskij and L. Mnih (Siedlce, 2019), 209.
6. Ibid., 212.
7. I. M. Bolotyan, "Novaya drama" ["New drama"], in *Eksperimental'nyi slovar' novejshej dramaturgii [Experimental Dictionary of New Drama]*, ed. S. Lavlinskij and L. Mnih (Siedlce, 2019), 215.
8. Ibid., 216–17.
9. B. Beumers and M. Lipovetsky, *Performing Violence: Literary and Theatrical Experiments of New Russian Drama* (Chicago: Intellect, 2009), xxxiii.
10. K. Serebrennikov, Foreword to *Performing Violence*, x–xi.
11. A. Sierz, *Rewriting the Nation: British Theatre Today* (London: Methuen, 2011), 15–16.
12. Bolotyan, 338.
13. Sizova, 6.
14. S. Dugdale, Preface to *Performing Violence*, xvi–xvii.
15. John Freedman, "Sasha Dugdale recalls the origins of New drama in Russia," *The Theater Times*, November 17, 2014, https://thetheatretimes.com/sasha-dugdale-russia/ (accessed August 10, 2018).
16. I. M. Bolotyan, "Verbatim," in *Eksperimental'nyi slovar' novejshej dramaturgii [Experimental Dictionary of New Drama]*, ed. S. Lavlinskij and L. Mnih (Siedlce, 2019), 45–54.
17. D. Desiateryk, ed. *Al'ternativnaya kul'tura*, Enciklopediya [*Alternative Culture. Encyclopedia*] (Yekaterinburg: Ultra Kul'tura, 2005), https://royallib.com/read/desyaterik_dmitriy/alternivnaya_kultura_entsiklopediya.html#225280 (accessed September 15, 2018).
18. A. Shenderova, Verbatim Inedita, Interview c glavnym geroem [Interview with M. Ugarov], *Teatr* [*Theatre*] No. 34 (2018): 18.
19. Ibid., 19.
20. A. Sierz, *In-Yer-Face Theatre: British Drama Today* (London: Faber and Faber, 2000), 4.
21. B. Beumers and M. Lipovetsky, xxxiii.
22. The year 2018 has become a really sad year for Russian theatre: Mikhail Ugarov, Elena Gremina, Dmitrii Brusnikin passed away, all in their early 60s; Kirill Serebrennikov, the artistic director of Gogol Center, has been under arrest. "Gogol Center is a place of freedom" is written on the website of the theatre.

23. D. Vasil'eva, D. "Vanya Vyrypaev—vazhnejshij hudozhnik iz vsekh moih sovremennikov" ["Vanya Vyrypaev is the most important artist among all my contemporaries"], *IA "Irkutsk online"*, 11 May 2017, https://www.irk.ru/news/articles/20170511/theatre / (accessed July 15, 2018).
24. Theatre critic Tatiana Moskvina criticizes Vyrypaev's plays for "using the Lord's name in vain." From the critic's point of view, the "unintelligible" plays and performances do not demonstrate a good aesthetic taste by their author. (T. Moskvina, "BDT podyhaet, Bol'shoj dramaticheskij teatr zhiv" ["BDT is dying. Bolshoi Drama Theatre is alive"], *Peterburgskij teatral'nyj zhurnal* [*St. Petersburg Theatre Journal*], February 11, 2016, http://ptj.spb.ru/pressa/bdt-podyxaet-bolshoj-dramaticheskij-teatr-zhiv/ [accessed August 21, 2018]).
25. A. Nesterenko, "Filosofiya Ivana Vyrypaeva" Interv'yu ["A philosophy of Ivan Vyrypaev"], *Glagol. Irkutskoe obozrenie* [*Verb. Irkutsk review*], July 30, 2018, https://glagol38.ru/text/30-07-2018/filosofija_ivana_vyrypaeva (accessed September 30, 2018).
26. I. Vyrypaev, *P'yanye* [*The Drunks*], Act 2, Scene 2, https://freedocs.xyz/docx-437600772 (accessed September 30, 2018).
27. Ibid., Act 1, Scene 1.
28. M. Lipoveckij and B. Beumers, *Performansy nasiliya: literaturnye i teatral'nye ehksperimenty "Novoj dramy"* [*Performing Violence: Literary and Theatrical Experiments of New Russian Drama*] (M.: Novoe literaturnoe obozrenie, 2012), 335.
29. Nesterenko.
30. Sigarev was called "Russian Ravenhill" in the 2002 article in *Kommersant* newspaper by P. Sigalov, "Otkrovennye priznaki hita v novoj p'ese Marka Ravenhilla" ["Some explicit features of a hit in a new play by Mark Ravenhill"], *Kommersant*, May 4, 2002, https://www.kommersant.ru/doc/316746 (accessed September 15, 2018).
31. Serebrennikov, xii.
32. O. Mukhortova, Vasilii Sigarev's *The Land of Oz* Program Notes, Revew "Strana O3" Vasiliya Sigareva, http://www.academia.edu/24563181/Vasilii_Sigarevs_The_Land_of_Oz_Program_Notes_Ревью_Страна_ОЗ_Василия_Сигарева (accessed September 25, 2018).
33. Information from Theatre.doc. website: "In an interview to the magazine *Bolshoy gorod* Elena Gremina said that the play about Magnitsky was the first performance in which the Theater.doc moved away from its traditionally neutral political position." See http://www.teatrdoc.ru/person.php?id=7 (accessed September 28, 2018).
34. J. Preston, "The playwright Mark Ravenhill talks about his upcoming adaptation of *Candide* for the RSC and how his cool, ironic years are over,"

The Telegraph, August 21, 2013, https://www.telegraph.co.uk/culture/theatre/theatre-features/10232821/Mark-Ravenhill-interview-I-feel-much-more-passionate-and-engaged-now.html (accessed June 16, 2018).
35. M. Ravenhill, "A touch of evil," *Guardian*, March 22, 2003, https://www.theguardian.com/stage/2003/mar/22/theatre.artsfeatures (accessed May 15, 2018).
36. M. Ravenhill, *Candide* (London: Bloomsbury Methuen Drama, 2001), 35.
37. A. Kiselev, "*Kandid*: spektakl'-trip s vos'mibitnym oformleniem ot vypusknikov Britanki" [*Candide:* performance-trip with 8 bytes decoration from the graduates of the British Higher School of Art and Design], *Afisha Daily*, October 4, 2016, https://daily.afisha.ru/brain/3149-kandid-spektakl-trip-s-vosmibitnym-oformleniem-ot-vypusknikov-britanki/ (accessed September 25, 2018).
38. O. Bagdasaryan, "Secondary Forms in Contemporary Russian Drama: Strategies of Literary Recycling," in *Russian Classical Literature Today: The Challenges/Trials of Messianism and Mass Culture*, ed. Y. Lyutskanov, H. Manolakev and R. Rusev (Cambridge: Cambridge Scholars Publishing, 2014), 108.
39. Ibid., 102.
40. "In fact, I've always loved the Bernstein musical,—Preston cited Ravenhill.—But then I thought, well, *Candide* has been adapted before and no doubt it will be adapted again, so there's not much point in worrying. Frankly, I suspect it's more of a concern for the musicians than it is for me" (Preston).
41. A. Voloshina, *Antigona: redukciya* [*Antigone: Reduction*], in *Luchshie p'esy 2013: sbornik* [*The Best Plays of 2013: a collection*] (M.: NF Vserossijskij dramaturgicheskij konkurs "Dejstvuyushchie lica", Livebook, 2014), 101.
42. Merkulova, 212.

CHAPTER 8

Surfing the Wave of In-Yer-Face Theatre on Australian Shores

Sandra Gattenhof

INTRODUCTION

The influence of In-Yer-Face on theaters outside Britain has been keenly felt on the antipodean shores of Australia. A number of Australian playwrights working in the United Kingdom at the time of the rise of In-Yer-Face in the early 1990s and in the years after demonstrate the need to use theater to interrogate and confront societal violence, victims of history or the media and a re-authoring of the histories. Most recently the legacy of In-Yer-Face has been seen on Australian stages through the work of Australian writer and director Daniel Evans. Using his two plays, *Oedipus Doesn't Live Here Anymore*[1] and *The Tragedy of King Richard the Third*,[2] as touchstones for the discussion, the latter part of the chapter will outline the critical commentary around the reception of these works that can at once interrogate, entertain and horrify. To understand how In-Yer-Face Theatre launched itself in Australian theater landscape, it is important to trace both the migration of the form and the nomenclature used for the Australian species. By this I mean, Australian theater did not merely trans-

S. Gattenhof (✉)
Queensland University of Technology, Brisbane, QLD, Australia
e-mail: s.gattenhof@qut.edu.au

plant In-Yer-Face from the British stage to playhouses in Australia. The arrival heralded an investigation of the In-Yer-Face moniker by playwrights and critics. With the Australian appropriation of the form, I suggest that the naming of the form is probably less important than what the plays set out to do. To help understand the influence of In-Yer-Face Theatre on Evans' work, it is important to outline the presence of In-Yer-Face on Australian stages prior to his two plays—*Oedipus Doesn't Live Here Anymore* and *The Tragedy of King Richard the Third*.

Locating In-Yer-Face Theatre on Australian Shores

In an article about the naming of In-Yer-Face Theatre and other theater forms, Yael Zarhy-Levo states that "[c]ultural groupings into theatre trends, schools or movements ... serve both to distinguish between and connect theatrical developments and to determine their significance."[3] Theater commentators who proffer universal names for perceived or real changes in the theatrical pantheon often try to determine a set of characteristics or tropes that can be seen across a number of playwrights and productions. More often than not, the attribution of a name for a new style, movement or approach is applied post-production or post-publication of the texts where historical hindsight is applied. The playwrights themselves do not try to place themselves into a siloed category, rather they might acknowledge the label, but they avoid using it as a defining characteristic of their oeuvre. Theater critic Alek Sierz is credited with applying the label of "In-Yer-Face Theatre" to playwrights and productions arising in Britain during the 1990s, although the term was first used in American sports journalism during the mid-1970s. No matter where the term came from, what Sierz was able to capture with the use of the phrase was a seismic shift in British theater making and theater sensibility, one that sought to rattle the audience, to question somewhat accepted societal norms around violence, abuse and power. Indeed, Sierz states that "In-Yer-Face theatre is blatantly aggressive or provocative, impossible to ignore or avoid and confrontational."[4] Before settling on the phrase "in-yer-face" to harness the zeitgeist of this theater movement, other phrases such as "new brutalism or theatre of the ennui"[5] and even "neo-Jacobeanism"[6] were applied to recall the violent stage images that were so much *de rigeur* of Jacobean theater. In Germany, the writers aligned to the In-Yer-Face esthetic were named the "Blood and Sperm Generation."[7]

From my vantage point as an Australian contemporary theater scholar, I am interested in exploring Australian playwrights and theater-makers, who, according to the tropes of the In-Yer-Face aesthetic, seem to align themselves to the form. The chapter does not concern itself with an exploration of how British In-Yer-Face Theatre playwrights made it to the stage, although as you will see the first production was not by an Australian playwright. In-Yer-Face Theatre did not arrive on Australian stages at the same time as it did in Britain and Europe. Theater works that could be described as having an In-Yer-Face aesthetic were seen in Australian theaters in the early 2000s, although it is hard to pinpoint an exact production or playwright that led the charge, unlike in Britain with playwrights Sarah Kane, Mark Ravenhill and Anthony Neilson being lauded as the wunderkinds of the style. In my view the first production of significance on Australian soil was by the German playwright Marius von Mayenburg. The controversial play called *Fireface* written by von Mayenburg was programmed as part of the Sydney Festival in 2001.[8] A play largely about incest, it was installed in the small Wharf Theatre 2 at Sydney Theatre Company. Australian performance critic Keith Gallasch described this intense and nightmarish chamber play for five actors. He wrote,

> Benedict Andrews' intense production provides a voyeuristic widescreen theatrical experience, an irregular letter-slot view of family life, so confining that even the family has to stoop at one constricted end of the stage. ... There are no tragic insights, no room for sympathy, a little for empathy. We watch the spread of an appalling condition.[9]

The production, as described above, has all the hallmarks of In-Yer-Face Theatre. I can recall being emotionally shaken by the work and assaulted with loud music by The Prodigy ("Firestarter") and Britney Spears ("...Baby One More Time") relentlessly. For me, this work displayed the rawness of sexual and self-abuse without any mediation. The work both confronted and intrigued me. The content of the piece was not where the confrontation resided. After all, the investigation of incest on the stage could be seen previously in plays such as the Greek tragedy of Sophocles' *Oedipus Rex* and in the early twentieth century in Ibsen's *Ghosts*. The confrontation was palpable in the rendering of the work, that is, how the stage is used to confine the action as though we, the audience, were peering through a letter-box slot. We were positioned as witnesses to violence, maltreatment and pain. The carnage was unrelenting in both word and deed. There was no pause for reflection or redemption for either the characters or the audience. For me, this was a most uncomfortable place to reside, but I also recognized the tone of the work as similar to the increasing news reportage of family violence in the suburbs near to where I lived. At the time of viewing the work, I was not aware of In-Yer-Face Theatre, yet in hindsight this is exactly what I witnessed. If we apply the tropes of In-Yer-Face Theatre or "Blood and Sperm" theater, von Mayenburg's *Fireface* had a

> feeling that your personal space [was being] threatened ... used explicit scenes of sex and violence to explore the extremes of human emotion ... [it] involved the breaking of taboos, insistently using the most vulgar language ... and [at] its cruel best, [it was] so intense that audiences feel—emotionally if not literally—that they have lived through the events shown on stage.[10]

But could this actually be called an Australian entry into the In-Yer-Face Theatre scene? Yes and no. A German writer's text rendered by an Australian director and cast—this was a halfway version of Australian In-Yer-Face Theatre.

ADAPTING AND ADOPTING IN-YER-FACE THEATRE FROM BRITISH STAGES TO THE AUSTRALIAN SCENE

As noted previously, the focus of this chapter rests how Australia playwrights and theater-makers adapt and adopt In-Yer-Face Theatre from British stages to the Australian scene. Australian theater director Benedict Andrews, who directed the 2001 version of von Mayenburg's *Fireface*, explains how he was yearning for a different form of theater than what he had previously seen and been involved with in Australia. Andrews says, "for my whole adult life I've looked to Britain and the Royal Court. ... When I was starting out I was so hungry to read plays that didn't look like other plays, by authors like Sarah Kane and Martin Crimp."[11] Another Australian playwright Angela Betzien (*The Kingswood Kids, Princess of Suburbia, Hoods, The Orphanage Project, The Dark Room*) was also influenced by her time at London's Royal Court where the In-Yer-Face zeitgeist was nurtured. In Betzien's case she undertook a residency at the Royal Court Theatre to get her dose of the new and develop the hallmark of her plays that "use the maltreatment of young people as a metaphor for the rankness and corruption of innocence in the broad Australian imaginary."[12] The tentacles of the British version of In-Yer-Face Theatre stretched to the Australian shores via young firebrand playwrights and directors as they traveled to London's Royal Court and back home to Australia.

In analyzing reviews of Australian versions of In-Yer-Face Theatre such as *Fireface*, it is uncommon to find the term applied. Keith Gallasch, in an overview of the Sydney Festival production of *Fireface*, used the term by saying the production employed "in-yer-face stylistic influences ... associated with the 1990s theatre scene."[13] A review of Angela Betzien's *The Dark Room* at Belvoir Street Theatre, Sydney, spoke of the production as being "80 minutes of extraordinary, in-your-face emotional and theatrical intensity ... that will ... unsettle you."[14] Both reviews note the movement and its aesthetic qualities but shy away from directly attributing the works to the In-Yer-Face Theatre genre. In 2011, Sydney Theatre Company published a short treatise on the movement but embraced the term "psycho-absurdism" to define the theater form on Australian shores. In writing the overview of the movement, Matthew Clayfield attempted to scope out the impact of the British renegade In-Yer-Face playwrights noting, "[i]n the decade-and-a-bit since, Australia's stages have seen their fair share of such productions."[15] He goes on to note two productions of Sarah Kane's plays—the 2001 production of *Blasted* for La Boite Theatre Company and Alyson Campbell's 2007 production of *4:48 Psychosis* for Red Stitch—but believes that largely the In-Yer-Face aesthetic had "moved on from the sensationalism of 'blood and sperm' to that of 'psycho-absurdism.'"[16]

This short history of In-Yer-Face Theatre in Australia shows that it is difficult to call this theater by a single moniker—In-Yer-Face, blood and sperm, new brutalism, theatre of the ennui, neo-Jacobeanism, psycho-absurdist, postmodern or even at a stretch postdramatic. What unites all the names for the aesthetic or movement, regardless of location—Britain, Germany or Australia—is a sensibility and series of theatrical techniques that break with conventional theatrical codes to "depart from naturalism, especially those of the well-made three-act drama."[17] This dismemberment of psychological realism in the theater forced a visceral engagement of sensation from the audience by taking them on journeys to delve into the dark, violent and transgressive corners of the human experience. For Sierz, "In-Yer-Face theatre is about emotion not shock tactics."[18]

Daniel Evans and In-Yer-Face Theatre in Australia

Unlike Aleks Sierz, who states that the In-Yer-Face movement is over in Britain, I believe that this theater form is very much alive on the Australian stage.[19] The Australian award-winning playwright, director and producer who is most strongly emblematic of In-Yer-Face Theatre is Daniel Evans. Before investigating what the remnants of In-Yer-Face look like on Australian stages, let me provide some insight to Daniel Evans. His professional biography tells us that "his theatrical work is about new mythologies for unreliable futures. Inspired by Pop culture, spurred on by the blur between performer-spectator."[20] My addition to the description of Evans would be that he is an eclectic pop culture referent who is able to speak directly to audiences about the times we live in or choose to turn away from. His works are both touching and traumatic, assaulting the senses and the sensibilities of the audience. Evans is aware of how to wield emotion on stage and he is not afraid to show it. He is familiar with the term In-Yer-Face Theatre and recognizes the tropes of the esthetic. He says that

> starting out as playwright means that you read everything you can get your hands on. I read Mark Ravenhill's *Shopping and Fucking* found out that it sat alongside a suite of works that began with Sarah Kane's *Blasted*. These plays were critiquing the state of affairs in the Cool Britannia years. I had never read plays before that were so economical in their dialogue or so radical and violent in their ideas. That violence shook me and made me really aware of what you could do on stage.[21]

Evans went onto investigate Kane's rationale for her writing that he described as a "wake up call for the middle-class theater going audience."[22] Evans relishes the idea of being able to aggressively rub the noses of his audience in something they may not want to observe. Like Kane, his work seeks to shock an audience to lead them into thinking something different. However, Evans does not aspire to rekindle In-Yer-Face in the shape of the British movement in the 1990s. He believes that the movement has waned, but in works by selected Australian playwrights there are still hallmarks of the In-Yer-Face genre or form that we can still see today.

The following two sections will excavate two of Evans' theater works—*Oedipus Doesn't Live Here Anymore* and *The Tragedy of King Richard the Third*, written in collaboration with Marcel Dorney—as contemporary illustrations of how In-Yer-Face aesthetic developed on Australian stages.

Both examples draw on a personal interview with Evans, production reviews, public interviews by journalists with the playwright, and the texts to develop a discourse on how both works could easily fit into the In-Yer-Face movement in 1990s Britain, but more importantly how the tropes of the form have been transplanted onto Australian shores almost thirty years since the founding of the movement.

OEDIPUS DOES SUBURBIA

Oedipus Doesn't Live Here Anymore won the Queensland Premier's Drama Award and had two professional seasons. One season was at Queensland Theatre Company in 2015 and the other programmed at Australian Theatre for Young People in 2017. The play pulls the ancient story of Oedipus, who kills his father Laius (unknowingly on a road outside Thebes) marries his mother Jocasta (again, initially unknowingly) and ultimately blinds himself with pins from his dead mother's dress after she hanged herself, into modern Australian suburbia. The Greek chorus is replaced by a group of young people who are left behind after "the chain of incest, murder and suicide has run its course ... and the adults have decided to never mention Oedipus and his family again."[23] *Oedipus Doesn't Live Here Any More* explores what happens after the tragedy of Oedipus. In the play Evans situates the action in a place "tattooed with tragedy, and what happens to the community that are left behind."[24] Evan's version of *Oedipus* transplants the happenings in Thebes to an outer suburb of an Australian urban center and transposes Theban royalty into a working-class family. The story is told through four young narrators all in their teens or early twenties. Somerville describes the production in a review as a "street wise anarchistic blend of modern-day horror and ancient Greek mythology."[25] By repositioning the site of unspeakable tragedies from ancient Thebes to Australian surburbia, the murders, abuse, suicides and bashings are placed in sharp juxtaposition to what audiences may see in the daily news stream. Using this framing device, the tale is placed as not so distant from the audiences' immediate experience. Evans is interested in using mythical stories to comment on contemporary times. The hook into Oedipus, for him, was about family. Evans notes, "[h]e was the original motherfucker. I loved that everyone's popular reaction to that myth is to say 'how could you ever do that'? And then my response is 'how can you ever normalize that?'"[26] A review of the production describes the aesthetic of the production as a "... delicate balance of graphic horror and broad comedy [that] allows us to safely engage one of the enduring problems of human existence."[27] The story of Oedipus even in its original form presents a dystopian future. Evans says, "that we need to look for where these myths and ancient figures come up in our society today."[28] In re-versioning the story of Oedipus, Evans was influenced by two murder-suicide events that occurred in his own home-town. He said, "it forced me to question how far have we come from Oedipus and how close to the surface are such violent impulses in each of us."[29] For the reviewer Robbie O'Brien, the work asks the audience to ponder on "how do we respond in the face of something, so many things, that are truly dreadful."[30]

Evans' story of a suburban Oedipus has no redemptive end. It imagines a scenario of familial and societal dysfunction by presenting a dystopian future that the audience has the power to change if they have the will to do so. In this tale of Oedipus, the audience is actively made complicit in the staged events as they are "cast as a party of rubberneckers drawn to the scene of the crime. Tragedy tourists, if you like," and the relationship between performer and viewer is described as "not a comfortable one."[31] In creating *Oedipus Doesn't Live Here Any More*, Evans wanted his audience to walk away and reflect on how fast we move through tragedies today, which was the original thesis for the play. Evans notes, "…this idea of the 24-hour news cycle is actually becoming more of a 4-hour news cycle where a victim tragedy and tragic event are kind of spun over and out by us so quickly that I wonder what that's doing for our levels of empathy and generosity."[32] In re-versioning *Oedipus*, Evans wanted to ask the question, "how do we deal with tragedy in the 21st century?"[33] Evans believes that when the tragedy was played out in the theaters of ancient Greece, there was time for the events to be considered and discussed, but in our 24-hour driven news cycle such contemplation is truncated and we, the audience, just churn through tragedy without the time for reflection. *Oedipus Doesn't Live Here Any More* asks the audience to think through the question of "who is the biggest motherfucker—the guy who did this to his family or the people who stood by and watched it happen?"[34] Evans is essentially asking the audience to reflect on how complicit they might be in devouring similar events played out daily in the media.

In keeping with the aesthetic frame of In-Yer-Face, the story does not adhere to the structures associated with realism. We do not see a street, a house or a backyard in outer suburbia rendered like a realistic set of a teledrama. Instead the "space is spare and functional (excluding the epic graffiti backdrop) and the lights starkly mark the scene changes, which pushes the focus to the script and the performers."[35] The choice of the pared-back set design is in keeping with the will of the earlier In-Yer-Face theatermakers to "transform the language of theatre, making it direct, raw and explicit."[36] Evans does not shy away from the fact that in taking the story of Oedipus and his family into a contemporary context that he was initially "drawn to the icky factor first and foremost."[37] However, in developing the text, Evans was aware of how the motive of In-Yer-Face was, as Aleks Sierz records, "not to titillate but to spread the knowledge of what human beings are capable of."[38] With this in mind, Evans sought to update the story with people and places that would be recognizable to his audience. Evans creates "a ghetto in city suburbia" replete with graffiti sprayed walls, detritus of everyday life and young people.[39] A place that news bulletins like to depict as places where horrors occur. Evans' aim is not to water down the horrors but to ensure that the ancient tale maintains all its power and still had the ability to shock. Thus, in keeping with the In-Yer-Face aesthetic to use language as power, the text is a "mix of direct address and dialogue related in the arid, profanity-strewn language of urban Australia."[40]

THE PAST IS NOT A WELL-MADE PLAY

Playing in the year of the 400th anniversary of the death of William Shakespeare, *The Tragedy of King Richard the Third* was commissioned by La Boite Theatre Company in Brisbane for the 2016 season. The play was created by Marcel Dorney and Daniel Evans not to celebrate the anniversary but rather to interrogate how history is made, propagated and needs to be challenged by the public. Evans describes this theater work as "the book of Richard."[41] He says that what an audience sees played out over ninety minutes are testimonies of a few historical and fictional figures who helped shape the character of Richard—his childhood sweetheart who becomes Lady Anne, his sworn family enemy Margaret of Anjou (wife of the dead and vanquished King Henry VI), William Shakespeare himself actively creating the story, and an unnamed servant sent to kill the two princes in the Tower. In taking such an approach Evans develops, as he says, "a multi-lens attack on one myth which is very deliberate as what [the play is trying to show] is that nobody knows history, least of all the characters involved with Richard."[42]

When asked why he wanted to adapt the text, Evans noted that it attracted him because through both history and tale Richard the Third is "widely acknowledged as one of the world's greatest villains."[43] Like the retelling of incest in *Oedipus Doesn't Live Here Any More*, Evans is once again interested in how tragedy, both real and imagined, is played out in ordinary circumstances. For Evans, tragedy is not something removed from the everyday experience. "At the heart of In-Yer-Face theatre" says Evans, "is the truth and the stories that people hold within themselves. Such truths are often more difficult to deal with than anything that can be invented."[44] Evans notes that in every process he has been involved with decisions had to be made about playing the truth for the audience. He says, it is "a delicate balancing act to ensure that the material doesn't become too exploitative or pornographic so he does not lose the audience."[45]

Evans did not initially think about how *The Tragedy of King Richard the Third* was a neat fit into the Australian In-Yer-Face pantheon. It was his co-writer Marcel Dorney who noted that the text reminded him of the In-Yer-Face movement. Buzacott's review of the production positioned it as "a phantasmagoria of theatrical shock tactics of the kind made notorious two generations ago by Howard Barker and Peter Handke, and still beloved by screw-the-audience, change-the-world drama majors today."[46] Just as Shakespeare provided King Richard the Third words of direct address to the audience in the original version, the version by Dorney and Evans has characters directly addressing the audience and exposing the fictive aspect of what is happening on stage. Sarah Kanowski characterized the production as postmodern or post-Brecht in that it repositions the emotional connection beyond an empathetic response to character and situation.[47] In a work that presents the audience with a sequence of moments seemingly without chronological order or logic *The Tragedy of King Richard the Third* questions where emotional connection is located. On the topic of emotional engagement by the audience, Evans notes, "… like the theater-goers of Brecht the audience is allowed to find emotional resonances in places and aspects which are not expected. … emotional response becomes part of the intellectual and ultimately political experience."[48]

One of the defining characteristics of In-Yer-Face Theatre is that it eschews closure. "In rebellion against the classic well-made play … nineties writers preferred to write work which didn't finish with a climax in the 'right' place."[49] Or, as Evans says in reference to his version of Richard the Third's story, "the past is not a well-made play."[50] The employment of a non-teleological structure can be disconcerting for an audience who regularly binges on Netflix crime dramas. They like to know who has done it and if good triumphs over evil. This disruption of a cause-and-effect plot structure commences from the moment the play opens. The narrator, Naomi, addresses the audience. She speaks the prologue on a large raised platform that will come to represent "a car park or a battlefield or a teenage bedroom, and so on."[51] Naomi outlines to the audience how they might like to engage their imaginations to place objects onto the platform as indications of places and spaces but carefully notes that "we know that you don't all know the same thing."[52] The opening, both imaginative and didactic, challenges the audience "on how we bring our interpretation to what we see, declaring that anyone who says they know history is lying or self-deceived."[53] The prologue also links the action throughout the production into Lehmann's idea that postdramatic theater "is a theatre of incompleteness," one that "retreats from meaning and synthesis."[54] As such it is theater form that demands a change in perception from audiences. At the end of *The Tragedy of King Richard the Third*, the audience is confronted with the idea that the story never happened or at least that the story of King Richard the Third changes depending on who tells it and from what time-anchored vantage point it is told. In this sense both history and reality are slippery beasts. The text plays as follows:

NAOMI	(*Our compere, our guide, our architect into the world begins to take us away from here, neatly... The others are in their own reverie, thinking about Richard, thinking about Henry, thinking about what they'll leave behind. Not NAOMI though: there's a sense that she—like ELIZABETH, like all leaders—have a job to do—give a story an ending:*)
	Let's say this is a car park.
AMY	And it changes.
NAOMI	It's not.
	But let's agree it is.
PACHARO	And it changes.
NAOMI	There are divots—holes—across the bitumen.
HELEN	And it changes.
NAOMI	And let's agree to fill those holes with dirt.
AMY	And it keeps changing.
NAOMI	Let's agree to smooth this whole place over with concrete.
KID	And changing again.
NAOMI	Let's agree that nothing/happened here.[55]

Like *Oedipus Doesn't Live Here Any More* the set is simple and flexible, but this time is in the round. It is a "central slab of marble-like stage with a raised lip (for containing the gore) that melds into the black pit surrounding it."[56] The actors are bombarded with water, fake blood and rain throughout the ninety minutes of stage action "and we [the audience], are always participating, as observer or protagonist. We experience both roles create the history."[57] Throughout the text, the players are variously named either by their real names or by the name of the historical character. It could be argued that this is a whiff of Hans Thies Lehmann coming through with the adoption of a postdramatic theater trait known as "irruption of the real" in which a situation or an event enters the fictive cosmos to deliberately disrupt the illusion.[58] Likewise, the text places historic figures often from differing periods of time in conversation with each other as well as the actors playing themselves in the present day. By using fragmentation in this way, Dorney and Evans provide a more augmented picture of who Richard the Third might be. Thus, the text forces the audience to engage with the notions of who writes history, who has permission to tell history and how violent events of the past refract on the violent present. As such, Marcel Dorney and Daniel Evans' *The Tragedy of King Richard the Third* is the kind of theater that finds a home in the Australian In-Yer-Face movement because it has "an unusual power to trouble the audience emotionally, to contain material that questions our ideas about who we are."[59]

Conclusion

Since the rise of the In-Yer-Face "aesthetic style" in Britain, the form has aimed to "kick down the door of complacency in the theatre."[60] Both in Britain and in Australia, the discussion in this chapter points to the notion that In-Yer-Face Theatre has never been about merely depicting explicit violent acts or exploring subjects understood as taboo. The theater aesthetic has been engaged by playwrights like Evans to unsettle and destabilize an audience's sense of safety and anonymity within the dark confines of a theater. In tracing the legacy of In-Yer-Face Theatre on Australian shores, it is easy to locate parallels between the Sarah Kane (the British writer credited with starting the form) and the work of Australian playwright Daniel Evans. Both Kane and Evans are interested in taking apart and innovating within the theater form. In particular, both writers eschew a teleological plot structure. Kane's *Blasted* employed a structure of two distinct halves using naturalism in the first act and symbolism in the second act.[61] Evans' innovation in both *Oedipus Doesn't Live Here Anymore* and *The Tragedy of King Richard the Third* reshapes ancient stories by placing action from the past into a present context. Evans achieves this through a process of re-versioning characters and the circumstances using dramatic time shifts and appropriating text from the original sources intermingled with contemporary conversation. These approaches have seen both Kane and Evans draw criticism with a particular focus on the use of explicit violence and depictions of abuse coupled with raw and sometimes profane language. Equally, comments about the work of Kane and Evan point to the engagement of humor as a device to unsettle the audience who is asked to question how levity could be possible. Critical reviews of the productions note Kane's use of "bleak humour"[62] and say that Evans' writing is "brutal, violent and often very witty."[63] The connection between Kane and Evans, writing twenty years apart, is the way in which their theater works are uncompromising in the use of brutal truth without redemption or closure for the audience. Mark Ravenhill described Kane's work as being "connected with a form of theatre that is quite confrontational because it doesn't reassure you … it doesn't explain things."[64] Evans describes his work in a similar way by saying that he is attracted to the In-Yer-Face Theatre form because, "you can still take the audience by the scruff of the neck and put their face in something and not let them go."[65] The potency of the form Sierz says is that "In-Yer-Face theatre is not a movement … it's an aesthetic style."[66] No matter how this theater form is named—In-Yer-Face, blood and sperm, new brutalism, theatre of the ennui, neo-Jacobeanism, psycho-absurdist—the unifying trope between the beginnings in Britain and the Australian adaptation of the form is the way In-Yer-Face Theatre seeks to break the shackles of naturalism and the well-made play to explore the darkness of the human condition. Or, to use the words of Sarah Kane, "[i]t is important to commit to memory events which have never happened—so they never happen."[67] In these uncertain times, In-Yer-Face Theatre productions are beacons that have potential to speak truth to power.

Notes

1. Daniel Evans, *Oedipus Doesn't Live Here Any More* (Brisbane: Playlab Press, 2015).
2. Marcel Dorney and Daniel Evans, *The Tragedy of King Richard The Third* (Performance Draft unpublished, 2015).
3. Yael Zarhy-Levo, "Dramatists under a label: Martin Esslin's The Theatre of the Absurd and Aleks Sierz' In-Yer-Face Theatre," *Studies in Theatre and Performance* 31, no. 3: 316.
4. Aleks Sierz, *In-Yer-Face Theatre: British Drama Today.* (London: Faber & Faber, 2001), 4.
5. Ibid., 30.
6. Aleks Sierz, "Still In-Yer-Face? Towards a critique and a summation," *New Theatre Quarterly* 18, no. 1 (2002): 18.
7. Ibid., 17.
8. *Fireface* (original German title: *Feuergesicht*) by Marius von Mayenburg was written in 1997 and first performed in 1998 at the Munich Kammerspiele.
9. Keith Gallasch, "Degrees of pathos: Sydney performance," *RealTime*, February-March 2001: 23, http://www.realtimearts.net/article/41/5567.
10. Sierz, "Still," 18–19.
11. Alice Saville, "In Conversation with Benedict Andrews," *Auditorium Magazine*, Spring 2014, https://www.auditoriummag.com/benedictandrews.
12. Stephen Carleton, "Scan 2003: Angela Betzien," *RealTime*, October–November 2003: 4, http://www.realtimearts.net/article/issue57/7176.
13. Gallasch, "Degrees," 23.
14. "Review: The Dark Room Belvoir Street Theatre Sydney," Crikey, https://blogs.crikey.com.au/curtaincall/2011/11/14/review-the-dark-room-belvoir-street-theatre-sydney/ (accessed February 10, 2018).
15. Matthew Clayfield, "Feature: In Yer Face," *Sydney Theatre Company Magazine*, June 2011, https://www.sydneytheatre.com.au/magazine/posts/2011/june/feature-in-yer-face.
16. Clayfield, "Feature: In Yer Face."
17. Sierz, *In-Yer-Face*, 6.
18. Sierz, "Still," 19.
19. Ibid., 18.
20. "Daniel Evans," The Good Room, https://thegoodroom.com.au/artists/ (accessed December 9, 2019).
21. Daniel Evans, Personal Interview with Sandra Gattenhof, January 12, 2018.

22. Ibid.
23. Robbie O'Brien, "A stunning play, immensely enjoyable for all its gruesomeness," *Arts Hub*, accessed February 10, 2018, http://performing.artshub.com.au/news-article/reviews/performing-arts/robbie-obrien/oedipus-doesnt-live-here-anymore-248250.
24. Kate Atkinson, "Oedipus Doesn't Live Here Anymore, But Dan Evans Does," *scenestr*, http://scenestr.com.au/arts/oedipus-doesn-t-live-here-anymore-but-dan-evans-does (accessed February 10, 2018).
25. Mel Somerville, "REVIEW: Oedipus Doesn't Live Here Anymore," *Alt Media*, https://altmedia.net.au (accessed February 11, 2018).
26. Evans, Personal Interview.
27. O'Brien, "A stunning play."
28. Evans, Personal Interview.
29. Ibid.
30. O'Brien, "A stunning play."
31. Jason Blake, "Oedipus Doesn't Live Here Anymore Review: Greek Tragedy Goes For Spin in 'Burbs," *Sydney Morning Herald*, June 13, 2017, https://www.smh.com.au/entertainment/oedipus-doesnt-live-here-anymore-review%2D%2Dgreek-tragedy-goes-for-spin-in-burbs-20170611-gwovj0.html.
32. Atkinson, "Oedipus."
33. Evans, Personal Interview.
34. Ibid.
35. O'Brien, "A stunning play."
36. Sierz, "Still," 20.
37. Evans, Personal Interview.
38. Sierz, "Still," 20.
39. Somerville, "REVIEW".
40. Blake, "Oedipus Doesn't."
41. Daniel Evans, "Richard III Out of the Car Park," interview by Sarah Kanowski, *ABC Radio Books and Arts Program*, June 8, 2016, audio, http://mpegmedia.abc.net.au/rn/podcast/2016/06/bay_20160608_1043.mp3.
42. Ibid.
43. Ibid.
44. Evans, Personal Interview.
45. Ibid.
46. Martin Buzacott, "La Boite's The Tragedy of King Richard III sets out to shock," *The Australian*, May 31, 2016, https://www.theaustralian.com.au/arts/stage/la-boites-the-tragedy-of-king-richard-iii-sets-out-to-shock/news-story/cadb20cfe3ddaf1b4d597efa6ff12514.
47. Evans, "Richard III."

48. Ibid.
49. Sierz, "Still," 19–20.
50. Evans, "Richard III."
51. Dorney and Evans, *The Tragedy of King Richard The Third*, 1.
52. Ibid., 3.
53. Kate Byrne, "The Tragedy Of King Richard III @ La Boite Review," *scenestr*, May 30, 2016, https://scenestr.com.au/item/7215-the-tragedy-of-king-richard-iii-la-boite-revie.
54. Hans-Thies Lehmann, *Postdramatic Theatre*, trans. Karen Jürs-Munby (London: Routledge, 2006), 88.
55. Dorney and Evans, *Tragedy*, 87.
56. Byrne, "The Tragedy."
57. Ibid.
58. Lehmann, *Postdramatic Theatre*, 86.
59. Sierz, *In-Yer-Face*, 30.
60. Sierz, "Still," 21–23.
61. Sarah Kane, *Blasted and Phaedra's Love* (London: Methuen, 1996).
62. Aleks Sierz, "The Nasty Nineties," accessed January 13, 2018, http://www.inyerfacetheatre.com/credits.html.
63. Ben Newtz, "Oedipus Doesn't Live Here Anymore." *Daily Review*, June 13, 2017, https://dailyreview.com.au.
64. Sierz, "The Nasty Nineties."
65. Evans, Personal interview.
66. Sierz, "Still," 21.
67. Sierz, "Still," 20.

PART III

A Movement's Aftermath

CHAPTER 9

The Hidden Dialogue Between Sarah Kane and Edward Bond: The Dramaturgy of Accident Time and Ethical Subjectivities

Chien-Cheng Chen

Since Sarah Kane admitted that Edward Bond's *Saved* (1965) was where she "learned to write dialogue" and that the baby-stoning scene in *Saved* made her realize that "there isn't anything you can't represent on stage,"[1] it is logical to assume that Kane was influenced mainly by Bond's early plays. Moreover, considering that the premiere of *Saved* also caused scandal at the Royal Court in 1965, it is understandable to regard Bond's initial support for *Blasted* (1995) as a sympathetic vindication for its radicalness. However, beyond these obvious associations, in the following I argue that it is the hidden dialogue between Kane's and Bond's later plays and theory that can be more fruitful in understanding the dramaturgical and theoretical relationship between the two playwrights. Although there are textual evidences that illustrate the mutual influence between Bond and Kane, what interests me more is the hidden dramaturgical and ethical logic common to their plays. Through exploring this often-neglected connection, we can understand the reason behind Bond's appreciation of Kane. Correspondingly, Bond's later theory can also shed

---

C.-C. Chen (✉)
Taipei National University of the Arts, Taipei, Taiwan

new light on Kane as a thinker who raises ethical questions through dramatizing violence and madness.

Apart from Greek tragedians and Shakespeare, Kane is the only contemporary playwright on whose plays Bond continues to make comments. Bond's observations on Kane suggest that his defense for Kane is not extemporary but presupposes his theoretical understanding of humanity and its relation to drama, as he states: "To understand Sarah Kane you must understand the origin and logic of drama, which is also the logic of imagination and humanness. [...] She is the crisis of modern drama"[2]— this "logic of drama" is what Bond seeks to formulate in his theoretical writings. During the late 1980s and early 1990s, there was a shift in Bond's theoretical writings from a Marxist understanding of the subject as determined by social-economic conditions to a post-Marxist understanding of the subject as structured by the development of the psyche. Bond's appreciation of Kane's plays is concomitant with his new theorizing about subjectivity and dramaturgy. In concluding his defense for Kane's *Blasted* at the Royal Court, Bond states: "The humanity of *Blasted* moved me. I worry for those too busy or so lost that they cannot see its humanity."[3] While Bond's use of "humanity" may seem humanistic, in Bond's theory of subjectivity, humanity remains a "gap" that cannot be filled by any predetermined values. In order to demonstrate what "the humanity of *Blasted*" means, my analysis of the hidden dialogue between Kane and Bond starts with Bond's theory of subjectivity in relation to dramatic imagination. I will proceed to argue that Kane's and Bond's dramatic imagination of violence and madness can be best understood through the dramaturgy of "accident time," and I will analyze the ethical implications of this dramaturgy to conclude this chapter.

IMAGINATION, VIOLENCE, AND MADNESS

According to Bond, in terms of development, the first stage of the subject is the "neonate," and the neonate cannot differentiate self from non-self at this stage. When the neonate becomes self-conscious, the pre-socialized self emerges. For the neonate and the pre-socialized self, the existential imperative is to seek justice, that is, the right to exist in this world. However, when the self enters the society and becomes socialized, the self must adapt to the injustice of society. In order to cope with social injustice, the self must use the power of imagination to imagine—through dramatic imagination, the socialized self can potentially return to the pre-socialized self and re-enter the gap of meaning in which the established social values are suspended. Bond uses "radical innocence" to designate this imperative to seek justice and the ability of creation. Although imagination may be "corrupted" by the dominant ideology in society, radical innocence operates as a relentless questioning about the legitimacy of the ideological status quo.

I contend that Bond's appreciation of Kane's dramaturgical use of violence and madness derives from his theory of subjectivity, in which the subject holds the potential to resist the status quo of society in order to reimagine reality. According to Bond's theory, the disruptive structure of *Blasted* corresponds to the working of subjective imagination, which redistributes the order of meaning of the "rationalized" normal world and reveals the hidden logic of reality, as demonstrated in the second half of the play. For Bond, in the second half of *Blasted*, "a self that in order to *be* must seek meaning, yet is abandoned in meaningless nothingness."[4] Bond by no means presupposes what new meanings can be gained in the world of meaningless nothingness. Rather, he proposes that, faced with the posthumous society dominated by totalizing reason, dramatic imagination must be activated to imagine otherwise.

This imagined dramatic world may abound in violence. However, for Kane and Bond, violence can serve as a means of disrupting the sanitized surface of social reality. As regards violence, Kane states: "I think Edward Bond is right in the sense that if we had a human need for violence—a kind of biological need for it we could die out as a species. […] So I suppose it comes from the situation we've created for ourselves."[5] In addition, Kane differentiates the infant's natural violence for survival from socially determined violent actions such as murder.[6] Both Kane and Bond oppose the idea that violent aggressiveness is intrinsic to humanity. For them, although human beings are potentially violent, humanity cannot be defined solely through violence. They never dramatize violence for the sake of violence, and neither do they use violence to demonstrate that some people are intrinsically depraved. Instead, extreme moments of violence in their plays are deployed to investigate how humanity can be defined.

Another method to examine humanity dramatically is through the structure of madness. In "Commentary of *The War Plays*" (1991), Bond states: "The brain's higher—now its lower—functions are the foundations of our psyche."[7] The brain's "higher functions" refer to radical innocence; however, since people need to adapt to society, these "higher functions" must be rendered inactive. Intriguingly, the speaker in *4.48 Psychosis*

(2000) also states that only by shutting down "the higher functions of the brain" can he or she be "capable of living."[8] The speaker is also troubled by the restraining effects of psychiatric institutions, in which the speaker's real mental state cannot be apprehended. Only when the speaker becomes what is defined as "mad" can he or she feel sane. The psychiatric hospital, instead of being a space for mental rehabilitation, becomes another traumatizing site.

Kane's articulation of concepts such as reason, madness, and sanity in this play discloses the logic by which she understands the relationship between reason and madness and that between sanity and insanity. In an interview, Kane makes explicit how she thinks about madness: "I think to a certain degree you have to deaden your ability to feel and perceive. In order to function you have to cut out at least one part of your mind. Otherwise you'd be chronically sane in a society which is chronically insane."[9] This subjective feeling of being alienated by the "chronic insanity" of society resonates with Bond's idea that the subject is destined to become socially mad since society itself is mad. For Bond, while we are faced with different forms of "social madness" such as Auschwitz and war, the function of drama is to enter insanity in order to examine our "cultural psychosis."[10] For Kane and Bond, "violence" and "psychosis" can be dramaturgically useful to disrupt the normal surface of everyday life and unearth the hidden aspects of social reality. This dramaturgy can be understood better through the concept of "accident time."

The Dramaturgy of Accident Time

In his letter to Kane on 15 September 1997, Bond writes: "*Cleansed* is even more powerful because it takes any two or three minutes from *Blasted* and subjects them to great pressure. [...] It's what I called 'accident time'. [...] It's not a matter of solution but of understanding."[11] In a letter to Stuart Seide, Bond discusses a production of *Blasted* in Paris, which he found lacked the power of "accident time" inherent in Kane's play: "*Blasted* was stylish. ... But the story had been slowed down in order to bring it to our attention: this is Brechtian and the opposite of *Accident Time*."[12] Interestingly, as Graham Saunders points out, Kane also uses the term "accident time" in *4.48 Psychosis*[13]: "In accident time where there are no accidents/You have no choice/the choice comes after."[14] How Kane describes "accident time" accurately captures the meaning of this Bondian term—accident time designates the moment in which the subject is faced with a necessary and inescapable event without being offered any possibilities of evasion. This concept also resonates with how Cate in *Blasted* describes the experience of her fit: "The world don't exist, not like this. Looks the same but—Time slows down. A dream I get stuck in, can't do anything about it."[15]

Bond's concept of accident time can be considered alongside with Bertolt Brecht's "street scene." According to Brecht, "the street scene," regarded as a basic model for epic theater, depends on an eyewitness who demonstrates to bystanders how a traffic accident took place. This demonstrator needs to imitate the action rather than the character, which means that helping bystanders form their opinions about the accident objectively is more important than making them subjectively re-experience what happened.[16] Bond also defines "accident time" by comparing extreme drama with a car crash.[17] From Bond's description of what happens in accident time, it is not accurate to state that the concept of accident time is completely different from Brecht's street scene. Both of the devices seek to create a theatrical experience in which meanings buried under the surface of everyday normalcy can be explored. However, Bond emphasizes the importance of the experiential aspect—for him, the extreme emotions provoked in accident time are essential for the spectator to enter the subsequent process of interpretation. Although Brecht by no means excludes the experience of emotions, he emphasizes that emotions can exist only insofar as they are subject to critical scrutiny. Another difference is that, while Brecht intends the spectator to understand the Marxist-inflected social meanings within certain situations, what concerns Bond is not how the subject's behavior and reaction are determined by class or other socialeconomic conditions, but how the subject, while being structured by ideological apparatuses, still retains the potential for resistance and self-reflection.

Notably, aggro-effects can be seen to be produced by the dramaturgy of accident time although Bond does not explicitly associate these two concepts. According to Bond, there are two kinds of aggro-effects: "It may shock the audience so as to disturb and bewilder them, disorientate them [...]. Or it may set them a dilemma—an either/or which requires a decision."[18] That is, "aggro-effects" can exert visceral impact and provoke critical reflections. These kinds of aggro-effects are also detectable in Kane's theater, as Joe Gill-Gibbins observes: "Kane wanted people to experience something emotionally before experiencing it intellectually. *Blasted* hits you so hard that you don't use your head until afterwards."[19]

The dramaturgy of accident time is best exemplified in the Palermo improvisation and the story of the Russian guard, both of which Bond discusses in "Commentary on *The War Plays*." During the improvisation, each student is required to play a soldier who must choose to kill either his mother's baby or his neighbor's. In the story, a Russian guard in a Nazi prisoner-of-war camp was ordered to kill his brother—if he refused to do so, both of them would be killed. Bond regards the decisions made in these ethical aporetic moments as expressions of radical innocence, demonstrating that humanness is created instead of being intrinsic.[20] As regards the constitution of the subject, Jacques Lacan's concept of the "divided subject" is pertinent here. For Lacan, the alienation of the divided subject at the advent of the introduction of language can be demonstrated in a dramatic structure: "This disjunction is incarnated in a highly illustratable, if not dramatic, way as soon as the signifier is incarnated at a more personalized level in demand or supply: in 'your money or your life' or 'liberty or death'."[21] While Lacan uses the "personalized" level to illustrate the relationship between the subject and the signifier, what interests us here resides precisely in the personalized dramatic level. The process of subjectivation always entails making choices, which function as the cause of the subject and determine the meaning of the world for the subject. This dramatic moment of choosing constitutes the pivot of the Palermo improvisation and the story of the Russian guard. For Lacan, by choosing, the subject is subjected to a certain meaning while the nonmeaning is simultaneously produced.[22] This process of choosing also necessitates the confrontation with "the ultimate" that Bond regards as the purpose of drama.[23]

Bond's later plays abound in such ethical moments of decision-making, through which characters are forced to define their "humanness"—since the distinction between meaning and nonmeaning is fluid, "humanness" remains a void to be defined. In *Coffee* (1995), in the forest scene, Nold encounters the Woman and the Girl, both of whom suffer from starvation and beg Nold for food. However, Nold cannot find any food; when he comes back, the Woman has killed the Girl in order to save her from the pain of hunger. Before the death of the Girl, the Woman asks the Girl to die and begs Gregory to kill the Girl for her: "Kill'er—the little madam!—One bit a' 'uman kindness."[24] It may seem paradoxical how the act of murdering can become "one bit a' 'uman kindness," but since in such extreme situations the criterion to define what is moral is suspended, the Woman chooses to kill the Girl so as to save her from the chronic pain of starvation. Later in the ditch scene, Nold defies Gregory's order and chooses to kill him in order to save the Woman and the Girl. This is another variation of the Palermo improvisation—instead of killing civilians, the soldier can choose to kill the commandant.

In *The Crime of the Twenty-First Century* (2001), the blinded Sweden kills Hoxton and Grace because they refuse to escape with him, making Sweden doubt whether they will tell the authorities about his whereabouts. Paradoxically, Sweden's murder is enacted out of his anxiety for help.[25] For Sweden, in order to ensure his "right to be," he can only murder them in order to remain human—this is how Sweden defines his "humanity." In *Born* (2006), what makes Luke hesitate before he kills the Woman and her baby is not the decision whether to kill or not to kill but his desire to know what takes place before one dies.[26] What Luke desires to experience is the moment of accident time—the extreme moment when he can understand what the human is. In Bond's later plays, the dramaturgy of accident time revolves around the moments in which humanity can be defined. Since Bond usually puts the perpetrator in such moments, the radicalness of this dramaturgy derives from the suspension of the violent moment in order to explore the ethical dimensions of violence.

In Kane's plays, we can also see the dramaturgy of accident time in operation. In *Blasted*, Cate is obsessed with Ian's gun—she keeps asking Ian if he can really shoot someone.[27] Cate's obsession with the possibility of shooting someone resonates with the Palermo improvisation. Moments of accident time can be extreme because they are the moments in which ethical decisions must be made. What concerns Cate is this kind of extreme moment, and she has firmly defined herself as non-violent. Later, she states again that she cannot imagine that Ian could kill anything or shoot someone. As Cate only speculates about the moment of accident time, it is the Soldier who forces Ian to enter accident time. The Soldier tells Ian that soldiers are "all like that,"[28] implying that when an individual becomes a solider, he or she must abide by military rules which leave no room for personal choice. This is illustrated later when the Soldier forces Ian to imagine that he is ordered to become a soldier: "In the line of duty. For your country. Wales."[29] In contradistinction to the Soldier, who is forced by the situation to kill, Cate insists that it is wrong to kill—including committing suicide. Faced with the blinded Ian, Cate still states: "It's wrong to kill yourself."[30] Cate's insistence on non-violence stands as a contrast to the Soldier's assertion that soldiers must kill and suggests the possibility of making choices in such moments of accident time.

Like *Blasted*, *Cleansed* (1998) also consists of a series of decision-making moments. As the spectacle of torture in *Cleansed* attests to "the violence of the symbolic,"[31] characters in this play are constantly forced to make choices, which then determine how they define themselves. "Love me or kill me"—both Grace and Graham use this form of choice to define their subjectivity. This form of choice denies the possibility of being "the self"—the subject can only choose between the annulation of the self and the incestuous unification. Both decisions destroy the socialized self and point toward the impossible. This form of impossible choice is also manifested in the relationship between Grace and Robin. Whether it is Grace's "imaginary identification"[32] with Graham or the "incestuous nature of the pre-Oedipal stage"[33] inherent in the relationship between Robin and Grace, this desire for the impossible harmony and disregard for symbolic constraints create an unthinkable terrain in which human subjectivity can be reimagined. This is where Grace/Graham eventually arrives at: "Here now. Safe on the other side and here."[34] The logic of "love or life" also operates in the relationship between Rod and Carl. Although Carl thinks he can love Rod unconditionally, when faced with extreme torture, he begs Tinker to torture Rod instead of him. Later it is Rod who chooses love and dies. As Kane states that the loss of the object of love can be as dehumanizing as what happens in concentration camps,[35] every character must undergo the trial of love to decide the real cause of the subject. The logic of "love or life" also exists in the relationship between Tinker and the Woman in the booth. However, different from Rod, who dies for love, or Grace, who absolutely transgresses the boundary of symbolic restraints, Tinker keeps his life but can never obtain love. He can only accept that the Woman, whose name is also Grace, can never be the one he loves.

In *4.48 Psychosis*, the speaker, who seems to remain depressed and unable to act, also constantly undergoes the process of being divided and alienated by the indifference of psychiatric rationality. The impulse to resist the socialized distinction between meaning and nonmeaning is expressed by the speaker's struggle to redefine the distinction between sanity and madness—only by being "insane" can the speaker feel "sane." However, this struggle can hardly reach any resolution, and the speaker always feels like a "fragmented puppet."[36] The experience of fragmentation is what takes place in accident time "where there are no accidents" because the subject cannot choose but enter and re-enter the process of necessary subjectivation.

Ethical Subjectivities

Although moments of accident time are often dramatized through scenes of violence and psychosis, these amoral shocking extreme moments can be ethical in the sense that they defy the norms of what can be represented. The shocking representation beyond the grasp of imagination can be compared to the sublime, which in Kant's aesthetics is reserved for nature. According to Theodor W. Adorno, who transposes the concept of the sublime to the sphere of art, the more art integrates "the nonidentical"—the sensually displeasing and culturally tabooed—the more art's content becomes forceful since its form remains indifferent regarding what to be included and what to be excluded.[37] In line with Adorno's argument, Karoline Gritzner argues that theater provides an imaginary space in which, due to the removing of the constraints of social reality, the conditions for subjective freedom can be presented and the negotiation with alterity can be made possible.[38]

The ethical radicalness of Kane's and Bond's plays derives from their "negotiation with alterity" by exploring the possibility of representing what may be ethically and representationally prohibited in theater. Kane is clearly aware of the ethical significance implied by the transgression of representational boundaries: "If we experience something through art, then we might be able to change our future, because experience engraves lessons on our hearts through suffering [...]."[39] For Kane, the experience of shock and suffering in theater can be ethical and educational not in the sense that this experience gives us direct moral lessons, but in the sense that it can arouse our awareness of the hidden violence in reality and heighten our ethical sensibilities.

In Bond's Palermo improvisation and the story of the Russian guard, the process of re-subjectivation is not only an extreme experience that involves violence but also a Levinasian face-to-face ethical encounter since the difficulty of making choices always already presupposes the existence of the face of the other. As regards the relationship between the face as a sensible datum and murder, Emmanuel Levinas states: "Murder still aims at a sensible datum, and yet it finds itself before a datum whose being can not be suspended by an appropriation. It finds itself before a datum absolutely non-neutralizable."[40] For Levinas, the non-neutralizable face that paralyzes the power to murder and exhibits itself in its vulnerable nudity also promises the hope of non-violence: "The relation with the Other as a relation with his transcendence [...] introduces into me what was not in me. But this 'action' upon my freedom precisely puts an end to violence."[41]

Levinas also maintains that, in opposition to the subject's egoism as the source of violence, the freedom of the subject implies responsibility, and it is this coincidence of freedom and responsibility that constitutes the structure of Eros: "The coinciding of freedom with responsibility constitutes the I, doubled with itself, encumbered with itself. *Eros* delivers from this encumberment, arrests the return of the I to itself."[42]

Therefore, choices made in accident time are ethical because they entail the negotiation between the subject's freedom and the subject's responsibility for the other. In *Coffee*, both Nold's impulse to help the Woman and the Girl from starvation in the forest scene and his later resistance to kill them in the ditch scene embody the logic of Eros—the subject's reach toward the other without returning to the logic of self-interest. However, these ethical moments remain "amoral" since they by no means provide any moral standards for us to judge the character. In *The Crime of the Twenty-First Century*, Sweden feels responsible for Hoxton and Grace and urges them to escape with him in order to find a better and safer place. However, when he feels rejected, he murders them consecutively. Sweden's decisions are ethically ambiguous since his impulse to kill coincides with his impulse not to kill—his stabbing of Hoxton's breasts symbolically represents the coexistence of his pre-Oedipal desire and the violence that originates from the impossibility of such desire. In *Born*, there are similar paradoxical gestures: Luke tortures the Woman and smashes her baby to death because he wants to know the truth about death. Later in a dream-like scene, Luke imagines that the dismembered baby's body parts are assembled again by the *Muselmänner*, but the Woman, instead of happily welcoming her baby back, takes the leftover in her baby's hands and eats it. At the same time, Donna, Luke's mother, keeps feeding other dead victims but refuses to feed Luke. Since these contradictory gestures, although situated within extreme situations, seem to lack clear moral messages, they force the spectator to enter a gray zone in which there are no definite ethical norms to rely on.

The ethical force of Kane's plays also originates from her exploration of these amoral but ethical moments. In *Blasted*, one of these moments is when the Soldier rapes Ian. Obviously, the Soldier feminizes Ian and treats him as a substitute for his girlfriend. When the Soldier rapes Ian, he is also crying, implying that this physical violence also reveals the Soldier's psychological truth—his desire for love. While the Soldier's paradoxical gesture can be compared to Sweden's murder of Hoxton, his desire to know what happens to Col when she was dying is akin to Luke's desire to know what happens to the Woman when she is about to die. Both Kane and Bond refuse to represent the perpetrator merely as an indifferent killing machine; instead, they suspend the moment of violence and extract the remains of what can possibly be defined as humanity, which is also the source of hope. As Aston argues, hope in *Blasted* stems from the feminist shift that situates the perpetrator in the aftermath of traumatizing violence.[43] As regards the role of Cate, her insistence on non-violence, care of the baby, and final gesture of giving Ian food embody what Levinas designates as the subjectivity of sensibility: "The subjectivity of sensibility, taken as incarnation, is an abandon without return, maternity, a body suffering for another, the body as passivity and renouncement, a pure undergoing."[44] Cate's ethical stance is demonstrated through concrete actions (caring and feeding) and a straightforward belief ("it's wrong to kill")—although the belief may seem naive and her actions tiny, through Cate, Kane suggests that the possibility of humanity resides precisely in these simple actions and ideas in a world of ruins.

This subjectivity of sensibility demonstrated through "an abandon without return" and the passive body is also what endows the characters in *Cleansed* with ethical weight. For Levinas, the ethics of Eros means the interruption of the return to the I, but this ethical demand is dramatized so extremely in *Cleansed* that it is doubtful if it can be satisfied. While in *Blasted*, we can state that the characters demonstrate what Levinas defines as ethical relations, in *Cleansed*, such ethical relations are suspended and cast into a series of trials. It is even doubtful whether the interruption of the return to the I, literally demonstrated through the total cancellation of the self and the nullification of the distinction between self and other, can be ethically desirable and possible. In this sense, the ethical power of *Cleansed* stems from the destabilization of what can theoretically be defined as ethical. In *4.48 Psychosis*, the speaker is also troubled by the potential of the human subject both as the source of violence and as the source of non-violence: "I gassed the Jews, I killed the Kurds, I bombed the Arabs, [...] I REFUSE I REFUSE I REFUSE LOOK AWAY FROM ME."[45] "I" can be the perpetrator who exerts violence on the other, but "I" can also refuse to do so. The ethical force of the other emanates from the other's gaze on the face, and this is why the speaker must demand the other should "look away." Kane keeps challenging and examining the boundary between the human and the inhuman and that between the ethical and the unethical—it is her unprejudiced examination of ethical aporetic moments that endows her dramaturgy of accident time with ethical force.

Coda

In his obituary of Kane, Mark Ravenhill states: "For those used to the reassurances of sociology or psychology in plays, the austere beauty of Kane's work was a shock to the system."[46] Aleks Sierz, in his reflection on the meaning of "in-yer-face," contends that "the in-yer-face approach is a matter of sensibility rather than of showing any specific acts. [...] In-yer-face theatre is about emotions, not about shock tactics."[47] Surely, Kane's plays cannot be reduced to a series of shock tactics, but we need to ask what shock means here. Shock is never only concerned with dramatic devices, but, as Ravenhill proposes, shock can be powerful because it is "a shock to the system." Bond's theorization about the dramaturgy of accident time and subjectivity explicates how drama can achieve the shock to the system. It is in this sense that I propose that "in-yer-face" sensibility always presupposes certain shock tactics, as can be seen in the theoretical and dramaturgical dialogues between Kane and the later Bond. This hidden dialogue sheds new light on how we understand In-Yer-Face "shock," which can be structured by the dramaturgy of accident time that appeals to our emotional receptivity and enhances our ethical sensibility.

Notes

1. Qtd. in Graham Saunders, *About Kane: The Playwright and the Work* (London: Faber and Faber, 2009), 48.
2. Edward Bond, "Epilogue: 'The mark of Kane,'" in *Sarah Kane in Context*, ed. Laurens De Vos and Graham Saunders (Manchester: Manchester University Press, 2010), 209.
3. Edward Bond, "A Blast at Our Smug Theatre: Edward Bond on Sarah Kane," *Guardian*, January 28, 1995.
4. Bond, "Epilogue," 216; original emphasis.
5. Qtd. in Saunders, *About Kane*, 101.
6. Ibid., 103.
7. Edward Bond, "Commentary of *The War Plays*," in *Plays: 6* (London: Methuen, 1998), 250.
8. Sarah Kane, *4.48 Psychosis*, in *Complete Plays* (London: Methuen, 2001), 221.
9. Qtd. in Graham Saunders, *"Love Me or Kill Me": Sarah Kane and the Theatre of Extremes* (Manchester: Manchester University Press, 2002), 114.
10. Edward Bond, "The Third Crisis: The Possibility of a Future Drama," *JCDE* 1, no.1 (2013): 17.

11. Ian Stuart, ed., *Edward Bond: Letters 5* (New York: Routledge, 2001), 167. Original emphasis.
12. Qtd. in Graham Saunders, "'Just a Word on a Page and there is the Drama.' Sarah Kane's Theatrical Legacy," *Contemporary Theatre Review* 13, no.1 (2003): 102. Original emphasis.
13. Ibid., 103, n. 33.
14. Kane, *4.48 Psychosis*, 230.
15. Ibid., 22.
16. Bertolt Brecht, *Brecht on Theatre*, trans. Jack Davis, et al. Ed. Marc Silberman, Steve Giles and Tom Kuhn. 3rd ed (London: Bloomsbury, 2015), 176–181.
17. Edward Bond, "Drama Devices," in *Edward Bond and the Dramatic Child: Edward Bond's Plays for Young People*, ed. David Davis (Stoke on Trent: Trentham Books, 2005), 90.
18. Ian Stuart, ed., *Selections from the Notebooks of Edward Bond: Volume Two 1980–1995* (London: Methuen, 2001), 267.
19. Qtd. in Saunders, *About Kane*, 30–31.
20. See Bond, "Commentary," 247–251.
21. Jacques Lacan, *Écrits: The First Complete Edition in English*, trans. Bruce Fink (New York: Norton, 2007), 713.
22. Ibid., 714.
23. Edward Bond, "Afterword: Sarah Kane and Theatre," in *"Love Me or Kill Me": Sarah Kane and the Theatre of Extremes*, by Graham Saunders (Manchester: Manchester University Press, 2002), 190.
24. Edward Bond, *Coffee*, in *Plays: 7* (London: Methuen, 2003), 156.
25. Edward Bond, *The Crime of the Twenty-First Century*, in *Plays: 7* (London: Methuen, 2003), 251.
26. Edward Bond, *Born*, in *Plays: 8* (London: Methuen, 2006), 45.
27. Kane, *Blasted*, in *Complete Plays* (London: Methuen, 2001), 20.
28. Ibid., 44.
29. Ibid., 45.
30. Ibid., 54.
31. Elaine Aston, *Feminist Views on the English Stage: Women Playwrights, 1990–2000* (Cambridge: Cambridge University Press, 2003), 90.
32. Laurens De Vos, *Cruelty and Desire in the Modern Theatre: Antonin Artaud, Sarah Kane, and Samuel Beckett* (Madison: Fairleigh Dickinson University, 2011), 127.
33. Ibid., 134.
34. Kane, *Cleansed*, in *Complete Plays* (London: Methuen, 2001), 150.
35. Qtd. in Saunders, *About Kane*, 76.
36. Kane, *4.48 Psychosis*, 229.

37. Theodor W. Adorno, *Aesthetic Theory*, trans. Robert Hullot-Kentor (London: Continuum, 2002), 196.
38. Karoline Gritzner, "(Post)Modern Subjectivity and the New Expressionism: Howard Barker, Sarah Kane, and Forced Entertainment," *Contemporary Theatre Review* 18, no. 3 (2008): 331.
39. Heidi Stephenson and Natasha Langridge, *Rage and Reason: Women Playwrights on Playwriting* (London: Methuen, 1997), 133.
40. Emmanuel Levinas, *Totality and Infinity*, trans. Alphonso Lingis (Pennsylvania: Duquesne University Press, 1969), 198.
41. Ibid., 203.
42. Ibid., 271; original emphasis.
43. Elaine Aston, "Reviewing the Fabric of *Blasted*," in *Sarah Kane in Context*, ed. Laurens De Vos and Graham Saunders (Manchester: Manchester University Press, 2010), 25.
44. Emmanuel Levinas, *Otherwise than Being or Beyond Essence*, trans. Alphonso Lingis (Pennsylvania: Duquesne University Press, 1998), 79.
45. Kane, *4.48 Psychosis*, 227.
46. Mark Ravenhill, "Obituary: Sarah Kane," *Independent*, February 23, 1999.
47. Aleks Sierz, "Still In-Yer-Face? Towards a Critique and a Summation," *New Theatre Quarterly* 18, no. 1 (2002): 19.

CHAPTER 10

From "In-Yer-Face" to "In-Yer-Head": Staging the Mind in Martin Crimp, Sarah Kane, and Anthony Neilson

Solange Ayache

INTRODUCTION

In the last chapter of his book *Rewriting the Nation: British Theatre Today*, Aleks Sierz underlines the renewed interest of a number of playwrights in exploring the alternative worlds of the human mind and creating "rival realities":

> The arts of the 2000s were rich in visions, imaginations and fantasy. It was the quantum decade, the metaphor-rich decade. If the notion of globalisation suggested a world that is shrinking ever more rapidly, British theatre seemed to have taken a mind-expanding drug, encouraging us to go beyond the normal confines of daily life. Sure, theatre usually reflects the economic, social and political life of the country but sometimes it does much more: it creates different realities; it explores imaginative worlds: it ascends to heaven or stumbles into hell.[1]

S. Ayache (✉)
Sorbonne University, Paris, France

Paradoxically, for the British stage, going "beyond the normal confines of daily life" into "mind-*expanding*" territories has meant going through a paradigm shift at the extreme end of a long historical process of *reduction* of the dramatic space. From the public spaces of Greek tragedies to the small spaces of European chamber plays, from the ancient *polis* to Beckett's rocking chair, the history of space in theater and drama is, first of all, a history of progressive shrinking and interiorization, in a way strikingly parallel to the death of distance characteristic of our globalized world. Examining the evolution of the dramatic space in relation to the place of women in theater, Hanna Scolnicov points out this evolution throughout the ages:

> The scene has shifted from the open air, the front of the palace, the street, the piazza, into the state-room, the parlor, the kitchen, the bedroom, narrowing down the scope and infringing on the privacy of intimate relations. Some contemporary playwrights have gone further, deconstructing the familiar naturalistic room to form a non-mimetic interior or abstracting space altogether.[2]

Pushing the limits of abstract, non-mimetic space to an extreme, a number of contemporary British playwrights, including the leading figures of In-Yer-Face Theatre, have undertaken to observe and display the inner workings of the mind. Often focusing on female characters, a number of recent plays indeed take place in undefined spaces open to infinite expansion, exploring inner and alternate realities through experimental forms and ways of dramatic writing, thus providing alternatives to "escape the ethical and aesthetic aporia postmodernism walled itself in," as Élisabeth Angel-Perez has shown.[3] As the main drama is now entirely delocalized in the mental space of the characters—or that of the viewers—such works provide new possibilities and directions for theatrical experimentation, marking the emergence of a theater no longer "In-Yer-Face" but, rather, "In-Yer-Head," in which the human mind has become the new frontier, as I will argue in the first part of this chapter. In these mental spaces, the character's speculative, reflexive, or dissociated mode of existence invites us to define the modalities of what could be called a "psychopoetics" of the stage that characterizes a trend interested in staging psychological indeterminacy, uncertainty, and instability by focusing on the troubled minds of disappearing female characters. The second part of this chapter will address this question by examining plays by Martin Crimp, Sarah Kane, and Anthony Neilson that portray women in pain.

"In-Yer-Head" Theatre: The Mind as the New Frontier in British Drama

Uncharted Worlds: Living Inside Our Heads

Examining the dramatic treatment of psychological and even psychiatric illness in former In-Yer-Face playwright Anthony Neilson's 2004 play *The Wonderful World of Dissocia*, theater critic David Jays provides a pertinent explanation for the growing interest in exploring mental spaces and the disturbed mind in contemporary British drama. Reflecting on Neilson's piece, which portrays the bipolar disorder of a young woman using a subjective, first-person perspective in the first act and an objective, third-person perspective in the second act, Jays notes:

> As everything plays out on the Discovery Channel, where can we find an uncharted world? The answer may be in our heads—the mind presents a landscape of madcap, baffling possibility, as in Anthony Neilson's alarming *Dissocia* wonderland. When there are few locations left to explore, the strangest undiscovered territory may be within our own troubled heads.[4]

With the unparalleled development of cognitive science, neuroscience, psychology, psychiatry, and philosophy of mind, the research on the mind has expanded further and faster than ever before over the past few decades. Post-traumatic stress disorder at the individual and collective scales has become an acknowledged phenomenon over the course of the twentieth century, especially in the post-Auschwitz era, and now in our post-9/11 culture. Mental health in general has become a major concern in a culture where the human subject suffers from various forms of psychological distress and the troubled mind has become a largely medicalized object. At the same time, unresolved mysteries such as the origin of consciousness and the mind-body problem continue to puzzle the scientific community, and quantum science asks the question of the role of the conscious mind in the determination of reality. In response, ultracontemporary British drama seems to have taken the human mind as a new frontier, leading to the development of a new expressionistic theater where the action takes place in a space which is mental rather than physical, thus moving from the In-Yer-Face aesthetic of the "Nasty Nineties" to an approach which could be called "In-Yer-Head."

In addition to approaching the mind and brain as a scientific, often pathological object,[5] contemporary British theater also looks into the ordinary psyche of the twenty-first-century citizen of the Western world, giving the metaphor of the "theatre of the mind" a literal dimension but in the renewed, postmodern context of late capitalist society. "In-Yer-Head" theater explores the way we think and the unprecedented importance of our private world in today's individualistic lifestyle. In a 2006 interview with Sierz, Martin Crimp suggests that this innovative kind of drama reveals a contemporary sensibility that speaks of our way of relating to the world and stresses the growing insular realities that we inhabit:

> I do think part of modern 'identity' is to live inside our heads (a bit like being shut in a car, endlessly driving). In the 19th century the theatre abandoned the street and moved into the tortured drawing-rooms of Ibsen and Feydeau; and in the 20th, Pinter and Beckett transformed it into a mental space, which some writers (the Kane of *Crave* and *4.48 Psychosis*) continued to explore.[6]

Although the visually dense fantasy land of Neilson's 2004 drama and its eventful, still rather In-Yer-Face narrative stands in stark contrast with the post-Beckettian vein and minimalistic settings of some of Crimp's and Kane's works, their respective styles highlight the variety of viewpoints and theatrical forms that support the "mentalization" of the British stage. Because the citizens of our consumerist and competitive world tend to live in their heads, Crimp's experimental theater looks for ways of staging the mind and its neurotic functioning as the very locus where our modern lives typically take place and our power relationships originate on a daily basis—with all the defense mechanisms and psychological complexes it implies. Reflecting on the dual nature of his work, Crimp insists on the specific nature of our times, accounting for this shift from a "head-on" to an "in-head" drama poetics by connecting mental space with the notion of "private choice": "The consumer-citizen of a liberal democracy generally experiences and is encouraged to experience the world as a set of private choices and personal pleasures (or grievances)—so perhaps this drama-in-the-head is simply a reflection of this state of affairs."[7] This, he says, explains why he has developed "a second kind of writing" in which "the dramatic space is a *mental* space, not a physical one," leading to a "form of narrated drama in which the act of story-telling *is itself dramatised*."[8]

Crimp's unconventional "drama-in-the-head" thus adds a decisive contextual dimension (social, economic, and ideological) to what can be regarded as the very nature of the human condition, as described by Finnish architect and philosopher Juhani Pallasmaa:

> We live in mental worlds in which the experienced, remembered and dreamed, as well as the present, past and future, constantly fuse into one another. We transform time and space through imagination and dreaming, into the specific human mode of existence—the world of possibilities. The self and the world mutually define one another in a perpetually intertwining process.[9]

It is precisely this inner "world of possibilities" that post-In-Yer-Face Theatre explores as the specific mode and plane of existence not only of the human subject, but of the citizens of a world both characterized by what American psychologist Barry Schwartz has identified as "the paradox of choice,"[10] which shows that the increase of consumer choice is a source of greater anxiety, and what Marc Augé has called "non-places,"[11] impersonal and transient physical places where the individual remains anonymous and lonely, such as hotel rooms, airports, and shopping malls. To these new configurations, one must add the chronic instability surrounding the threat and proliferation of traumatic events on a global scale. Crimp wrote the first two short plays of his 2005 trilogy *Fewer Emergencies* the day before the September 11 attacks. In these satirical mini-plays, which precisely take place in an unspecified, non-physical location ("*Time*: Blank / *Place*: Blank"[12]), just like his 1997 play *Attempts on Her Life*, he denounces the illusion of safety and a growing sense of threat in our Western world by playing with uncertain voices who have internalized the anxiety of our times.

States of Uncertainty: From the Eye to the Ear

This "mentalization" of the stage goes along with a renewed emphasis on language, voice, and storytelling. Writing about this kind of "post-post dramatic theatre," Angel-Perez notes that, on the British stage, "the beginning of the 21st century is marked by a revival of verbal drama: a theatre '*In-Yer-Ear*' rather than '*In-Yer-Face*.'"[13] Insisting on "the return of the word" as the main drama,[14] she notes:

> Caryl Churchill, Martin Crimp and Sarah Kane in her last two plays allow us to hear a new form of dramatic writing based on the return of the word and the renewed command of language. Instead of attacking the eye and opting for the *opsis*, this new verbal theatre moves from *In-Yer-Face* to *In-Yer-Ear*. Violence resonates in the power of a language where aggressive and raw images alternate with failing words and ellipses, which make violence even more salient.[15]

In a number of plays, including those by Tim Crouch and debbie tucker green, the stage empties itself as the mind invades the space, a movement intrinsically linked to the decreasing importance of visual density in favor of a growing reliance on the aural. It is precisely this kind of theater which is "carrying other visions" for "a new eye" able to see potentialities that French director Claude Régy was interested in staging, as he explained in his 2002 book *L'État d'incertitude* [*The State of Uncertainty*]. Alluding to his creation of *4.48 Psychosis* in Paris that same year, in which Isabelle Huppert embodied the mentally ill female patient of Sarah Kane's play in a strikingly motionless performance, he wrote:

> It's about working on all that which is produced by a body but is not necessarily visible or communicated through direct exchange.
> It then becomes obvious that staging the play in semi-darkness and talking very softly moves the threshold of perception for the eye and the ear. ... There is another way to use language, and thus probably another perception of the world which could be explored beyond our own usual thresholds. By developing a more subtle and less utilitarian form of hearing, maybe we will hear differently. Maybe we will hear something else.
> A new eye would be invented, carrying other visions.
> It would suffice to open a field for all the potentialities stored in the nonexistent. It would suffice to let the nonexistent hover around. One would realize ... that what has not been really done, what has not been really said, still has an effect.[16]

Régy's insistence on the imperceptible confirms the connection between the spectral mode of existence of "in-yer-head" characters and stories (the "nonexistent" which "still has an effect"), the voice (which is able to move the "thresholds" of the real for the ear), and the unconscious mind (which can be staged in "semi-darkness"). In Crimp's unconventional theater as well as in other recent plays exploring mental processes, "the action is nowhere on the stage. The only 'drama' taking place in front of the audience is that of speaking."[17]

This obviously jars with Sierz's description of a theater "rich in visions." As Neilson's theater shows, the fascination for the mind on the British stage exceeds the limits of this definition and has also given rise to plays that possess a persistent visceral and confrontational quality, exploring disturbed mindscapes with emotional rawness and visual aggressivity. In Mark Haddon's *Polar Bears* (2010), for instance, the main character, Kay, also suffers from bipolar disorder, and the chaotic structure of the play, which provides a puzzling alternation of contradictory scenarios, becomes a metaphor for the protagonist's subjective perceptions and delusions and the possible fantasies and projections of her partner. In the end, both approaches—visual and aural—converge in that most fantasies are created on the stage using the performative power of language, and both mark the emergence of a theater "in-yer-head," as we will now see in more detail. Regardless of the aesthetic they used, all the leading figures of 1990s In-Yer-Face Theatre have played a major role in the rise of "In-Yer-Head" drama, developing a "psychopoetics" of the stage which still bears the mark of a provocative writing style and includes visceral narrative elements, yet generally tends to focus on what the ear hears and what the mind says, rather than what the eye sees and what the body does. This is what Mark Ravenhill's *pool (no water)* (2006) and Philip Ridley's *Tender Napalm* (2011), for instance, also suggest, where anonymous characters onstage either tell themselves stories to deal with unpleasant truths, as in Ravenhill's 2006 drama, or tell each other exotic fantasies to build sexual tension, as in Ridley's 2011 piece.

STAGING THE (FEMALE) MIND: WATCHING HER VANISH

Martin Crimp and Sarah Kane's Theaters of Absence

With its poetic, even musical quality and the crystallization of the drama around voices lost in a non-local, abstract space, Sarah Kane's *4.48 Psychosis* carries out the process of exhaustion of the self, which first appeared in *Crave*. Her two "voice plays" reach beneath the surface of the faceless subject into the dark territory of the human psyche where the self, "whose face is pasted on the underside of [her] mind,"[18] remains unattainable. With its first-person fragmented narrative, Kane's posthumous "drama-in-the-head" can thus be described as an In-Yer-Face dramatic experiment turned inward, displayed for everyone to see.

Diving into a female patient's subjective experience of disconnectedness between her mind and body, *4.48 Psychosis* stages a confused mental space where anonymous and unspecified voices come and go in an undetermined way. Largely inspired by Crimp's *Attempts on Her Life* in this respect, it also mentions—and acts out—the absence of a woman reminiscent of the invisible character of Anne (or Anya, Annie, Anushka, etc.) whose life is being fantasized about, commented upon, dissected, ignored, alienated, or negated in Crimp's "Seventeen Scenarios for the Theatre." Kane indeed held Crimp as "one of a small number of living dramatists whose plays inspire[d her] to push [her] own work in new directions,"[19] and the female characters' need to speak combined with their disappearance from the stage in their plays actually allows us to see *Attempts on Her Life* and *4.48 Psychosis* as a diptych. Providing, to a certain extent, a first-person sequel to Crimp's play created two years earlier, Kane's play reverses the passage from the first person to the third in Crimp's theater after the eviction of the protagonist at the end of his 1993 play *The Treatment*, a troubled and confused character already named Anne who is shot offstage in the last scene. With the passage from *The Treatment* to *Attempts on Her Life*, which corresponds to the transition from a theater In-Yer-Face to a theater "In-Yer-Head," the dramatic space in Crimp's writing moves from physical to mental, as the post-traumatic stage gives way to a post-sacrificial stage where the woman only exists in our heads. While Anne is psychologically and sexually abused in *The Treatment* and her story is stolen, rewritten, and staged by art facilitators, in scenario 11 of *Attempts on Her Life*, Anne, an artist, is absent: she has committed suicide after turning her own previous attempts into performances staged in a morbid installation. This leads an art critic to comment that she "should've been admitted not to an art school but to a psychiatric unit"[20]—a condemnation very similar to the remarks Kane received from theater critics Jack Tinker and Charles Spencer in their infamous reviews of her first two plays, *Blasted* and *Phaedra's Love*.[21] Thus, Kane's *4.48 Psychosis* not only restores Anne's voice and presence onstage but also dramatizes Anne/Kane's very process of self-erasure in response to the trauma of her voice being alienated and misunderstood by her contemporaries, a trauma which is thus re-enacted—Kane's own suicide shortly thereafter reinforcing this reading.[22] Through the voice of an anonymous female patient effectively receiving "treatment" in a "psychiatric unit" before "attempting to her [own] life," Kane provides the reader-spectator with the subjective, introspective point of view precisely erased in Crimp. In doing so, however, she follows the injunction in *Attempts on Her Life*: "—And now she speaks. /—Yes, because she *must*,"[23] bringing Anne back from the dead onto the stage, until, once again, "No one speaks."[24]

Even though center stage, Kane's patient—a resurrected "Anne" speaking in the first person again, though not for long—remains absent to herself. In *4.48 Psychosis*, the spectral mode of existence of the subject is voiced through words that express a hollow sense of self inhabiting a body experienced as an "alien carcass,"[25] as when she declares: "nothing can fill this void in my heart,"[26] or "my legs are empty."[27] The absence of the loved one, highlighted when she mentions "a song for my loved one, touching her absence"[28] or declares herself "built to be lonely / to love the absent,"[29] is eventually revealed as her own absence to herself, as suggested when she confesses "I miss a woman who was never born"[30] and then "It is myself I have never met."[31] This absence is performed as a dramatic and textual process with the ultimate disappearance of the patient herself, vanishing with the words of the play which used "to fill [her] space"—and the dramatic space—and which are now being engulfed in the widening gaps on the page:

   watch me vanish

   watch me

            vanish

   watch me

   watch me

            watch[32]

Both Crimp and Kane have developed an alternative, unconventional writing style, which "delineate[s] a new phenomenology of the stage that reconfigures the modalities of seeing and of not seeing in the theatre," as Angel-Perez has shown.[33] After Crimp (and Beckett), Kane borrowed from European modernist influences to create a "spectropoetics" of the stage,[34] where the fundamental trauma of absence plays a central role and invisibility has become a structural modality of existence for (what remains of) the character. That which is disappearing sheds light on the rhythm, music, and interaction between the interlaced voices that remain—on what is heard rather than seen—and on the punctuating and underlying silences in the dialogues. Whether the voices on stage perform the violent act of occultation through the use of the authorial third person—the storying of the other—which objectifies the absent woman (in Crimp), or denounce this obliteration through the use of the first person whose fragility testifies to the erasure of the subject (in Kane), the character is put into question.

Anthony Neilson's Theater of Dissociation

Citing Anthony Neilson alongside with Kane in the last chapter of *Rewriting the Nation*, Sierz notes that "after laying aside his original In-Yer-Face style, Neilson spent most of the decade 'exploring the internal life of the mind,' which presents a challenge to traditional notions of form because 'the mind works on so many levels.'"[35] Interested in debunking the stigma around mental illness, Neilson's "In-Yer-Head" drama investigates the fictional worlds of the psyche, first from a pathological point of view—in *The Wonderful World of Dissocia*—then from a non-pathological one, two years later—in *Realism*—addressing the impact of mind disorders and repressed impulses in social and domestic settings. Using more conventional dramatic forms than Kane, Neilson resorts to identified characters to enact a story and focuses on embodying the visual fantasies going on in one's head using vivid metaphors and theatrical images on stage. Based on symbolic and visual representations of the protagonists' inner experiences and perceptions, his plays dramatize conflicting situations that result from the confrontation of their private worlds with the objective and external reality that other characters stand for.

The Wonderful World of Dissocia however also offers a thematic exploration of psychosis from an inner perspective, in an attempt to "look at mental illness in a more lateral, subjective way than we're used to," as Neilson explains.[36] In his own words, "What the piece is trying to illuminate is why people who are mentally ill find it difficult to take their medication, but it's not aiming at depicting a particular mental state. Instead, the play will move in the same way the mind does, through association."[37] Despite its dichotomic, "bipolar" structure, the play thus still provides a recognizable narrative. Going down the rabbit hole of her delusional mind, the protagonist, a modern Alice named Lisa, takes us to the weird and colorful land of the disturbed imaginings that haunt her troubled mental space. As she meets a series of carnivalesque and fantastical beings in absurdist settings who take her through heightened sensuous experiences and intense emotions of terror and excitement, she is led by events into an increasingly menacing journey. The people of the "Divided States of Dissocia," who are at war, have lost their Queen, Sarah of the House of Tonin, the only one able to defeat the armies of the Black Dog King—a metaphor for the war raging in Lisa's brain between her serotonin levels and her depression. Portraying her descent into madness, the first act of the play thus appears as a stylized immersion into the main character's mind, where cultural and literary references ease the viewer into Lisa's inner experience. Neilson explains:

> I wanted to find a form that would enable people to participate and enter into the psychological space of the protagonist. I could have used a more individualistic experience in the first half of the play but I would then have had to set up what her life was so that the audience could understand where all that stuff came from. I went for more common cultural elements so there are hints of *Alice in Wonderland* and *The Wizard of Oz*.[38]

By contrast, the short, often silent scenes in Act Two—Act One's polar opposite—adopt an external point of view showing Lisa surrounded by anonymous nurses and occasional doctors who come and go, interned in the restricted space of a hospital white room where she is being treated for her illness in a sterile environment.

For Sierz, who views it as "one of the best" plays of the 2000s "that explored the inner space" of the human subject,[39] *The Wonderful World of Dissocia* marks "a turn towards more surrealistic, anti-realist or absurdist ways of staging subjective reality" in Neilson's writing.[40] While emblematic of the movement from In-Yer-Face to "In-Yer-Head" just like *4.48 Psychosis*, its aesthetic stands in stark contrast to the vocal psychopoetics developed by Kane, although they tackle similar issues around a suffering female character's journey told from within, both plays addressing the question of the inner perception and treatment of reality by the troubled mind as well as the perception and treatment of psychotic disorders by the outer world. With its familiar quest structure, Neilson's play looks at the tension between the protagonist's free will, as Lisa refuses to take her pills, and the toll her illness has on her relationships with her family and partner. When her boyfriend Vince visits her at the end of the play, Lisa explains why she is regularly tempted to get off her medication—just like the female patient in Kane's play—and to go back to Dissocia. The mythical image she uses sheds light on the universal odyssey of our shared humanity, allowing Vince to relate to her experience and express his own inner drama:

Lisa   You know what it is: it's like the Sirens.
       Pause.
Vince The Sirens?
Lisa   You know. They sit on the rocks and they sing to the sailors. And what they sing is so lovely it's like... they're hypnotised. They know if they sail to them their ship's going to get all smashed up. But they think it's worth it, you know—for the song.
       Long pause.
Vince I should go.
       ...
       That thing you said. About the Sirens.
       Pause.
       I understand that. That's how it is for me, with you.[41]

Dissocia, as a result, appears as an "alternative space" while "the play itself becomes a space for alternatives," as Diane Gagneret points out.[42] Compared to Crimp's spectral *Attempts on Her Life*, Neilson's spectacular play is thus at the other end of the spectrum, which he calls "experiential," rendering the invisible not only visible, but graphic and picturesque with epic proportions through theatrical images of exacerbated senses. At the end though, while "colour lights play *on her face*, swirling around her head," Neilson's In-Yer-Face play literally gives way to an "In-Yer-Head" drama to be continued, as "Dissocia still exists, caged *within her head*"[43] (my emphasis). The psychopoetics of the stage developed by Kane and Neilson thus offers a theater possibly more "in-*her*-head" than "in-*yer*-head." In any case, by "adapting the structure and aesthetics of the plays to the protagonists' inner reality,"[44] Neilson contributes to the radical use of psychological realism that Christina Wald has identified as a main feature of what she calls the "Drama of Performative Malady."

Conclusion

Looking at the metaphors of madness in British theater, Anna Harpin explains the link between madness and the trope of place. She indirectly provides a relevant description of the blank mental space where "In-Yer-

Head" plays take place, and of the process of disappearance or displacement that the mentally ill female characters in *4.48 Psychosis* and *The Wonderful World of Dissocia* go through:

> To be mad is, according to common idiom, to be out-of-place. One has lost the plot, gone out of one's mind, taken leave of one's senses; you are out to lunch, round the bend, away with the fairies, round the twist, in a dark place. A person descends into madness or is driven there. Two things are apparent here. Firstly, there is the recurrent sense of journeying that attends on madness. Secondly, the dominant notion of place renders "mad" experience an inherently geographical encounter. Madness, then, is figured as a location, as site. Or, perhaps more accurately, as simultaneously site and non-site. To be mad is to be both somewhere and yet nowhere, or at least not here, that is to say "reality." It is, then, to be displaced, dislocated, gone. Indeed, as Peter Barham and Robert Hayward have noted, this language of absence and disappearance "is recapitulated in the traditional psychiatric account of schizophrenia as a narrative of loss in which the pre-illness person goes missing, seemingly abandoned by the force of the disorder."[45]

This process of dislocation in contemporary British drama explains why, paradoxically, "shade, shadows and obliteration might well come out as the unexpected guarantees of the *ontos*."[46] Angel-Perez shows that the "spectropoetics" at play in Crimp's and Kane's dramatic experiments with absence (following Beckett) allows the subject to be freed from the determinism of the body and revealed through the "nomadism" of inner and outer voices.[47] Because the dramatic space is no longer physical but mental, this spectropoetics is also a psychopoetics, relocating reality in the mind, where the self and the world are subjectively perceived and altered. From *The Treatment* to *Attempts on her Life* and *Fewer Emergencies*, and from *Cleansed* to *Crave* and *4.48 Psychosis*, the significant shift in Crimp's and Kane's writing style plays a pivotal role in the emergence of "In-Yer-Head" drama, a concept that sheds light on a growing interest in staging the mind in ultracontemporary theater, and which often implies the fragmentation and disappearance of the conventional character along with the dissolution of the traditional structure of the well-made play, thus giving rise to a form of post-realism. The dramatic indeterminacy characteristic of their plays (unassigned lines, nameless speakers) indeed supports, mirrors, and points to the "psychological indeterminacy" constitutive of our intersubjective interactions, which Michael Ter Hak defines as the inherent (i.e. not epistemic) uncertainty concerning the mental contents and processes in another person's mind.[48] Trying to make the uncertain spectacularly palpable even if metaphorically, Neilson opts for an antagonistic approach but shares the same concern for that which cannot be seen but through displacement.

In the end, this dramatic exploration of the human psyche often speaks of the anxiety, uncertainty, and internalized violence that is constitutive of postmodern subjectivity and involved in the growth of mental disorders. "In-Yer-Head" theater blurs the boundaries between fantasy and reality, presence and absence, the self and the other, the personal and the impersonal, and questions the nature of objective and subjective reality to the point of renewing the possibilities of the dramatic form. In a context of global agitation internalized on the individual scale and possibly reflected through one's instable sense of self, it paradoxically opens unprecedented horizons for psychological realism and stage realism.

Notes

1. Aleks Sierz, *Rewriting the Nation: British Theatre Today* (London: Methuen Drama, 2011), 195.
2. Hanna Scolnicov, *Woman's Theatrical Space* (Cambridge: Cambridge University Press, 1994), 1.
3. Élisabeth Angel-Perez, "Introduction," *European Journal of English Studies* 7, no. 1 (2003): 3.
4. David Jays, "Theatre's landscape of the mind," *Guardian*, March 12, 2009.
5. In addition to Neilson's *The Wonderful World of Dissocia*, plays focused on the mysteries of the mind from a scientific or psychiatric viewpoint include Michael Frayn's *Copenhagen* (1998), Joe Penhall's *Blue/Orange* (2000), Peter Brook and Marie-Helene Estienne's *The Man Who* (2002), Mick Gordon's *On Ego* (2005), Lucy Prebble's *The Effect* (2012), and Tom Stoppard's *The Hard Problem* (2015).
6. Martin Crimp in Aleks Sierz, *The Theatre of Martin Crimp* (London: Bloomsbury, 2006), 140.
7. Martin Crimp, "*Into the Little Hill*: A work for stage by George Benjamin and Martin Crimp," interview by Ensemble Modern, *Ensemble Modern Newsletter* no. 23, October 2006, https://www.ensemble-modern.com/en/mediatheque/texts/2006-10-01/into-the-little-hill-a-work-for-stage-by-george-benjamin-and-martin-crimp.
8. Ibid.
9. Juhani Pallasmaa, "The Space of Time," *Oz* 20 (1998): 54.

10. See Barry Schwartz, *The Paradox of Choice: Why More Is Less* (New York: Harper Collins, 2004).
11. See Marc Augé, *Non-lieux. Introduction à une anthropologie de la surmodernité* (Paris: Le Seuil, 1992).
12. Martin Crimp, *Fewer Emergencies* (London: Faber and Faber, 2005), 5, 23, 39.
13. Élisabeth Angel-Perez, "Back to Verbal Theatre: Post-Post-Dramatic Theatres from Crimp to Crouch," *Études britanniques contemporaines* 45 (2013), https://journals.openedition.org/ebc/862.
14. Compare with Sarah Kane's statement, "Just a word on a page and there is the drama." Sarah Kane, *4.48 Psychosis*, in *Complete Works* (London: Methuen Drama, 2001), 213.
15. "Caryl Churchill, Martin Crimp et Sarah Kane dans ses deux derniers textes donnent à entendre une nouvelle écriture scénique fondée sur le retour du verbe et sur la puissance retrouvée du langage. Plutôt que d'agresser la vue et d'opter pour l'opsis, ce nouveau théâtre verbal délaisse le *In-Yer-Face* au profit du *In-Yer-Ear*. La violence résonne dans la force d'une langue où alternent les images agressives et brutales (le cru) et, à l'inverse, le manque à dire, l'ellipse qui rend la violence plus prégnante encore." (Élisabeth Angel-Perez, "Du *In-Yer-Face* au *In-Yer-Ear*: les 'solo-symphonies' de debbie tucker green," *Coup de Théâtre* 29 (2015): 175. Author translation.)
16. "Il s'agit de travailler sur tout ce qu'un corps émet qui n'est pas forcément visible et qui ne passe pas forcément par l'échange direct. | On tombe alors sur une évidence: mettre le spectacle dans l'ombre et parler très bas, c'est faire bouger pour l'œil, pour l'oreille, les seuils de perception … y a une autre manière d'utiliser le langage, et donc une autre perception du monde sans doute qui pourrait s'explorer en dehors des seuils qui sont les nôtres habituellement. En faisant travailler une ouïe plus subtile et mois utilitaire, peut-être entendra-t-on autrement. Peut-être entendra-t-on autre chose. | Un œil s'inventerait, porteur d'autres visions. | Il suffirait d'ouvrir un champ à toutes les potentialités stockées dans l'inexistant. Il suffirait de laisser flotter l'inexistant. On s'apercevrait … que ce qui n'a pas été vraiment dit, que tout ça agit." (Claude Régy, *L'État d'incertitude* [Besançon: Les Solitaires Intempestifs, 2002], 17–18. Author translation.)
17. Élisabeth Angel-Perez, "Sounding Crimp's Verbal Stage: The Translator's Challenge," *Contemporary Theatre Review* 24, no. 3 (2014), http://www.contemporarytheatrereview.org/2014/sounding-crimps-verbal-stage/.
18. Kane, *4.48 Psychosis*, 245.
19. Sarah Kane in Caroline Egan, "The Playwright's Playwright," *Guardian*, September 11, 1998.
20. Crimp, *Attempts*, 53–54.

21. "Some will undoubtedly say the money might have been better spent on a course of remedial therapy," wrote Jack Tinker following the 1995 premiere of Kane's debut play. (Jack Tinker, "This Disgusting Feast of Filth," *Daily Mail*, January 19, 1995.) Reviewing *Phaedra's Love*, Charles Spencer called himself seriously concerned about Sarah Kane's mental health and concluded, "it's not a theatre critic that's required here, it's a psychiatrist." (Charles Spencer, "Review of Phaedra's Love," *Daily Telegraph*, May 21, 1996.)
22. In her 2007 book on women and sacrifice, psychoanalyst and philosopher Anne Dufourmantelle explains that a woman's sacrifice is a means for her to attempt to repair the traumatic experience she has been through by restaging it in a way that allows her to somehow become not only a victim but also an agent. She paradoxically describes suicide "as an ultimate recourse to not vanish, as if one could at least be acknowledged afterwards, from one's death. From death itself." (Anne Dufourmantelle, *La Femme et le sacrifice: d'Antigone à la femme d'à côté* [Paris: Denoël, 2007], 39. Author translation.)
23. Crimp, *Attempts*, 20.
24. Kane, *4.48 Psychosis*, 243.
25. Ibid., 213.
26. Ibid., 219.
27. Ibid., 227.
28. Ibid., 218.
29. Ibid., 219.
30. Ibid., 218.
31. Ibid., 245.
32. Ibid., 244.
33. Élisabeth Angel-Perez, "Éloge de l'ombre: les paradoxes du corps spectral dans le théâtre anglais contemporain," *Miranda* 8 (2013), https://journals.openedition.org/miranda/3354.
34. Ibid.
35. Sierz, *Rewriting the Nation*, 197.
36. Anthony Neilson in Dominic Cavendish, "Edinburgh reports: 'I want to disturb people,'" *Telegraph*, August 1, 2004: 6.
37. Ibid.
38. Anthony Neilson, interview by Caroline Smith, *Brand Literary Magazine* 2 (2008), 77–79, http://www.brandliterarymagazine.co.uk/editions/02/contributors/01/extract.pdf.
39. Sierz, *Rewriting the Nation*, 197.
40. Aleks Sierz, "Whatever happened to in-yer-face theatre?" Aleks Sierz website, April 1, 2016, http://www.sierz.co.uk/writings/what-ever-happened-to-in-yer-face-theatre/.

41. Anthony Neilson, *The Wonderful World of Dissocia* (London: Methuen Drama, 2007), 89.
42. Diane Gagneret, "'A country called Dissocia': Anthony Neilson's Heterotopian Exploration of Madness," *Savoirs en prismes* 8 (2018), https://savoirsenprisme.com/numeros/08-2018-textualites-et-spatialites/a-country-called-dissocia-anthony-neilsons-heterotopian-exploration-of-madness/.
43. Neilson, *Dissocia*, 89.
44. Christina Wald, *Hysteria, Trauma and Melancholia: Performative Maladies in Contemporary Anglophone Drama* (Basingstoke: Palgrave Macmillan, 2007), 216.
45. Anna Harpin, "Dislocated: Metaphors of Madness in British Theatre," in *Performance, Madness and Psychiatry: Isolated Acts*, ed. Anna Harpin and Juliet Foster (Basingstoke: Palgrave, 2014), 187.
46. Angel-Perez, "Éloge de l'ombre."
47. See Élisabeth Angel-Perez, "La Voix nomade dans le théâtre anglais contemporain," *in 'Où est ce corps que j'entends?' Des corps et des voix dans le théâtre contemporain*, ed. Sandrine Le Pors and Pierre Longuenesse (Arras: Artois PU, 2014), 149–160.
48. See Michel Ter Hark, "Uncertainty, Vagueness and Psychological Indeterminacy," *Synthese* 124, no. 2 (2000), 193–220.

CHAPTER 11

Philip Ridley: Still In-Yer-Face

Thomas A. Oldham

The title of this collection, *After In-Yer-Face Theatre: Remnants of a Theatrical Revolution*, invites us to consider whether In-Yer-Face Theatre remains relevant today. Nearly two decades ago, Aleks Sierz described In-Yer-Face Theatre as "a theatre of sensation: it jolts both the actors and spectators out of conventional responses, touching nerves and provoking alarm.... In other words, it is experiential, not speculative."[1] Though Sierz has been highly influential, artists and scholars have since reexamined this label, forming complementary and contesting narratives and providing much-needed revision and reinterpretation. Even so, Sierz maintains that because it "describes not just the content of a play but the relationship between the writer and the public, or (more accurately) the relationship between the stage and the audience,"[2] In-Yer-Face remains a perfect descriptor for the writing of the 1990s. What about theater since the 1990s? The long-term viability of the "In-Yer-Face" label appears uncertain. A new production of Sarah Kane's *Cleansed*, for one, made headlines with its graphic imagery in 2016. Perhaps more shocking than any faints and walkouts, however, was the venue: The National Theatre. Erstwhile

T. A. Oldham (✉)
Department of Theatre and Dance, Texas A&M University-Corpus Christi, Corpus Christi, TX, USA
e-mail: Thomas.Oldham@tamucc.edu

© The Author(s) 2020
W. C. Boles (ed.), *After In-Yer-Face Theatre*,
https://doi.org/10.1007/978-3-030-39427-1_11

bad boys Martin McDonagh and Jez Butterworth have become even more respectable, writing plays that have won Oliviers and Tonys, while maintaining successful film careers. Perhaps the standard-bearer for the idea of In-Yer-Face theatre today, then, is a playwright who still courts controversy with squirm-inducing sexual and violent imagery—a playwright who still manages to divide critics and disturb audiences profoundly. Iconoclastic and impossible to pigeonhole, Philip Ridley is unquestionably still In-Yer-Face, and his plays merit wider acclaim and further critical study.

In-Yer-Face Dramaturgy: Ridley Through the Years

After its introductory material, Sierz's *In-Yer-Face Theatre* begins with an analysis of the work of Philip Ridley, whose breakthrough play, *The Pitchfork Disney* (1991), "kicked off the decade," introducing the world to a playwright who "is fascinated by the simultaneous attraction and repulsion of the gross and the grotesque."[3] The book concludes by saying that Ridley uses violence "to electrify sensibilities and leave the emotions open to other sensations."[4] Sierz has kept Ridley in high esteem, referring to him as "a pivotal figure in the history of 1990s playwriting because *The Pitchfork Disney* introduced a new sensibility into British theatre"[5] and detailing his influence on later playwrights from Mark Ravenhill to Butterworth to Kane.[6] While Sierz's *Rewriting the Nation* acknowledges that most theater has "moved on" from an In-Yer-Face aesthetic, concerning itself more with "global issues, social issues, and personal issues,"[7] the book still devotes significant space to Ridley. If there is any doubt that Philip Ridley is, as the title of this chapter suggests, still In-Yer-Face, it is clear that Sierz thinks so. He singles out three playwrights as continuing to use such aesthetic techniques: Dennis Kelly, debbie tucker green, and Philip Ridley.[8]

A useful theoretical paradigm for examining the power and significance of Ridley's In-Yer-Face dramaturgy is Ken Urban's "Theory of Cruel Britannia," which cites Nietzsche, Artaud, Bataille, and Heidegger, among others. Analyzing the larger implications of In-Yer-Face theatre, Urban finds "the ethical possibilities of an active nihilism"[9] and "the ground in which an ethics can take root."[10] A "cruel" dramaturgy "violently awakens consciousness to a horror that has remained unseen and unspoken, or willfully repressed" and "makes a space for ethical possibility, for change, even joy, but such possibility does not allow any escape or metaphysical hope."[11] With this paradigm, Urban activates In-Yer-Face Theatre with a political imperative, describing how "playwrights of the 1990s critique and intervene in their historical moment,"[12] forcing audiences to "reflect on the possibility of change, even if ... change cannot be imagined as a complete escape or overcoming."[13] Urban's theory, thus, is a powerful tool to analyze In-Yer-Face Theatre not merely for its sensationalism, but as profoundly, cruelly effectual. Philip Ridley, a playwright who once said that his plays emerge from asking, "How do we live in a godless world?"[14] may be the perfect example of this cruel aesthetic.

At one point in *The Pitchfork Disney*, the character Cosmo Disney gives a vivid speech describing his "vocation" as a geek show performer:

> It's a ghost train. People love it. Sitting there in the dark. Having the living daylights scared out of them. Tell someone there's a photograph of a car crash in the newspaper and what's the first thing they do? Buy the fucking newspaper. They all say, 'Oh, I don't want to see it.' But you know what that means? 'I *do* want to see it.' You know what we should do? Televise public executions. A Saturday-night fry-up of all the murderers, rapists, child-molesters and homosexuals. What a show that would be. Have the biggest audience in the history of entertainment. And why? Because mankind has loved to watch stuff like that since mankind began. Public flogging, the Roman Coliseum, bear-baiting, torture, crucifixion, Bedlam, bull-fighting, hunting, snuff movies, the atom bomb. They're all part of the same thing. Man's need for the shivers. Afraid of blood, wanting blood. We all need our daily dose of disgust. That's all. Nothing incredible ...[15]

While it would be disingenuous to see this quote as a thesis statement summarizing Ridley's outlook, it does provide an apt example of what a Philip Ridley play does: virtuosic monologues combine poetic language with horrific imagery into what Ridley calls an "image-aria,"[16] which serves as "a kind of captivator of emotion."[17] Ridley's first three plays earned him a place in *In-Yer-Face Theatre*: Sierz devotes the most space to *Ghost from a Perfect Place* (1994) and the resulting critical contempt, but *The Fastest Clock in the Universe* (1992) and *The Pitchfork Disney* were similarly impactful. These plays do not utilize the same on-stage violence as Kane's or McDonagh's works. Ridley's plays rarely are more violent than when a cigar is extinguished on an old man's face in *Ghost*, a finger is broken in *Disney*, or a pregnant woman is punched in *Clock*. Nonetheless, highly disturbing imagery and language wreak sufficient psychological damage: a violation of nostalgia and sentimentality creates an ominous sense of foreboding.[18] Ridley often frames the violence in a way that heightens its potential for disturbance; in making violence strange, Ridley approaches the uncanny. In *Ghost*, there are incestuous overtones; Cosmo Disney violates the sleeping Haley by thrusting his finger into her mouth; Sherbet's miscarriage in *Clock* is paralleled by a haunting monologue about the slaughtering of animals for fur. Providing theater audiences with profoundly impactful sensory experiences, Ridley finds the strange in the familiar and vice versa, drawing on his vivid imagination while dissecting elements of contemporary culture. As Urban's theory would suggest, this can lead to audience self-awareness, reflection, and the possibility of change.

Even though the 1990s, the decade of In-Yer-Face Theatre, ended, Ridley continued to provoke. As Dan Rebellato indicates, the dramaturgy shifted somewhat, featuring a "stronger sense of psychological depth to the characters."[19] Gone are characters with names such as Cosmo Disney, Foxtrot Darling, and Torchie Sparks that populated his first three plays. Sierz claims that Ridley "muffled"[20] the more sensational aspects of his dramaturgy in later plays, and Andrew Wyllie finds "in-yer-ears"[21] to be a more appropriate label for these plays, because they privilege the power of dialogue. The plays, however, are still "rich in metaphor and verbal imagery: and sensory and cognitive disturbances remain prominent."[22] In this modified style, Ridley appears to have drawn inspiration from his childhood, even though the plays are not remotely autobiographical. Tropes that echo Ridley's life appear repeatedly: plots feature homosexual men, artists, and complicated familial relationships, especially between brothers. His plays continue to depict the East End of London, where he was born and raised. An inward-looking turn also dominates the prefatory material to his two volumes of collected plays, which eschew the typical critical essays that introduce most of Methuen's offerings in favor of impressionistic sketches written by Ridley himself. While these entries are fragmentary and aestheticized, enough details match Ridley's biography to call them autobiographical.[23] In the Introduction to *Plays: 2*, time passes via Ridley's first-person present narration detailing his age ("I'm ten years old").[24] As a child, he encounters violence at home and at school but manages to find strange beauty in unexpected places, from insects to tombstones. A tantalizing yet obscure clue to future work appears in an anecdote involving his father, who reads racehorse names aloud from the newspaper: "Shrapnel Midnight," "Cactus Snow."[25] These colorfully nonsensical names suggest an early inspiration for apparently nonsequitur titles like *Mercury Fur* and *Daffodil Scissors*. The Introduction to the revised edition of *Plays: 1* covers a more expansive period: impossibly early memories from the age of one, childhood struggles with asthma, art school, early career, and budding same-sex attraction. Dominating both Introductions is the development of Ridley's artistic sensibility, as narrative breadcrumbs trace the path of a burgeoning In-Yer-Face aesthetic: sadistic treatment of bugs, fascination with the beauty of death, and obsession with turning experience into stories. There are nascent versions of characters seen in *The Pitchfork Disney* (a sequined-jacket-wearing performer eating cockroaches for audience titillation) and *Ghost From a Perfect Place* (a tough gang of pre-teen girls and an old woman nostalgic for the East End of the Krays).

Ridley's post-1999 work shows a newly realistic approach to character and recurring employment of selective autobiography, but this does not result in naturalistic plays. Philip Ridley continues to merit the label "In-Yer-Face": horrific action still dominates, though largely from offstage; trauma from past events, or those occurring just out of sight, lingers and manifests itself onstage. In *Vincent River* (2000), a mother pines for her deceased son by bonding with Davey who, she learns, was his lover. As in earlier plays, extended monologues feature prominently, but there is no onstage violence: Davey's image arias reveal that bigots murdered the son in a derelict public toilet used for clandestine homosexual assignations. The words come close to hypnotizing both characters and audience through their swirling virtuosity. *Leaves of Glass* (2007) approaches autobiography by depicting an artist who creates disturbing work and his relationship with his straitlaced brother.[26] The fictional fraternal bond turns dark, however, with the revelation that the artist was the victim of sexual abuse, leading to emotional trauma, alcoholism, and death. *Piranha Heights* (2008), another play about family, presents abnormal maternal and fraternal relationships in the characters of two quarreling brothers. They encounter a puzzling, ersatz family: a woman of subversively ambiguous racial, ethnic, and linguistic identity; her tattooed, profanity-spewing partner; and a baby doll, which they treat as a real child. In the end, the action devolves into a series of brawls and gunplay. Even *Tender Napalm* (2011), an ostensibly simple play about love and sex, defies expectations with language and imagery as paradoxically disturbing as its title. Two lovers, alone on stage with no scenery or props, create violent spectacle simply by reenacting their intensely passionate courtship with elaborate monologues and stichomythic dialogue comparing love to warfare. *Shivered* (2012) utilizes many of Ridley's characteristic dramaturgical features and thematic strands in addition to a structural novelty:

out-of-sequence chronology. A disreputable faith healer, paranormal activity, a viral video of terrorists beheading a soldier, and multiple variations of family strife among working-class British people contribute strands to the elaborate plot, which climaxes in a brutal onstage beating at the end of the first act. *Radiant Vermin* (2015), Ridley's most overtly satirical play, brings violent humor to the topics of fair housing, gentrification, and poverty. A young couple receives a fixer-upper house gratis, with one caveat: they must renovate it into their dream house. They quickly discover that such renovations magically occur when they kill homeless people on the property.

Mercury Fur

Over the course of Ridley's long career, he has written plays that have garnered controversy, featured disturbing violence, divided critics, and alienated audiences. In many ways, he has been the consummate In-Yer-Face playwright. The ultimate expression of Ridley's cruel, In-Yer-Face dramaturgy, however, is almost certainly *Mercury Fur* (2005). Its premiere "was greeted by a press hysteria that echoed the reception of *Blasted* a decade" prior.[27] Faber and Faber even refused to publish it. Like many of Ridley's plays, its plot unfolds in real time without any scene or act breaks. This structure is integral to audience reception of *Mercury Fur*; the gruesome plot's relentlessness heightens the feeling of claustrophobia, making it difficult, if not impossible, for the squeamish to walk out of usually small performance spaces. Despite its compact structure, *Mercury Fur* takes place in an elaborately wrought, dystopian near future, where two typically Ridleyean brothers work for a disreputable venture, supplying psychotropic butterflies to a narcotized public. On certain occasions, like the evening depicted in the play, Darren and Elliot also work to provide more illicit fantasy-fulfillment, mounting carefully staged events in which wealthy clients kill street urchins to their detailed specifications. In a feverish nightmare scenario, the current client pays to portray a soldier in the Vietnam War killing Elvis Presley, played by a young stand-in known only as "the Party Piece." The preparation for this "party" and its aftermath make up the bulk of the play.

For a play so caked in blood, the brutality of language dominates *Mercury Fur*, as it does in many In-Yer-Face plays. Several characters rattle off lengthy insults, stringing together profane series of racial epithets and ethnic slurs: "you nigger, Paki, wop, spic, Chinky, Muslim, Christian cunt!"[28] After the audience experiences several of these diatribes, the initial (intended) shock wears off, as the highly specific individual instances of hate speech aggregate into a numbed conglomeration that transcends specific offense. The incendiary eventually becomes mundane, and the audience becomes as accustomed to it as the characters are. These mini-rituals of profanity are paralleled by mini-rituals of storytelling, a fixture for the playwright, and which Sierz has stated, is "characteristic of Ridley's playwriting style."[29] This goes as far back as *The Pitchfork Disney*, where, in Urban's analysis, "the telling is a shared experience, a ritual in which both participants know their roles."[30] In *Mercury Fur*, this trope is especially powerful. As a result of society's addiction to butterflies, its collective memory is decimated. Knowledge of history is elusive, and Elliott is considered wise because of his ability to recite stories from the past, both private and public. At one point, he recalls the Minotaur myth, and Ridley draws parallels between Theseus's guiding thread and the role storytelling plays in his work: characters use stories to guide them through disintegrating history and as linguistic rituals expressing emotion.[31] Ritual has always held a primary place in In-Yer-Face Theatre, from the ready meals in Ravenhill's *Shopping and Fucking* to the recitation of medications in Kane's *4.48 Psychosis*. Sierz has analyzed the ritualistic character of *The Fastest Clock in the Universe*,[32] and Ridley has eloquently described ritual's importance:

> That's been part of the work from the very beginning. And theatre itself is very ritualised; I've always seen theatre as a piece of alchemy. You know, it's like a tribe in the middle of the jungle being afraid of the forest because of the monsters or wild animals. And it's the witch doctor's job to tell a story to make them less afraid, or at least feel that they can deal with the monsters. I'm the witch doctor and the story around the tribe's camp fire is theatre. The story aims to make sense of fear. And so it's a very simple kind of ritual; theatre for me is a very primeval activity. It's very sweaty, bloody, and I'm really fascinated by that kind of alchemy when I get it—not just in my own work but in other people's too—when it's a real transformative exploration.[33]

A more succinct summation comes from Ridley's acknowledgment that his work owes a debt to Jean Genet: "we can't truly experience something until we have found a ritual."[34]

These rituals provide a foundation in which a cruel ethics, in Urban's words, can form. As David Ian Rabey points out, Ridley creates situations "whereby a character attempts to (re-) order their past through a repeated activity of storytelling which willfully obscures any reliable boundaries between truth and fiction."[35] Ridley explains, "*Mercury Fur* is about what happens to people when you take away their history. The first thing that goes is a sense of identity. And once your identity and storytelling start to go, the next thing that goes is a sense of morality: you cease to be able to decide what is right or wrong. That's something that I've always been passionate about in the writing. Storytelling is our morality."[36] The end of the play is a precipice for Darren and Elliot: they kill their client and let the victim escape. Elliot contemplates mercy-killing Darren so that he will suffer neither the inevitable, painful consequences of their actions nor the increasingly dire state of the world crumbling around them. In the face of this, Darren attempts one last ritual: a recapitulation of earlier dialogue when the brothers expressed their love for each other in a back-and-forth litany of ritualized sentiments.

Darren: I love you so much I could grab you and grab you.
Elliot: I love you so much I could grab you harder and harder.
Darren: I love you so much I could make you scream and scream
Elliot: I love you so much I could kick you and punch you.[37]

Ridley ends the play in the middle of the crucial decision, though: Elliot refuses to respond to Darren's prompts and holds the gun to his brother's head; Darren repeatedly screams, "Say it!"[38] Blackout denies resolution but indicates the possibility for a new ethics, a new path forward, through Urban's cruelty.

The production history of *Mercury Fur* reads like a template for In-Yer-Face Theatre in general: initial shock followed by hard-won (though far from universal) acclaim. During John Tiffany's 2005 production, audience members walked out on a regular basis, and critical opinion was predominantly negative, even openly hostile, with accusations of depravity on the part of the playwright. Ridley defended the play, saying, "I don't think there's anything wrong in people being disturbed in the theatre."[39] In the same interview, he denigrated critics who judge plays "purely on their subject matter, regardless of the theatrical experience," singling out Michael Billington, "going home to warm slippers and cocoa" as particularly out-of-touch with the experience of most people in this world.[40] While trying to avoid overly simplistic exegesis, Ridley drew attention to the seriousness of the play, with its political message of governmental attempts to rewrite history and monopolize truth; for him the play is remarkably liberating, with characters finding new morality and regaining human qualities. In short, he wanted people to "experience it as an experience" and appreciate "the sensation it causes," but see it as a "deeply moral play in what's it trying to say."[41] In this one interview, Ridley perfectly captured both Sierz's original parameters for In-Yer-Face Theatre and Urban's definition of the cruel aesthetic of active nihilism.

By the 2012 revival directed by Ned Bennett, the play had indeed undergone a critical reevaluation, becoming something of a modern classic and receiving critical praise both in daily newspapers and from scholars like Anna Harpin, who utilizes trauma theory to make a case for the moral efficacy of the play.[42] The Off-Broadway premiere by the New Group in August 2015, however, received mixed reviews, with many critics still focused on what the *New York Post*'s critic saw as "provocation for provocation's sake."[43] This is perhaps unfair to Ridley, who, far from fetishizing provocation, sees the need for direct action: "I've always maintained that any play, if it has any merit at all, fills you with a greater passion for life, no matter the subject matter. I want audiences to come out of my plays with a passion for life. That's what it's all about really. Passion."[44]

RIDLEY'S LASTING SIGNIFICANCE

One reason Ridley's work is divisive is the young age of many of his characters: the fifteen-year-old object of lust in *The Fastest Clock in the Universe*, the twelve-year-old gang member in *Ghost from a Perfect Place*. The extreme example is *Mercury Fur*'s brutalized Party Piece, who is ten. Ridley cannot, however, be dismissed as a sadistic child butcher. Helen Freshwater, for one, sees this as dramaturgically significant to the play: "the figure of the child drives and focuses experiments with form."[45] Furthermore, some of Ridley's most successful writing is for children, including a series of plays for young audiences, which sheds further light on Ridley's grand design. With common themes and motifs, five of these plays appear as a single volume, fittingly titled *The Storyteller Sequence* (2015). The prominence of storytelling is significant for both content and form: characters tell each other stories in order to forge connection, and the theater audience is both witness to and participant in the sharing. In these plays, the storytelling impetus that informs much of Ridley's dramaturgy manifests itself metatheatrically. His biography again provides a parallel, proving story's long-standing importance: "Carl [Ridley's younger brother] was a very nervous child, afraid of all sorts of things: cold pillows, dust, the sound of next door's TV. I made up stories to send him to sleep."[46] Of these Storyteller plays, *Sparkleshark* (1997) is an illustrative example, exploring some of the playwright's preoccupations from a comparatively wholesome perspective. A group of fourteen- to sixteen-year-olds unexpectedly bond by sharing a communal storytelling experience on the roof of a rundown tower block in Ridley's East London. The main character is the Ridleyean Jake, an outcast youth of artistic temperament, who escapes isolation using the fantastical power of words. One by one, a cast of characters straight out of any coming-of-age story of cliques, bullies, and geeks intrudes upon his sanctuary. When the alpha male and two hangers-on threaten physical violence, Jake pulls them into his world of make-believe, like an adolescent Scheherazade, and the charming fantasy leads to empathy, reconciliation, and growth. *Sparkleshark* displays the true nature of Ridley's dramaturgical endeavor: a staggering call to human connection. His plays for young audiences provide a greater appreciation for Ridley's In-Yer-Face offerings: the sex, the violence, and the grotesque are not sensationalistic horrors, nor do they espouse a specific political belief. Instead, they display the extremes of human behavior, pushing the audience to its limits in order to make the world anew, with the knowledge of past atrocities, but with the possibility of a new perspective for all. Ridley has called several of his plays "hopeful" and has even said, "*Mercury Fur* is a thing of great tenderness."[47] For him, "there has to be this sense of redemption at the end."[48]

As of this writing, his most recent full-length play is *Karagula* (2016), which, perhaps unsurprisingly for a new Ridley offering, opened to scathing reviews. Also unsurprisingly, the play tweaked expectations of the theatrical form and audience convention: it made headlines even before its opening, because the venue location was kept secret. As throughout his career, though, most initial reviews of Ridley's experimentation were simplistically dismissive. The headline of the review in *The Telegraph* asked, "Is *Karagula* the Worst Play of 2016?"[49] while *The Guardian* concluded that the play had been "sunk by its own excesses."[50] This combination of self-consciously odd presentation and critical disdain suggests a profound misunderstanding of Ridley's project; the play warrants a closer look. Analyzing *Karagula* in the context of his decades-long career provides a key to deciphering the seemingly confusing text, as it contains several of his dramaturgical hallmarks. Featuring an out-of-sequence chronology and a profoundly misplaced nostalgia for popular culture, the play at first glance seems a confused mishmash of a disjointed, post-apocalyptic sci-fi thriller where Prom Night in "Mereka" gives way to ritual sacrifice, powerful cabals, and nuclear holocaust. It is with the final scene that everything comes together, although many reviewers seem to have run out of patience long before then. The ending of the play seems to suggest (although the obscurity of the action perhaps prevents any fully satisfactory exegesis) that everything that has come before was the fractured mythologizing of a decrepit old man, establishing a foundational historical text that explains fragmentary evidence from the pre-annihilation world: ritual storytelling once again. It may be the ultimate example of this facet of Ridley's aesthetic.

If *Mercury Fur* occupies the space immediately prior to oblivion, *Karagula* occurs long after the conflagration subsides. Then, the need for storytelling is paramount; every object, relic, and memory is literally meaningless without it. This is the defining motif of Ridley's oeuvre; it unites the In-Yer-Face sex and violence, the childlike curiosity and innocent empathy, the necessary darkness, and the all-consuming work of the Renaissance man of many arts. He has said:

> I don't have many eureka moments; I'm always making notes, drawing images, writing down ideas and pieces of dialogue in a notebook... The easiest way to describe "inspiration" is "it's like a bomb explosion in reverse". You start with lots of broken up shrapnel all over the place and you can't see how it all fits together, but gradually it comes together and forms something. So I suppose you could say I have lots of mini eureka moments—eurekaettes—rather than one big one.[51]

Ridley often works by collecting: taking Polaroids[52]; jotting down overheard conversations.[53] He then draws them all together. *The Times*'s review of *Piranha Heights* could apply to almost any of Ridley's work in any media over the past three decades: "The extravagance of Ridley's dark vision suggests a dangerously confused society in which individuals seize on random gobbets of semi-digested information and use them to construct their own personal narrative."[54] This is how meaning is created in Ridley's world.

It should be clear that time has not diminished Philip Ridley's relevance. The 2016 repertory pairing of *Dark Vanilla Jungle* and *Tonight with Donny Stixx*, two monologues from lost souls recreating their troubled histories as self-aware mythology, caused the reviewer from *The New York Times* to remark that Ridley's ability to endow "his blighted characters with an instinctive gift for poetry" allows you to "know where they're coming from. And that's likely to be closer than you'd think—or hope—to a place that you occupy, too."[55] This identification is key to Ridley's work; these terrible In-Yer-Face actions are perpetrated on and by people like us. That is why his writing continues to disturb, yet avoid the pitfalls of shock for shock's sake. With both Sierz's definition of In-Yer-Face Theatre and Urban's Cruel Britannia, the ultimate responsibility lies with the audience; we must take moral stands. As Ridley says, "We have entered a period where the world is astonishing and terrifying and…the old world doesn't apply any more and as an artist that is very exciting…. How can you rationally and intellectually react to something that isn't intelligent or rational…?"[56] Three decades on, Philip Ridley is still In-Yer-Face and all that the label entails: gruesome, sensational, vitally theatrical, and absolutely necessary.

Notes

1. Aleks Sierz, *In-Yer-Face Theatre: British Drama Today* (London: Faber and Faber, 2001), 4.
2. Aleks Sierz, "'We All Need Stories': The Politics of In-Yer-Face Theatre," in *Cool Britannia? British Political Drama in the 1990s*, ed. Rebecca D'Monté and Graham Saunders (Basingstoke: Palgrave, 2008), 24.
3. Sierz, *In-Yer-Face*, 40–41.
4. Ibid., 209.
5. Aleks Sierz, *Modern British Playwriting. The 1990s: Voices, Documents, New Interpretations* (London: Methuen Drama, 2012), 89–90.
6. Sierz, *In-Yer-Face*, 111.
7. Aleks Sierz, *Rewriting the Nation: British Theatre Today* (London: Methuen Drama, 2011), 11.
8. Sierz, "We All Need Stories," 34.
9. Ken Urban, "Cruel Britannia," in D'Monté and Saunders, *Cool Britannia?*, 39.
10. Ibid., 49.
11. Ibid., 43.
12. Ibid., 45.
13. Ibid., 50.
14. Ken Urban, "Ghosts from an Imperfect Place: Philip Ridley's Nostalgia," *Modern Drama* 50, no. 3 (Fall 2007): 328, https://doi.org/10.1353/mdr.2007.0063.
15. Philip Ridley, *The Pitchfork Disney*, in *Plays: 1* (London: Methuen Drama, 2012), 67.

16. Sierz, *In-Yer-Face*, 43.
17. Philip Ridley and Aleks Sierz, "'Putting a New Lens on the World': The Art of Theatrical Alchemy," *New Theatre Quarterly* 25, no. 2 (2009): 113, https://doi.org/10.1017/S0266464X09000207.
18. For a further discussion of nostalgia, see Urban, "Ghosts from an Imperfect Place."
19. Dan Rebellato, "Philip Ridley," in *The Methuen Drama Guide to Contemporary British Playwrights*, ed. Martin Middeke, Peter Paul Schnierer, and Aleks Sierz (London: Methuen Drama, 2011), 427.
20. Sierz, *Modern British Playwriting*, 226.
21. Andrew Wylie, "Philip Ridley and Memory," *Studies in Theatre and Performance* 33, no. 1 (January 2013): 2, https://doi.org/10.1386/stap.33.1.65_1.
22. Rebellato, "Philip Ridley," 427.
23. See Ridley and Sierz, "Putting a New Lens"; Lucy Powell, "And When He is Good He is Horrid," *The Times*, February 25, 2010, The Times Digital Archive; Alexis Soloski, "A Macabre Vision Takes Many Forms," *The New York Times*, August 16, 2015, https://www.nytimes.com/2015/08/16/theater/philip-ridley-writer-of-mercury-fur-is-all-over-the-media-map.html.
24. Philip Ridley, introduction to *Plays: 2* (London: Methuen Drama, 2009), ix.
25. Ibid., x.
26. Rebellato, "Philip Ridley," 427.
27. Urban, "Cruel Britannia," 52.
28. Philip Ridley, *Mercury Fur*, in *Plays: 2* (London: Methuen Drama, 2009), 83.
29. Sierz, *Modern British Playwriting*, 92.
30. Urban, "Ghosts," 327.
31. Philip Ridley, "Controversial Playwright Philip Ridley Defends His Work," interview by Rachel Halliburton, *Theatre Voice*, March 4, 2005, http://www.theatrevoice.com/audio/interview-philip-ridley-the-controversial-writers-latest/.
32. Sierz, *Modern British Playwriting*, 100.
33. Ridley and Sierz, "Putting a New Lens," 112.
34. Ridley, "Controversial Playwright."
35. David Ian Rabey, *English Drama since 1940* (London: Longman, 2003), 196.
36. Ridley and Sierz, "Putting a New Lens," 114.
37. Ridley, *Mercury Fur*, 91.
38. Ibid., 202.
39. Ridley, "Controversial Playwright."
40. Ibid.
41. Ibid.

42. Anna Harpin, "Intolerable Acts," *Performance Research* 16, no. 1 (March 2011), https://doi.org/10.1080/13528165.2011.561681.
43. Elisabeth Vincentelli, review of *Mercury Fur*, *The New York Post*, August 21, 2015, https://nypost.com/2015/08/21/its-physically-impossible-to-leave-new-play-mercury-fur-early.
44. Philip Ridley, "Karagula: An Interview with Playwright Philip Ridley," by Laura Foulger, *The Upcoming*, June 6, 2016, http://www.theupcoming.co.uk/2016/06/06/karagula-an-interview-with-playwright-philip-ridley.
45. Helen Freshwater, "Children and the Limits of Representation in the Work of Tim Crouch," in *Contemporary British Theatre: Breaking New Ground*, ed. Vicky Angelaki (Basingstoke: Palgrave, 2013), 170.
46. Soloski, "A Macabre Vision."
47. Ibid.
48. Ridley and Sierz, "Putting a New Lens," 112.
49. Dominic Cavendish, review of *Karagula*, *The Telegraph*, June 16, 2016, https://www.telegraph.co.uk/theatre/what-to-see/is-karagula-at-the-styx-the-worst-play-of-2016%2D%2D-review.
50. Lyn Gardner, review of *Karagula*, *Guardian*, June 19, 2016, http://www.theguardian.com/stage/2016/jun/19/karagula-review-styx-london.
51. Ridley, "*Karagula*: An Interview."
52. Soloski, "A Macabre Vision."
53. Dina Rabinovitch, "Author of the Month: Philip Ridley," *Guardian*, April 27, 2005, http://www.theguardian.com/books/2005/apr/27/booksforchildrenandteenagers.familyandrelationships.
54. Sam Marlowe, review of *Piranha Heights*, *The Times*, May 27, 2008, The Times Digital Archive.
55. Ben Brantley, review of *Dark Vanilla Jungle* and *Tonight with Donny Stixx*, *The New York Times*, January 29, 2016, https://www.nytimes.com/2016/01/30/theater/review-in-tonight-jungle-by-philip-ridley-darkness-rules.html.
56. Philip Ridley, interview by Emily Jupp, *The Independent*, June 2, 2016, https://www.independent.co.uk/arts-entertainment/theatre-dance/philip-ridley-on-how-to-combat-donald-trump-his-love-of-jude-law-his-new-fantasy-play-karagula-and-a7061911.html.

CHAPTER 12

Tales from the East End: Dialogic and Confessional Storytelling as Therapy (?) in the Plays of Philip Ridley

Cath Badham

INTRODUCTION

Storytelling is an enduring trope in Philip Ridley's plays, but its form and emphasis changes throughout his work. In his earlier plays, such as *The Pitchfork Disney* (1991) and *The Fastest Clock in the Universe* (1992), the stories are nostalgic in nature, helping to consolidate the identities forged by the characters who tell them. Ken Urban and Andrew Wyllie suggest that Ridley's nostalgic storytelling is either a sickness or a therapy, respectively.[1] Ridley's early plays can be seen as drawing on the traditions of dramatic realism where the stories that are told between the characters on stage in a dialogic manner create and reinforce a rupture in identities and relationships resulting in a state of Aristotelian catharsis. His recent work sees a shift to a confessional style of storytelling, where the stories are told in direct address to the audience. Thus, the audience are positioned as either a therapist listening to a patient or as the audience for a television

C. Badham (✉)
University of Derby, Derby, UK
e-mail: c.badham@derby.ac.uk

program such as *The Jeremy Kyle Show* or *Jerry Springer* in which public confession becomes entertainment.

I argue that both the dialogic and confessional styles of storytelling that Ridley utilizes offer opportunities for therapy, confession and catharsis. I focus my discussion as follows. *Vincent River* (2000) is an example of Ridley's earlier dialogic style. It is the story of two strangers, Anita and Davey, meeting for the first time. They are connected through the death of Anita's son, the eponymous Vincent, and their conversation leads to the truth of his life and death being revealed. *Dark Vanilla Jungle* (2013) and *Tonight with Donny Stixx* (2015) are both examples of a confessional style of storytelling employing direct address. In *Dark Vanilla Jungle* Andrea tells us the story of her dysfunctional home life, how she is groomed and then abused, eventually taking advantage of somebody more vulnerable than herself. In *Tonight with Donny Stixx* Donny entertains us with the story of his life and the fatal consequences of his desire to be famous.

Storytelling and Therapy

The term "talking cure" was coined by Joseph Breuer's patient Anna O. Breuer's technique of using "a sort of hypnosis" allowed his patient to talk about the "fancies" that were occupying her mind.[2] "Whenever she had related a number of such fancies she was, as it were, freed and restored to her normal mental life."[3] Freud's initial work in this area capitalized on Breuer's cathartic use of hypnotism to recall repressed trauma and the emotions that memory aroused. Freud later rejected this, opting instead for a process that started with asking the patient if they could recall "…what had originally occasioned the symptom concerned…"[4] John McLeod states that "[t]he great advance made by Freud [...] was to discover that patients could be cured by someone listening to them. If the patient was given an opportunity to tell his or her story, they appeared to get better."[5] McLeod also argues "that stories and storytelling represent the primary point of connection between what goes on in 'therapy' [...] and what goes on in the culture as a whole. From a cultural perspective, a therapy session is a site for telling stories in a certain way."[6]

This concept allows for the possibility that using storytelling and narrative as a form of therapy is not restricted to formal sessions with a professional. Indeed, McLeod considers how narrative was used therapeutically before ideas of psychotherapy were developed.[7] "The telling of personal stories, tales of 'who I am', 'what I want to be', or 'what troubles me,' to a listener or audience mandated by culture to hear such stories, is an essential mechanism through which individual lives become and can remain aligned with collective realities."[8] Theater offers the opportunity of just such a mandated audience. Like the therapist, a theater audience is delegated to hear these stories offering a potential site in which a "talking cure" might be available. This is especially the case if we remember that through Aristotle's idea of catharsis, which Stephen Halliwell suggests "entails both an expenditure of emotion, and an amelioration of the underlying emotional disposition," theater and therapy can be connected.[9]

For a cure to be affected some type of disease, illness or addiction needs to be treated. In all of the plays under consideration here some cause of dis-ease can be identified. It is also possible to recognize two different styles of therapeutic narrative across the three plays. In *Vincent River*, we can see a traditional dialogic form of storytelling that imitates the question and answer form of a session between therapist and patient, with, in this case, Anita and Davey acting in both roles over the course of the play. In *Dark Vanilla Jungle* and *Tonight with Donny Stixx*, the overwhelming form of storytelling is confessional direct address from protagonist to audience. In *Dark Vanilla Jungle*, Andrea seems to be confessing to a group in a therapy session, recounting her biography to begin a healing process. Donny Stixx, who also suggests he is engaged in some form of rehabilitation, draws us into the world of the TV/celebrity confessional, where everybody wants their shot at being famous. All our protagonists have a need to talk to enable them to be rid of their emotional dis-ease.

Aristotelian Catharsis in *Vincent River*

Ken Urban identifies nostalgia as a disease that holds Ridley's characters in a cycle of reminiscence trapping them in the past. Urban contrasts a modern definition of nostalgia as "sanitized memory, the past without the pain" with seventeenth and eighteenth century notions of nostalgia as an illness.[10] In identifying both Johannes Hofer's location of "nostalgia's source in a longing for place" and Immanuel Kant's further positioning of nostalgia "to include a temporal element" Urban suggests that "adherence to a nostalgic vision leads to a dismissal of the present and an abdication of the future."[11] Andrew Wyllie, in contrast, proposes that Ridley's later plays "[dramatize]...the need to recapture the past as therapy for a sick present."[12] In *Vincent River*, Ridley's fourth play, Davey and Anita use storytelling, much of which is reminiscent and nostalgic, not only to deal with the death of the title character, Vincent River, but also to reveal the truths about themselves. In the process, their joint reminiscences also create a more honest identity for Vincent than their own separate notions of who he was, resulting in catharsis for both characters. Set in Anita's new home, the domestic location fulfils Fred Miller Robinson's proposition identifying the room as a space in which the subjective nature of characters can be revealed.[13] One of the modes of revealing this subjectivity is through the ritual of storytelling.

At the start of the play, Davey is a stranger to Anita, but her identity as a mother figure is quickly established by her concern over his black eye. However, they are wary of each other and the short sharp statements by both characters indicate a desire to reveal as little as possible.

Anita   You thirsty?
            Slight Pause
            I'm offering. You want a drink?
Davey   No. Thank you.
Anita   What you after, then?
Davey   Wh-what d'ya mean?
Anita   Why you here?
Davey   You...you opened the door. You called me in.
Anita   And why'd I do that?[14]

Anita and Davey are curious about each other and ask questions that act as a means of eliciting narrative.[15] However, this early exchange makes it feel that they are unwilling to give away their secrets.

It is through telling stories about their lives that we begin to get a picture of not only who they are but who Vincent, Anita's only son, was as well. As Anita and Davey begin to talk, we learn that Vincent has been murdered in a homophobic attack. Davey explains he found the body and his girlfriend made the call to the police. One outcome of the murder was the revelation to Anita that her son was gay. Throughout the play they trade stories of their current situation and of their history. Slowly a picture is built up of two people who are struggling not only with their grief for someone they both loved but with their position in society. We discover, with Davey, that Anita became pregnant with Vincent through an affair with a married man and was subsequently disowned by her family, that she is not afraid of her sexuality and she doted on her bookish, shy, artistic son who, as a young boy, created necklaces out of dead insects found on the local bomb site. In a final ignominy, she has been driven out of her home by bigoted neighbors after Vincent's homosexuality is described as "sordid" by the papers. We learn, with Anita, that Davey has a girlfriend called Rachel and that he got engaged to her to make his mum happy; nurses taught him to do reflexology to help his mum, but she has died of cancer. He also states that he was walking Rachel home when he found Vincent's body. These stories reveal the underlying dis-ease that both characters possess. Anita has presented a hard, defensive front to the world to negate the hurt felt by the rejection she has suffered. Davey has endured the pain of seeing his mother die and, we discover later, the murder of his lover. Information is revealed because one character demands it of the other or because either Anita or Davey wish to get something off their chest, as might happen in a therapy session. They tell each other stories that reveal the traumas that they have both suffered and repressed, beginning a healing process.

As with a Greek tragedy, where the spectators would hear news at the same time as the protagonists, Davey reveals the truth to Anita and the audience at the same moment. His disclosure that he and Vincent were lovers, that he witnessed the murder and, by extension, his life with his girlfriend has been one long deception changes the dialogic form of the storytelling. It now becomes entwined with role-playing, building the tension later released in a cathartic climax. Davey reveals that he and Vincent met at the hospital when Davey was visiting his mum and Vincent was visiting Anita. He gives Anita enough information about his other gay sexual encounters for her to realize that Davey picked up Vincent. He tells Anita about their meetings and finally gets to the night where Davey persuades Vincent to take him home to the flat he shared with Anita. With Anita's encouragement, Davey manages to find the words to begin to tell the final part of the story initially recalling his astonishment at Vincent's use of internet porn. For Davey, this is an inadequate replacement for the feel of another human body. As Davey unbuttons his shirt, he addresses Anita as if she is Vincent saying, "'Feel my heart, Vince.'"[16] She does not move but after Davey asks twice more she finally places her hand on his chest, acknowledging she can feel his heart beating. In becoming Vincent, Anita "take[s] on character for the sake of action" and becomes part of Davey's story as well as being the listener.[17] Her taking on this role allows Davey to relive an intimate moment with Vincent. In the same way that a therapist might allow a quiet moment to linger, Anita's empathy and eventual silence creates the space in which Davey can finally tell the truth of Vincent's death. His final narrative produces the pity and fear necessary to generate catharsis.[18] We witness Anita's growing dread as she hears the truth of her son's death. We feel this along with her allowing us some degree of empathy. We are taken, with Anita, along the sickening journey of the vicious beating that killed Vincent and it is only in her "long painful cry" that any release is found.[19] No more words are spoken between Davey and Anita. They are not needed. Their repressed truths and the reasons for their dis-eases have been revealed through the narratives they have told. Most important is the truth about Vincent, who he was and how he died. This relieves Davey of the burden of knowledge he was carrying; he now shares it with Anita. At the same time, she is freed from the burden of denying the truth about her son. In the final moments Anita returns to mothering Davey as she did at the beginning. This time they are both silent as she hands him his jacket and straightens his collar.[20] Anita is able to say goodbye to her son, now represented by Davey, and in return Davey can say goodbye to his mother, displaced onto Anita. As Davey leaves and the lights go down, we are left with a cathartic sense of closure and the expectation of recovery.

The catharsis felt by Anita, Davey and the audience at the end of *Vincent River* is not unexpected. The play follows a form that allows for a feeling of purgation and relief for both the onstage characters and the audience. Stephen Halliwell states that catharsis is "tied to a conscious, cognitive experience of a work of mimetic art and the emotions involved [...] are properly and justifiably evoked by a portrayal of events which, if encountered in reality, would call for the same emotional response."[21] If Davey and Anita were real, then the stories that they encourage each other to tell would lead to the same freeing of their emotions as we see on stage. Similarly, as Halliwell suggests, if the audience were to witness Davey and Anita's conversation in real life, they would feel the same relief and hope as they do at the end of the play. In both cases, the catharsis is not due to the presence of the audience, but a product of the interaction between two characters and how it affects themselves and those watching. Through the truths they eventually commit to there is the belief that Anita and Davey will both move forward rather than being stuck in their pasts.

Confessional Storytelling

There is a shift in theatrical form in *Dark Vanilla Jungle* and *Tonight with Donny Stixx*. In these plays, the naturalistic dialogic style of *Vincent River* is replaced by direct address; the characters talking to the audience rather than to other each other on stage. In turn, the narrative style, whilst maintaining the sense of a beginning, middle and end, takes on a confessional tone.[22] As with *Vincent River*, the protagonists have a dis-ease caused by a trauma but in these plays the audience are not eavesdropping on a private process. Instead the use of direct address demands that they listen and make judgement on the stories they are told.

Confession is often associated with private situations: confessing to God in the sanctity of the church confessional or admitting to a crime in the privacy of a police interview room. Sharon Hymer states that "[r]eligious confession binds us to the larger community."[23] Here she is suggesting that by making a confession in a religious context one is connected to a community which has longstanding "cultural and historical roots" as well as "a worldwide community of the faithful."[24] John McLeod traces some of the earliest uses of public confession to the traditional rural cultures that existed in pre-industrial European society.[25] He notes that the treatment of psychological illnesses fell to priests and pastors but that a "collective ritual" was used to help those suffering with, what would be identified today as, mental health issues.[26] This communal treatment would involve the "patient" telling their story in the fullest manner possible in a public arena.[27] In this type of public confession, we see the link that Hymer makes between the individual and community. Revealing one's secrets in a public setting immediately opens the individual up to peer judgement but also the possibility of help from that community. Where, then, are the opportunities for public confession in the present day? Perhaps it is possible to substitute forms of communal communication, such as theater or television, for religion. Is it possible that theater provides opportunities for public confession leading to some form of healing or redemption in conjunction with one's community as suggested by Hymer?[28]

Dark Vanilla Jungle and *Tonight with Donny Stixx* sit within the concept of public rather than private confession because the protagonists directly address the audience. We become their community. In the rest of this chapter, I will argue these plays align with contemporary notions of public confession and that the audience are positioned as "therapists." However, I also suggest that a theater audience is impotent to intercede due to conventions of spectatorship that prevent them from intervening and that results in an incomplete catharsis.

Dark Vanilla Jungle

Dark Vanilla Jungle is an emotionally challenging monologue charting the journey of Andrea, from manipulated teenager to manipulator and the psychological toll that takes on her. She wants to love and to be loved, but previous experiences have been traumatic leading to anger issues and a psychological breakdown. It is not surprising that the play takes on the air of a session between a therapist and their patient, set as it is on a bare stage with no furniture and only a plain back wall defining the playing space.[29] "I was stung by a wasp once—Shall I tell you about this? Well, it's something you don't know. And I have to start somewhere."[30] These opening lines indicate that a story is coming but Andrea is struggling to know how to start her narrative. Beginning wherever she desires gives Andrea control and echoes the invitation often given by therapists to their patients, as suggested by John McLeod: "Well, you can start wherever you want to, whatever thing you want to talk about."[31] Andrea acknowledges the need to tell the truth asking for "a few words of well-intentioned reprimand if they help to keep me on track."[32] Her awareness that she is talking to more than one person is confirmed in her line "I'm talking to the women now."[33] She knows her story is being heard in a public forum made up of both sexes. This is not a one-to-one session between two characters as seen in *Vincent River* but a public revealing of her story, a confessional and therapeutic narrative told in a group situation.

Andrea's narrative changes in tone as she tells her story. In the beginning we see her as the abused teenager she is, unloved by her parents then groomed, raped and left pregnant by a married man, Tyrone. We identify her as the victim and we sympathize with her. Her trauma is manifested in bursts of anger which, in the two performances I have seen, were directed at individual members of the audience. She is angry that other people are telling her story and distorting her truth which only she can relate. "Well, if you *have* fucking heard this before I'd like to know how because *I* didn't fucking tell you!"[34] She believes that we, her audience, only want to hear about what happened to her baby rather than allowing her to "tell this exactly how I wanted to."[35] Nevertheless, the premise of Andrea as patient and the audience as therapist/listening ear is established and Andrea's initial vacillation between stories about her parents and her abuser help us to draw parallels between these two formative, but uncaring, relationships. It is as if she is finding her feet, collecting her story together to try and make sense of it, just as a therapist or counselor might encourage their patient to do the same. In the second half of the play, Andrea's narrative becomes more linear in format as if her story and how she should tell it is becoming clearer to her. She talks to us in the present tense, reliving events as she tells us about them. This reveals how the trauma of her experiences has affected her behavior. Andrea takes Mrs. Vye, her foster carer, to the hospital after she has had a stroke. Whilst there, she overhears the medical staff talking about Glenn, a soldier left in a vegetative state after being injured by a landmine. By the time she leaves the hospital that night, she believes that she is meant to be with Glenn. She has even begun to exhibit a form of selective amnesia forgetting who Mrs. Vye was as if drawing a veil over her previous life.[36] In this amnesia she is actively repressing the trauma of the abuse suffered at Tyrone's hands.

Using the present tense allows us to see Andrea's descent into paranoia, imagining that men are only seeing her as a sexual object, as if it is happening in front of us. She tells of her belief that one of the male nurses wants to suck her nipples and when she describes getting on the bus her thoughts become more disturbing.

Andrea   I sit at the back. I'm the only passenger. Is the driver looking at me in his mirror? Does he want to rape me? Probably. It's one of the perks of the job these days. [...] Two men get on. [...] One of them looks back at me. He says something to his friend. [...] Do *they* want to rape me? Probably. They're going to collude with the bus driver and commit gang rape.[37]

This paranoia results in "*a violent fit*" a physical manifestation of her psychological problems.[38] The audience can see how much she is suffering emotionally in the violence of the seizure. It also compounds the break that she is making with her former life. By lying about her status as his girlfriend Andrea wormed her way into the lives and home of Glenn and his mother, Renee. She also shows how her grasp on reality broke down. Talking about wearing Mrs. Vye's shapeless dresses and how she would do anything for Glenn, Andrea casts herself as subservient. This submissive attitude can be seen as learnt behavior from her time with Tyrone, as she struggles to maintain a hold on her self-worth. However, the audience can see that although she is still telling her story, she is actually lying to herself, believing herself to be the perfect partner for Glenn. We see through the untruths, for example, that her insistence that baby is Glenn's rather than Tyrone's, and as we do so the concern for her mental health grows.

In the final section, Andrea breaks down completely. What sends her out of control is her account of how she was unmasked as Glenn's sexual abuser. After her violent exile from Glenn's house, she walks to Epping Forest. She is talking to herself now, no longer acknowledging us as her audience: "If a man looks at me I'll poke his eyes out," and "It's times like this I wish I had a veil."[39] The pace is getting quicker, building to the climatic birth of the baby in the woods. This is the final incident that has brought her the need to tell her story for therapeutic purposes. Unlike *Vincent River*, though, in the calm after this moment it does not feel like a catharsis has been achieved. Instead, her belief that her baby has grown into a man overnight and that he is "[t]he lord of everything" leaves us feeling that Andrea's healing process has only just begun.[40] In *Dark Vanilla Jungle* Andrea uses the audience as her listening ear suggesting she is treating this session as an opportunity to unburden herself. When her moment of breakdown comes, it is a purgation for her but not for us. Her final act of kneeling, of quasi-religious contrition is just the start of her healing process. As the community that she has chosen to confide in, we should be a part of this. Instead, we are prevented by the conventions of audience and character from assisting Andrea further. Andrea's confession fails to provide the type of catharsis that Davey and Anita achieve because we are unable to fulfill the role of community suggested by Hymer or McLeod. Davey and Anita act for each other but no-one acts for Andrea leaving us with a sense of unease and discomfort in our own shortcomings as we leave the theatre.

TONIGHT WITH DONNY STIXX

Tonight with Donny Stixx is a confession in a different type of public forum: the TV/celebrity revelation. The title itself suggests an entertainment rather than a therapy session and has echoes of *An Audience with...* the name of a series of TV specials shown on ITV and Channel 4 between 1980 and 2011.[41] A celebrity, usually a comedian, singer or raconteur, performed in front of an audience of other celebrities, answering questions asked by those spectators. These shows were designed to allow the celebrity to show their talents whilst permitting both the studio audience and the audience at home to know some (carefully orchestrated) personal information. *Tonight with Donny Stixx* opens with one such question.

Donny   My favourite time? You mean my favourite time in my *whole life*?... Mmm, good question—What's your name, my friend? ... *Bob*! Let me have a little think about that one, Bob [...] This is my favourite time. Being on stage. Entertaining an audience.[42]

Donny is much more confident in front of an audience than Andrea was. It is where he wants to be. Andrea was nervous and unsure where to start, whereas Donny is in his element; he wants to perform. Like Andrea, he wants to tell his story on his terms, but his invited audience may not allow him. After only a few minutes his showman persona disappears, and his anger comes through as he responds to a heckle.[43]

Who said that? 'Just tell us about the shooting.' I was told I could do this session exactly how I fucking wanted. That's what we agreed! You're no better than the fucking paparazzi. 'Why did you *kill* them, Donny?' 'How long had you been *planning* it, Donny?' You make me sick! *All* of you. Fuck it, I'm not carrying on! Get my agent on the phone! DO IT! I WANT TO SPEAK TO MY AGENT NOW! *NOW!*[44]

Donny is not only angry about being heckled, but also because he is not being allowed to tell his story in his way. By calling for his agent and suggesting he will stop the show, Donny also shows traits that are associated with "diva-ish" behavior, perceived to be common among performers and celebrities.[45] This behavior is not associated with the format of the *An Audience With...* specials which are classified as light entertainment, but can be seen to fit more with programs such as *The Jeremy Kyle Show* or *Jerry Springer*, where conflicts between protagonists are aired in front of an audience and where tempers often flare.[46] David W. Hill suggests that the premise of this type of talk show "hinges on the participants' willingness to confess domestic and emotional failures or conflicts in front of an audience."[47] In combining the confessional talk show and the celebrity entertainment show into one, Ridley gives Donny the opportunity to tell his story whilst living his dream of being an entertainer.

Donny can tell his story however he wants, but the format opens up the possibility that his truth is still hiding the real trauma he has experienced. Sean Redmond states that "[t]hrough the confessional text [...] the star or celebrity seemingly attempts to speak openly and honestly about where they have come from."[48] Often talking in the present tense Donny, like

Andrea, relives the events that have led to his need for confession. He tells us about his wonderful relationship with his mother, who he always refers to as Yvonne, portraying her as a "delicate flower" too good for her working-class roots.[49] Donny looked after her when she was ill doing magic shows for her and for his Aunt Jess, with whom he eventually lives. He tells us how he develops his magic act, doing birthday parties and family gatherings and even engages the services of an assistant, a girl his own age called Sharmi. They eventually enter a talent competition at the local shopping center illustrating Donny's willingness to do anything to achieve his goal.

As with Andrea we see hints that we are not being told everything, only the truth Donny wants us to hear. Like Andrea, he does not tell his story in the "frank and open manner" that McLeod suggests was necessary for a collective ritual of confession.[50] Instead we see flashes of anger and a complete loss of control. He is seemingly nonplussed talking about his mother's death, is unable to cope with sex or masturbation and the messy nature of those activities, and insists that he is correct about everything. What finally tipped him over the edge was when the truth of himself was revealed by Sharmi's brother Corey, a successful model and the subject of Donny's first crush. "Donny! Listen to me. *Someone* has to tell you this. [...] They were laughing *at* you. They thought you were a joke."[51] Dismissed as an embarrassment by the object of his desire only made Donny more determined to succeed. Underneath the calm exterior he showed to Corey is a seething anger.

Donny Time to do my warm-up exercises. I've got a show to do. Mustn't let a tiny setback like that deter me from—IF YVONNE WAS HERE SHE'D PUT YOU IN YOUR FUCKING PLACE, YOU FUCKING BASTARD.[52]

Our suspicions are raised further when Donny refers to The Stupendous Santini, a magician who killed himself when a sword swallowing trick went wrong leading to "ETERNAL ADORATION."[53] Jennifer L. Murray notes how mass shooters often "reference/discuss their well-publicized prior homicidal role models in self-created archival documents they leave behind. They do not just copycat prior killers, they often relate to them, are inspired by them, and want to outdo them."[54] Thus, when Donny reveals he has his cousin's gun we understand that his intention was to commit suicide in front of an audience, aping his idol.

Donny acts out his final show, which was in front of an elderly audience in an old people's home, for us. Donny wanted this audience of OAPs to film him and post the videos online, thus giving him fame through viral sharing of the videos but they had no capacity to make this happen. The ever-increasing frenzy of the storytelling in this section builds to a climactic scream and, finally having had his moment in the spotlight, Donny tells us the truth. "*He is calm, very relaxed*," when he explains to us how he was born with a club foot, and that, after the operation to correct this, it was his father who bought him the box of tricks.[55] His insecurities stem from the fact his mother "didn't like imperfect things."[56] As Donny starts telling us the truth of his life rather than the celebrity version of it, he says "I don't mind talking about this. I... I want to. These sessions we've been having since ... you know ..."[57] Donny's entertainment show has been set up as part of his therapy. Returning to Donny's first outburst about being heckled, we see he refers to this being a session. This performance was not necessarily the celebration of notoriety it is presented as. We, the theatre audience, have been part of Donny's healing process providing the link to community that Hymer and McLeod suggests public confession needs. We have given Donny the fame he craves, allowing him to feel he has achieved his goal, rather than the infamy of the newspaper headlines.[58]

As with *Dark Vanilla Jungle*, the ending of *Tonight with Donny Stixx* is problematic in terms of the catharsis achieved. Again, the use of direct address shifts the focus of the storytelling from an act between the characters on stage in which the audience are observers, to one where they become the primary recipients of the narrative through direct address. This shift then offers the possibility of a route to healing and catharsis through public confession. Creating a connection with a community permits judgement by one's peers but, because it is a theatre audience as opposed to a religious organization or civic community, it fails to allow help and support directly from that community. Donny's admission at the end of *Tonight with Donny Stixx* suggests he is finding the sessions useful and is further along in his healing process than Andrea by acknowledging the truth of his life rather than the truth of his story. As with Andrea, we as the audience are prevented from offering our communal help, but in this case, we are left with a sense that Donny has taken some solace from our presence and may be able to work his way through his trauma.

Notes

1. See Ken Urban, "Ghosts from an Imperfect Place: Philip Ridley's Nostalgia," *Modern Drama*, 50, no. 3 (2007): 325–345; and Andrew Wyllie, "Philip Ridley and Memory," *Studies in Theatre and Performance*, 3, no. 2 (2013): 65–75.
2. Sigmund Freud, "The Origin and Development of Psychoanalysis" in *The American Journal of Psychoanalysis*, 21, no. 2 (1910): 184; see also Josef Breuer and Sigmund Freud, *Studies in Hysteria*, ed. James Strachey and Anna Freud (Harmondsworth: Pelican Books, 1974).
3. Freud, "The Origin," 184.
4. Freud, "Psychotherapy of Hysteria" in Josef Breuer and Sigmund Freud, *Studies in Hysteria*, 351.
5. John McLeod, *Narrative and Psychotherapy* (London: Sage Publications, 1997), 14.
6. Ibid., 2.
7. Ibid., 7.
8. Ibid., 2.
9. Stephen Halliwell, *Aristotle's Poetics*, 2nd ed (Chicago: University of Chicago Press, 1998), 198.
10. Urban, "Ghosts," 325.
11. Ibid., 328–329.
12. Wyllie, "Philip Ridley," 74.
13. Fred Miller Robinson, *Rooms in Dramatic Realism* (New York; Routledge, 2016), 27.
14. Philip Ridley, *Vincent River*, in *Plays: 2* (London: Methuen Drama, 2009), 11.
15. Kristin. M. Langellier and Eric. E. Peterson, *Storytelling in Daily Life* (Philadelphia: Temple University Press, 2004), 1; Joanna Thornborrow & Jennifer Coates (eds), *The Sociolinguistics of Narrative* (Amsterdam/Philadelphia: John Benjamins, 2005), 4.
16. Ridley, *Vincent River*, 63.
17. Aristotle, *Poetics*, ed. and trans. Michelle Zerba & David Gorman (New York: W.W. Norton & Company, Inc), 10.
18. Ibid., 46.
19. Ridley, *Vincent River*, 69.
20. Ibid., 69–70.
21. Halliwell, *Aristotle's Poetics*, 200.
22. Aristotle, *Poetics*, 48; and Thornborrow & Coates, *The Sociolinguistics of Narrative*, 3–5.
23. Sharon Hymer, "Therapeutic and Redemptive Aspects of Religious Confession," *Journal of Religion and Health* 34, no. 1 (1995): 50.

24. Ibid., 50.
25. McLeod, *Narrative and Psychotherapy*, 3.
26. Ibid., 7. Original italics.
27. Ibid., 7–8.
28. Hymer, "Therapeutic and Redemptive Aspects," 50–51.
29. I saw productions of *Dark Vanilla Jungle* at the Royal Exchange Theatre Studio, Manchester on July 27, 2013, and at the Soho Theatre, London on April 6, 2014.
30. Philip Ridley, *Dark Vanilla Jungle* (London: Bloomsbury Methuen Drama, 2014), 3.
31. McLeod, *Narrative and Psychotherapy*, 37.
32. Ridley, *Dark Vanilla Jungle*, 3.
33. Ibid., 10.
34. Ibid., 5. Original italics.
35. Ibid., 9.
36. Sigmund Freud, *Case Histories 1*, ed. Angela Richards (London: Penguin Books, 1977), 46, 47.
37. Ridley, *Dark Vanilla Jungle*, 25. Original italics.
38. Ibid., 26.
39. Ibid., 35.
40. Ibid., 36–37.
41. https://www.comedy.co.uk/tv/an_audience_with/episodes/ (accessed June 17, 2018).
42. Philip Ridley, *Tonight with Donny Stixx* (London: Bloomsbury Methuen Drama, 2016), 5. Original italics.
43. As with *DVJ* the heckles are imagined by the theatre audience but the protagonist reacts as if they have actually been shouted out.
44. Ridley, *Tonight with Donny Stixx*, 5–6. Original italics/emphasis.
45. Just a quick Google search reveals several articles on demanding behavior and exacting riders. *The Guardian* website has an interesting article on the changing nature of celebrity riders (https://www.theguardian.com/life-andstyle/2015/feb/11/rock-stars-riders-jack-white-guacamole-square-melons), whilst thesmokinggun.com (http://www.thesmokinggun.com) has a whole section devoted to the riders and demands of the rich and famous. Iggy Pop's is particularly entertaining. However, having been a stage manager for 25 years, I'm pleased to reassure you I've rarely come across such behavior and reports of it are often blown out of all proportion.
46. *The Jeremy Kyle Show* was shown at 9:25 a.m. on weekdays on ITV. Presented by Jeremy Kyle it was a talk show in which people were encouraged to discuss and resolve their issues often using technology such as lie detector tests. It was regularly confrontational. https://www.itv.com/jeremykyle.

It ran from 2005 and was cancelled in May 2019 after the revelation that a guest on the show had committed suicide prior to the airing of the episode in which they had appeared. See also D.W. Hill, "Class, Trust and Confessional Media in Austerity Britain," *Media, Culture and Society* 37, no. 4 (2015): 566–580. *The Jerry Springer Show* ran from 1991 to 2018. Predating *The Jeremy Kyle Show* it used many of the same techniques. The episode titles were often provocative in themselves. See Hill, op cit., and https://www.theguardian.com/tv-and-radio/2018/jun/19/farewell-to-the-jerry-springer-show-27-years-of-fights-bleeps-and-outrage (accessed June 29, 2018).
47. Hill, "Class, Trust," 567. See also Sean Redmond, "The Star and Celebrity Confessional," *Social Semiotics*, 18, no. 2 (2008): 109–114.
48. Redmond, 110.
49. Ridley, *Tonight with Donny Stixx*, 7.
50. McLeod, *Narrative and Psychotherapy*, 8.
51. Ridley, *Tonight with Donny Stixx*, 32. Original italics.
52. Ibid., 34. Original emphasis.
53. Ibid., 35. Original emphasis.
54. Jennifer L. Murray, "Mass Media Reporting and Enabling of Mass Shootings," *Critical Studies – Critical Methodologies* 17, no. 2 (2017): 114. See also Adam Lankford, "Fame Seeking Rampage Shooters: Initial Findings and Empirical Predictions," *Aggression and Violent Behavior* 27 (2016): 122–129.
55. Ridley, *Tonight with Donny Stixx*, 40.
56. Ibid., 40.
57. Ibid., 40.
58. Ibid., 11–12.

CHAPTER 13

Joe Penhall's Fatherhood Plays: Escaping the Influence of Sam Shepard and the Lad

William C. Boles

In his 2012 article for *The Guardian* Joe Penhall revealed a major influence on his successful playwriting career: Sam Shepard's *True West* (1980). More specifically, it was the 1994 Donmar Warehouse production of *True West*, featuring Mark Rylance and Michael Rudko alternating nightly the roles of Lee and Austin, the play's squabbling brothers. Penhall saw Rylance play Lee, the edgy brother with a criminal past who constantly irritates and challenges his straight and narrow, attempting to write a screenplay sibling. Penhall admitted that Rylance's "performance lit such a furnace underneath me that I immediately went home and started writing. I didn't want to go to the theater again after that. I was busy. Most of my work came out of that. It fueled me for the next 15 years."[1] Shepard's play, depicting a fraternal battle fueled by jealousy and an intense, competitive history, relies on one set (living room and kitchen) and offers a slow-fuse burning narrative. Penhall discovered an invigorating muse in Rylance's performance, which highlighted the energetic nature of Shepard's language and the headstrong, testosterone influenced conflict between the two brothers. This influence is palpable when looking at the

W. C. Boles (✉)
Rollins College, Winter Park, FL, USA
e-mail: WBoles@Rollins.edu

ensuing fifteen years of his argumentative plays filled with "desperate characters, baffled losers and lonesome oddballs,"[2] many of whom would fit comfortably within the confines of a Shepard play (if it were set in London). Penhall wrote about the strained relationship between brothers in *Some Voices* (1994); the tense relationship between two male best friends competing for the attention of the same woman in *Love and Understanding* (1997); an adult son struggling with his recently made redundant father in *The Bullet* (1999); two male doctors battling over the medical diagnosis of a patient in *Blue/Orange* (2000); the manipulation of a celebrity by a journalist in *Dumb Show* (2004); and the competitive, angry, violent brothers in *Landscape with Weapon* (2007).[3]

Using Penhall's calculation, the influence of Shepard's play lasted from 1994 until 2009, which was after *Landscape with Weapon* had premiered. In one sense that play, produced at the National Theatre, could be seen as the culmination of what Penhall had been exploring for the previous decade and a half through the staging of his "cock fighting males."[4] *Landscape with Weapon* proved to be a perfect final homage to *True West*, especially as it too depended on one set (again a living room and kitchen) and revolved around a familial and political dispute between two brothers, including a scene where Indian food is angrily thrown all over the kitchen. (Penhall substitutes Shepard's aromatic smell of toast in *True West* with the sweetness of korma.[5]) Despite these similarities between the two plays, Shepard's influence would still have one more appearance in Penhall's work, where it would smoothly overlap with his next inspiration. What was that next fiery inspiration for Penhall? Interestingly, it did not come from the theater nor the world of television and movies, where he had spent so much time after the international success of *Blue/Orange*, but some place much closer and more personal: his own family, more specifically, the birth of his two sons.

This new responsibility of being a father would be highly influential on his next two plays: *Haunted Child* (2011) and *Birthday* (2012). Prior to his playwriting success, Penhall was a journalist in Shepherd's Bush and his plays were, in part, driven by what he saw on the London streets he covered. With these two new plays, produced within months of one another at the Royal Court Theatre Downstairs, this core member of In-Yer-Face Theatre found himself exploring a new direction from his formerly argumentative focus on brothers, best male friends, co-workers, single men, and the hyper-masculine attitude of the omnipresent Lad, who dominated the 1990s popular culture media from television to the movies to magazines to pop music. Instead, his new interest turned to parenting, with an interest in the reflexive definition of what it means to be a parent in the first decade of the new century, as he wrote two plays back-to-back about a middle-aged married man struggling with the responsibilities that come with family life.

Penhall acknowledged that becoming a father had positive and negative influences on his writing: "I talk to Simon Stephens a lot about kids, he's got kids too, and it's a big, big, big, big thing and it's very hard to find the time and headspace but it does a thing to your brain, to your soul and your consciousness, it bestows upon you a wisdom and an ability to see what you couldn't see before."[6] This insight provided Penhall with a new creative impetus, allowing him to find a replacement for the one he found with *True West*. Interestingly, the "fire" imagery he used to describe the influence of Shepard's play on his writing—"lit such a furnace"—is echoed in his description of fatherhood's effect on his writing. Having children, he said, "fires you up. You work everything out: your morality, your sense of what matters, what's happening to the world. Until you have kids you don't feel it viscerally. You feel it instantly, viscerally and overwhelmingly in a way you're removed from prior to that so it doesn't affect you."[7] His role as a parent plays a dramatic role in the creation of the different father figures he writes for these two plays. Prior, he only had written one play with a father in it: *The Bullet*, which was inspired by Arthur Miller's *Death of a Salesman* (1949), where Penhall aimed to explore the difficulty inherent in a father-son dynamic, when the adult son and father are both facing job struggles. In these two more recent plays his focus is on the behavior of a father with a young son (*Haunted Child*) and the emotional and physical struggles of a father about to go into labor (*Birthday*). The two works, though, offer diametrically opposed characterizations of fatherhood. The former presents a father character who shares similar laddish characteristics with Penhall's earlier male characters, suggesting that Shepard and the Lad's influences had not completely waned, while the latter play explores a New Man father who goes the extra distance for his family. Through the two plays Penhall captures the overpowering, enticing, enrichening, frightening, and self-conceited feelings that accompany being a father through two disparate portrayals.

HAUNTED CHILD: FATHERHOOD AS SELFISHNESS

Opening at the Royal Court on December 2, 2011, *Haunted Child* highlights a constant dilemma associated with fatherhood: the absent father. Having recently completed the screenplay for the film version of Cormac McCarthy's *The Road*, which focuses almost exclusively on a father teaching his young son how to navigate through and survive in a post-apocalyptic world, Penhall found himself drawn to exploring the father/son dynamic on stage. The writing, though, for *Haunted Child* went slowly, including a period where he did not touch the play for a year, which places its drafting process still within the fifteen-year influence of Shepard's touch. He finally was able to jumpstart the story after he merged the father/son story with another interest of his: cults. During a visit to Japan, he became interested in the Aum cult after reading Haruki Murakami's *Underground: The Tokyo Gas Attack and the Japanese Psyche* (2000). Penhall explained: "They were these engineers, scientists, journalists, ordinary people who were bright and you wouldn't imagine them joining a death cult. So two ideas collided."[8]

Haunted Child is a three hander, set in the living room and kitchen of a Victorian house. As the play opens, we learn that Douglas has disappeared without a trace and Julie, his wife, and Thomas, his young son, are slowly coping with his absence. However, Douglas suddenly returns, only to reveal that he is not there to rejoin his family. Instead, he discloses that he has joined a cult, whose mission is never fully explained in the play, and he has returned home to convince Julie to sell their house, so he can use his half of the proceeds to pay the required tithe. Unable to convince her to sell their home as well as come and join him, he leaves, only to return at play's end disheveled and beaten by the cult members, and not knowing where to turn, having been rejected by both his adopted community and former family.

Even though Penhall's focus has changed to a married family dynamic, the laddish behavior of his previous characters, which put him at the heart of Sierz's In-Yer-Face designation,[9] has not been completely abandoned in *Haunted Child*. Arguably, Douglas is a perfect extension of Penhall's earlier male characters if they became husbands and fathers. Like the plays of the 1990s, where, as Sierz wrote, "the family became a no-man's land of missing fathers,"[10] Douglas is focused on himself and his own sense of place and mind. In addition to this overlap with Penhall's earlier work, Shepard's influence is still present. The title itself *Haunted Child* immediately calls to mind Shepard's Pulitzer Prize winning play *Buried Child*, which at its heart is about the disruptive, violent, and fraught relationships between grandfathers, fathers and sons, where the killing of a baby haunts an entire family. In an interview Penhall conducted with Sam Shepard for *The Guardian*, the American playwright opined on the interconnectedness of fathers and sons, telling Penhall: "You know, Flann O'Brien has this great quote ...'I am my own father and my son.' There have been moments when I've been with my oldest son, Jessie, where I feel that he's the father and I'm the son. Or he's my brother, you know what I mean?"[11] This fluidity between familial generations of men is a driving thematic element for Shepard in *Buried Child* and is best articulated during a speech by the youngest male member Vince, who has returned to claim the family homestead as the patriarch Dodge lays dying. Vince describes driving down the road and looking in the rearview mirror and staring at his face and then seeing his face morph into someone else's:

> His face became his father's face. Same bones. Same eyes. Same nose. Same breath. And his father's face changed to his Grandfather's face. And it went on like that. Changing. Clear on back to faces I'd never seen before but still recognized. Still recognized the bones underneath. The eyes. The breath. The mouth.[12]

This concept of generational recycling through the ages that Shepard captured in his interview with Penhall and in Vince's quote also appears in *Haunted Child*. After Douglas returns home, he shares a similar concept with his eight-year old son.

Douglas My father's soul is in me. My soul is in you.... Also: I believe that when Grandpa died he was reincarnated and he came back as you. So, really, you're my dad....
Thomas ... *looks up at him, bewildered.*
Douglas Why not? You're a natural striker—he was a good striker. You're a leftie just like him—he used to get holes in the same shoe. You can hear things no normal person can hear just like he could—you can hear sounds which are miles away. (*Pause.*) You were born a year after he died...it's very weird for me.[13]

Despite this professed connection he sees between his son, father and himself (even though he fails to see the distress he is causing his son through this pronouncement), Douglas, similar to the fathers in *Buried Child*, is not a hands-on father. Instead, he has rejected his fatherly duties and obligations to his family as a whole. He seeks a personal and communal recognition that does not exist within his current domestic arrangement, and he believes he has found a replacement in the interpersonal dynamics of a cult. He prefers being part of the multitude, where the individual obligations of taking his son to school and picking him up, his presence at family dinners, and the familial exchanges between his wife and himself are not required. Douglas has categorically rejected the societal role to which he had previously agreed and aligned himself with the members of the group with whom he only has a cursory relationship, since he still has not been fully indoctrinated into their membership.

Julie contests his rejection of their family, especially when it comes to his replacement of their relationship with the cult members. She tells him: "Stop calling them your people—they're not your people—*we're* your people."[14] In addition, she reminds him of his responsibilities in marrying her, purchasing a home, and having a child. All are requisite elements of the process of being an adult, something she challenges him about consistently when he returns home and the importance of which he refutes.

Julie	As 'grown ups' we protect children from all our darkness and strangeness and delusion and dysfunction—
Douglas	Why?
Julie	So that they can be children.
Douglas	It's neurotic.[15]

Family and its requisite roles on each member are at the heart of their dispute. Julie believes in the status quo, as she prepares food for the family, takes her son to school and after school activities, consoles him when he is sad, and punishes him when he misbehaves. Through the scenes between Julie and Thomas, Penhall captures the frustrations and successes of how a parent and child negotiate their way through every day challenges, but Douglas has rejected those tenets of everyday behavior, and she chastises him for his break from the established norm: "We're a family...we're already one. You can't undo it—you can't just renounce it suddenly because it doesn't suit your beliefs."[16] Douglas only defines family through the economic value attained through the selling of the family's home. He has returned to obtain the financial reward of selling their Victorian house and not to rekindle the emotional values found in his relationships with his wife and son. Unlike his relationship with Julie and Thomas, which was previously based on a mutual loving and emotional connection with one another, with the cult he has to pay for his place within the community. Family places immediate value on the multiple, concurrent roles of husband, father, lover, friend, breadwinner, and confidante, but within the cult his only value resides through the amount of money he can provide. Because of Julie's refusal to sell their home, he is beaten up and cast out of the community when he returns to the cult without any funds. Douglas' selfish behavior ultimately leaves him bereft of any type of community and emotional support, as he stands on Julie's doorway with no place else to go, joining other Penhall men from previous plays who equally have found that their behavior leaves them separated from friends, family, co-workers and lovers.

What is telling in *Haunted Child* and will be influential to his next play is Penhall's interest in disrupting the usual roles associated with parenting. Even though Douglas fulfills the usual stereotype of the distant, absent father (albeit not because of work responsibilities, the usual reason for distancing), Penhall's characterization of Julie highlights the blending of gender roles. *Haunted Child* presents the complicated nature of parenting, when new roles must be played by one parent when the other one goes missing. In this case Julie has become the sole caregiver to Thomas. She struggles to play both roles in the family and acknowledges the difficulty inherent in such a position.

Julie	As long as we stick together we'll be all right. We have to help each other now. I have to be your dad now.
Thomas	What do you mean?
Julie	I'll do the things he used to do. Take you to school and play football with you.[17]

It is precisely that challenge to stereotypical familial roles, as she enunciates that she will "have to be your dad," that becomes the heart of Penhall's next play, where the roles associated with men and women in the family dynamic are disrupted. Penhall takes this idea further by creating a world where scientific advancements have made it possible for men to give birth, allowing them to become their child's "mom." With *Haunted Child*, the final remnants of the influence of Sam Shepard and lad culture had run its course. Penhall was now entering new territory when it came to his playwriting.

BIRTHDAY: FATHERHOOD AS SACRIFICE

Blue/Orange, Penhall's most well-known work, is his State of the Nation play, as he provided not only a damning glimpse into the treatment of immigrants and blacks in London by the Metropolitan Police Department but also a scathing indictment of the National Health Service's failure to treat bipolar patients. The play transferred to the West End and catapulted Penhall to the status of Olivier Award Winner.[18] In *Birthday* once again Penhall focuses his ire on the National Health Service (NHS) due to his wife's horrendous experience when she gave birth to their second child. He acknowledged that "*Birthday* was straight autobiography. It was me, my wife in labour for seventeen hours fighting tooth and claw."[19] Penhall presents a system at the NHS that is indifferent to families, arguing that the NHS "count on the fact that there is no repeat custom. ... It's a neatly concealed problem. They use your child as leverage. 'Here's your lovely new baby. Now stop complaining about the mutilation you've experienced.'"[20] Penhall is direct about the unprofessional, irresponsible, and dangerous behavior of the NHS when it came to his wife's arduous labor: "They wouldn't give her an epidural because there was no one there to give her one. It went on for 17 hours and it turned into an emergency. It was dramatic and frightening and farcical. We both went to a very dark place afterwards. Our first baby was the same. He nearly died as well. I had a lot to get off my chest,"[21] especially as he admitted that the experience "completely traumatized" him.[22]

In contrast to the longer gestation period in the writing of *Haunted Child*, *Birthday* came quite quickly, perhaps the fastest of all of Penhall's plays, taking three days to write.[23] He acknowledged that what drove the energy behind the play was conveying how much he understood and sympathized with the two awful deliveries that his wife experienced.

> I wanted to show my wife that I understood viscerally, deep down, the humiliation, degradation, boredom, horror and fear that she'd somehow managed to surf with incredible dignity. So it was partly a kind of present for her but it was also partly because I was curious as to how men would be able to handle it. I was absolutely sure that no man I knew would be able to handle it with the same class and grace as my wife did.[24]

Birthday models their maternity ward experience but inverts the natural birthing process, creating a scenario where science has made it possible for a man to gestate and give birth. Penhall's intention behind the biological switch was to "wake people up."[25] The Penhall's struggles now become Ed and Lisa's as they find the hospital staff less than accommodating to Ed's ever-growing discomfort as he prepares to give birth to their daughter. Because of the unbelievability of the play's premise, Penhall felt that in order for Ed's condition to be accepted by the audience, the "geographical and political context had to be super real" and the location had to be embedded in reality,[26] so he set the play in Queen Charlotte Hospital, which is in Shepherd's Bush, where his wife gave birth, and he even offers the same view out of the hospital window to his characters that he and his wife had, the room "overlooking the prison."[27]

Penhall's interest in disrupting gender and reproductive roles echoes a larger societal perspective about the changing role of men in the family and their greater participation in domestic and parental duties. The rise of the New Man espousing the softer side of masculinity in the late 1980s began the contemporary challenge to the stereotypical expectation and behavior of men in romantic relationships (Hugh Grant's appearances in countless romantic comedies at this time document the change) as well as an uptick in a greater involvement in raising children. However, by the mid-1990s a pushback against the softening of male social roles occurred with the rise of the Lad and the embracing of bad boy behavior (*Men Behaving Badly*, a British sitcom, captured this shift). After Lad Culture had run its course, redefining fatherhood once again became a prominent feature in gender studies, academic studies by sociologists, and political actions. For example, "in Britain the Fatherhood Institute was set up in 1999 to promote the idea of shared parenting and, in particular, to involve the father more in the domestic care of children."[28] However, a struggle existed for men between the long held masculine behavior of familial distancing with this new mindset of engagement. As Stephen Williams noted, "[I]t might be said that fathers are squeezed between the 'new man' models on the one hand, and, on the other, the traditional cultural models of fathering. That is to say, squeezed between wishing to play a more involved role and the more removed father who simply 'provides for' his family."[29] While the attitude of Douglas in *Haunted Child* fulfills the stereotype of the "traditional father as overly authoritarian, disinterested, absent and emotionally distant,"[30] Ed in *Birthday* reflects the sympathetic and empathetic perspective expressed by Penhall toward his wife's labor. In a sense,

Penhall's representation of Ed shares the same characteristic of popular media representations of a "good father" as "caring, nurturing, emotionally involved co-parent actively taking on domestic responsibilities and participating in family life,"[31] but Penhall raises the medical stakes through Ed choosing to carry and give birth to their next daughter because of his love for Lisa and not wanting her to go through the hellish experience of her first delivery, which "mutilated" her.[32] He tells Lisa:

> You didn't have to stand there listening to the ear-splitting screams while one congenital fuckwit after another came in, rummaged around inside you and then fucked off for a smoke. No epidural. No doctors. You didn't see them at the end, stitching you back together, legs akimbo, marinating in your own blood and shit, great strings of blood like drool.[33]

In becoming pregnant he takes on the physical, economic and social stigma that such a decision by a male would provoke. His parents are embarrassed and refuse to talk to him; his alcohol intake is next to nil; his wife, as his advocate, makes decisions about his and their daughter's medical condition, despite his protests, including scheduling his caesarian around her busy days at work; and he undergoes embarrassing, emasculating and torturous medical procedures during his delayed labor. His decision to carry their child has made him the "female" in the relationship, and he has lost his male entitlements and privileges, a position with which he is not completely comfortable, as he makes clear to Joyce, the nurse caring for him.

Joyce   It's nice for men to break their waters.
Ed   Is it absolutely necessary?
Joyce   No, but it's liberating. It makes you feel like a woman.
Ed   I don't need to feel like a woman.[34]

While the female characters all can leave the hospital room, Ed remains confined to his hospital bed and reliant upon the aid of others. Considering the diminished power of this male Penhall character, it is significant to note that the cast list for *Birthday* reifies this lessened male status as females outnumber male characters by a three to one ratio, which is the first time in all of Penhall's plays where females are in the majority.

By eschewing the laddish, selfish qualities of Douglas and other Penhall men, Ed instead embraces tenets associated with the "ideas of caring masculinities," where men take on more of a caretaker role and focus less on the role of economic provider.[35] Even though Ed chooses to take on such a new, feminized role, he still struggles in losing his masculine privileges, demonstrating that "men can feel marginalized if they want to take on the primary caring role as a full-time father."[36] After the birth of their first child, Ed has become a stay-at-home parent, while Lisa becomes the primary earner. Numerous times Ed manifests a macho posture against the feminine role he now embodies, but Lisa skewers his attempts to reclaim his masculine position. Where Julie in *Haunted Child* has actually taken on both roles of mother and father due to the abandonment of Douglas, Ed's claims to be the main caregiver *and* the economic head of the family are punctured by Lisa.

Ed   Yes well as taxpayers we have a right to… A certain standard of care. I pay a lot of tax so I'll be looked after when I go into the hospital.
Lisa *I* pay a lot of tax.[37]

When he argues early on that he can handle the pain of childbirth because he is a man, Lisa remarks, "No you can't. That's just the myth they sell you."[38]

Despite his failed attempts to claim supremacy in their relationship, one could still argue that Penhall has created a "gender rebel" through his characterization of Ed, who is emotionally affected by the hormones he has taken throughout his pregnancy, bemoans his wife forgetting to bring a magazine to the hospital because there was a diet he wanted to read, and worries greatly about his body and its look.[39] He tells Lisa: "Don't talk to me about hormones. I'm like a Bernard Matthews turkey. You don't know what I've been through with this; the tears the swollen ankles, you have no idea."[40] While these examples indicate Penhall's reliance on the predictable comedy of a pregnant man parroting comments usually said in media depictions of pregnant women, he also highlights the physical difficulties women face during delivery, by putting Ed through incredibly uncomfortable medical procedures, including the insertion of an anal suppository, the insertion of a catheter, the breaking of his waters with an amniotic hook, and the preparation (with lots of lube) of a hand being inserted through his anus to adjust the position of the baby. These scenes, while humorous due to Ed's reactions, also allow for male audience members to comprehend the difficult, invasive but also routine nature of childbirth for women through witnessing the male form exposed to these same procedures, which now become horrific when enacted on the male body. Penhall drives the point home further for his audience later in the play after Ed has given birth. Ed complains to Lisa of what he has just experienced and she provides the counterpoint to his male privileged perspective.

Ed This shouldn't happen to a man. It's just not fair.
Lisa But it should happen to a *woman*? Because it's quote unquote "normal" for a woman. Which bit of it do you think feels *normal* for a woman. You're lucky you didn't wind up in stirrups![41]

Partly driving Ed's complaint is the uncertainty of the health of their newly born child, who may have any number of infections (Penhall's digs at the incompetence of the NHS arises again within this section of the play). Once they learn that their daughter is healthy, Ed's masculine posturing melts away as he shares why he chose to carry their second child. Ultimately, despite the socio-economic and familial challenges to his masculinity, Ed, Penhall's most feminine male character, reveals his empathy for and worry about the health of his wife and future unborn child. He tells Lisa: "I wanted to die when we couldn't have babies when you had all the miscarriages. I wanted to die when we were having Charlie and you were in here in the same bed and I thought you were going to die and I thought he was going to die, I wanted to die after you had him and you couldn't have any more we couldn't sleep he couldn't sleep he was always sick."[42] The nature of care, concern, and vulnerability comes through in Ed's confession and, based on interviews, no doubt reveals Penhall's own frustrations and fears in reaction to his wife's two deliveries. The cult of masculinity, so prevalent throughout Penhall's plays, is replaced in *Birthday* by sympathy and love, where the societally dictated gender roles become secondary to the healthiness of one's family.

While Penhall's plays have always reflected his view of the world that surrounds him in London, he has always had at their center a masculine world filled with laddish, boorish, selfish, and privileged male behavior. When Penhall turned his analytical lens to his own life and family, a new type of male character appeared, a conglomerative representation of the New Man, who is emotionally available for his spouse and family and embraces the role of being the "mother" in the family from childcare to childbirth. Penhall, who has professed that "I think that men should be made to feel like women,"[43] has successfully presented that view in *Birthday* and in the process underlines his divorce from the influence of Shepard's *True West* and the badly behaving male who have dotted his oeuvre. However, *Birthday* would not be the end of Penhall's exploration of this new type of male character. His next play, *Mood Music* (2018), while returning to his normal ratio of male characters outnumbering female characters, continues to question the behavior of men in their interactions with the opposite sex. In this case, he moves from the privacy of the delivery room to the privacy of the recording studio, as the play, inspired by the #MeToo Movement, takes aim at a powerful record producer's exploitative relationship with a young female protégé. Clearly, this once In-Yer-Face, Sam Shepard inspired writer has found a new focus as his plays continue to get "in-yer-face" but with a focus now on critiquing male privilege and power.

Notes

1. Gemma Kappala-Ramsamy, "Joe Penhall: the best performance I've ever seen," *Guardian*, June 17, 2012, https://www.theguardian.com/stage/2012/jun/17/joe-penhall-mark-rylance-performance (accessed March 15, 2018).
2. Aleks Sierz, *In-Yer-Face Theatre: British Drama Today* (London: Faber & Faber, 2000), 214.
3. See William C. Boles, *The Argumentative Theatre of Joe Penhall* (Jefferson, NC: McFarland, 2011).
4. Alice Jones, "Guess who's having a baby," *The Independent*, June 28, 2012: 40.
5. After being dared by his convict brother to commit a crime, Austin steals toasters throughout the surrounding neighborhood and then proceeds to make toast during the play's final scene. Like Shepard, Penhall is fascinated by the power of food on the stage. Citing the effect of simply peeling an orange in *Blue/Orange*, Penhall said: "You could smell the zest and see the spray. My favourite part of Landscape with Weapons is where the characters have a food fight, throwing curry at each other. There's something about those purely physical moments." (Mark Lawson, "Regrets? Too few to mention," *Guardian*, November 30, 2011: Sec. G2, 19.)
6. Sarah Tejal Hamilton, "Joe Penhall—the interview Part 1," *Writerly*, March 31, 2017, https://writerlyblogblog.wordpress.com/2017/03/31/joe-penhall-the-interview-part-1/ (accessed July 5, 2018). Simon Stephens has

three children, but unlike Penhall, Stephens has been a father for the majority of his playwriting career.
7. Ibid.
8. Ibid.
9. See Sierz, 153–177. See also Boles, *Argumentative*, 25–39; and William C. Boles, "Rise and Fall of the Lad: Joe Penhall's Early Plays," in *Drama and the Post-Modern: Assessing the Limits of Metatheatre*, ed. Daniel K. Jernigan (Amherst, NY: Cambria Press, 2008): 307–325.
10. Sierz, 153.
11. Joe Penhall, "The Outsider," *Guardian*, June 14, 2006, https://www.theguardian.com/film/2006/jun/14/theatre (accessed March 15, 2018).
12. Sam Shepard, *Buried Child*, in *Seven Plays* (New York Bantam, 1986), 130.
13. Joe Penhall, *Haunted Child* (London: Methuen, 2011), 25–26.
14. Ibid., 56.
15. Ibid., 62.
16. Ibid., 60.
17. Ibid., 8.
18. While Penhall was the first of the In-Yer-Face writers to win the Olivier for Best Play, two others have also won since *Blue/Orange*'s victory. Martin McDonagh won for *The Pillowman* in 2004 and *Hangmen* in 2016, while Jez Butterworth won for *The Ferryman* in 2018.
19. Hamilton, "Joe Penhall."
20. Viv Groskop, "He's having my baby," *Evening Standard*, June 26, 2012: 32.
21. Ibid.
22. Jones, 40.
23. Penhall described the gestation period for the play. "*Birthday*… took six days to write, in fact it took three days to write—I wrote it day and night and didn't *stop*. And then I gave it to director Roger Michell who said I really like it but the second half, does the baby have to die? I was like look man, I've been up all night for about four days drinking brandy! I could give it another three days, I'll see, I dunno. So I went back, rewrote the second half, the baby didn't die, gave it to him. I think it's shit but you're the boss, and he loved it." (Hamilton, "Joe Penhall—the interview Part 1.")
24. Jones, 40.
25. Groskop, 32.
26. British Library Sound Archive, *Birthday* Post Show Talk, Royal Court Theatre, July 7, 2012. C1209/171.
27. Joe Penhall, *Birthday* (London: Methuen, 2012), 4.
28. Angela Smith, "'New Man' or 'Son of the Manse'? Gordon Brown as a Reluctant Celebrity Father," *British Politics* 3 (2008): 561.

29. Stephen Williams, "What is Fatherhood? Searching for the Reflexive Father," *Sociology* 42, no. 3 (2008): 540.
30. Mark Finn and Karen Henwood, "Exploring Masculinities within Men's Identificatory Imaginings of First-time Fatherhood," *British Journal of Social Psychology* 48 (2009): 548.
31. Ibid.
32. Penhall, *Birthday*, 37.
33. Ibid., 36.
34. Ibid., 13.
35. Tina Miller, "Falling Back in Gender? Men's Narratives and Practices around First-time Fatherhood," *Sociology* 45, no. 6 (2011): 1100.
36. Ibid., 1101.
37. Penhall, *Birthday*, 18.
38. Ibid., 7.
39. Finn and Henwood, 554.
40. Penhall, *Birthday*, 9.
41. Ibid., 68.
42. Ibid., 71.
43. Jones, 40.

CHAPTER 14

"Experiential, not speculative": Love In and After In-Yer-Face

Korbinian Stöckl

Introduction: In-Yer-Face Theatre's Aesthetics of Directness

When Aleks Sierz set out to delineate the characteristics of the theatrical revolution that had dominated the new writing of the 1990s in his seminal *In-Yer-Face Theatre* in 2001, he suggested that "[t]he widest definition of in-yer-face theatre is any drama that takes the audience by the scruff of the neck and shakes it until it gets the message."[1] The paragraph starting with this definition ends on a notion of In-Yer-Face theatre which contains what I take to be its most crucial attribute, namely that it is a kind of theatre that addresses the sensory apparatus more than the intellect, that touches the audience more on an affective and subconscious than on a cognitive level,

---

Some of the ideas and parts of the argumentation put forward in this chapter appear in my dissertation Concepts of Love in Contemporary British Drama, which contains detailed interpretations of the three plays discussed here and their treatments of romantic/erotic love.

K. Stöckl (✉)
University of Augsburg, Augsburg, Germany
e-mail: korbinian.stoeckl@philhist.uni-augsburg.de

© The Author(s) 2020
W. C. Boles (ed.), *After In-Yer-Face Theatre*,
https://doi.org/10.1007/978-3-030-39427-1_14

that asks not so much for interpretation than for perception. "In other words," as Sierz puts it borrowing a phrase from Sarah Kane, "it is experiential, not speculative."[2] In what follows, however, Sierz narrows down his wide definition with a list of shocking ingredients such as filthy language, nudity, sex, humiliation, and violence,[3] which make the concept both more specific and more exclusive and urge him to put forward a further distinction between "hot and cool versions of in-yer-face theatre" that either do or do not make use of an "aesthetics of extremism"[4]—a distinction that never really took off. Seven years later, in an essay titled "We All Need Stories," Sierz recounts how in the world of literary criticism, reversing his own initial progress from a wide to a narrow definition, the notion of In-Yer-Face theatre developed from being defined by a "menu of ingredients" to a broader conception as a theatre of "emotional intensity" that "makes you squirm inside"[5] to the most inclusive approach that "conceptualized the term as a general sensibility, one that is characterized by a new directness and that carries a mix of personal feeling and public ideas typical of the 1990s."[6] This broadest conception, with its central characteristic of a "new directness," comes close to Sierz' original "widest definition," and it is most promising as a lasting description of the phenomenon, as it is neither too exclusive nor too unspecific to do justice to the variety of plays it seeks to comprise.

In this chapter, I will try to elaborate on the element of "directness" that is integral to this definition through a comparison of two plays that are commonly regarded prototypical representatives of In-Yer-Face theatre—Mark Ravenhill's *Shopping and Fucking* and Sarah Kane's *Cleansed*—with Dennis Kelly's *Love and Money*, which shares many of their thematic concerns but differs considerably in its mode of presentation. The aim of this chapter is to test the workability of an approach that considers not the provocativeness and shock value of its content, language, and imagery as the most characteristic features of In-Yer-Face theatre, but the "directness" with which it presents its themes. I argue that the directness and declarative nature of character speeches are part and parcel of an aesthetics that prioritizes the combination of language with powerful images and metaphors over the naturalistic imitation of reality and the subtleties of everyday speech. Frequently, speech utterances are "in-yer-face" not only because they are obscene and confrontational (which they often are) but because they are forthright and declarative in a way natural speech usually is not. Moreover, they are tied to the eloquent images produced by these plays, for which the characters' words often serve merely as explanatory captions designed, it seems, to make sure that the audience "gets the message" the images are supposed to communicate on a pre-discursive level.[7] "Experientiality" thus means "directness" in the sense that these plays try to talk to the sensory apparatus rather than to the intellect. If this can be seen as the attempt to provide a more direct, "purer" access to the realm of affects and emotions, one that does not take the "detour" of rational understanding or analysis, Kelly's play returns to a more indirect and more cognitive approach. While the In-Yer-Face plays minimize language to a form of unrealistic declaration and rely instead on the experiential effect of their metaphorical and symbolic images, Kelly's play relies almost exclusively on the images created by language and on the emotional effects produced mainly by the imaginative and interpretive skills of the spectator or reader.

This difference becomes tangible by comparing the way Ravenhill, Kane, and Kelly treat intense emotional states as their content matter. Sierz describes In-Yer-Face Theatre as "the kind of experiential theatre where audience members felt as if they were actively sharing the emotions being depicted by the actors."[8] The audience is not supposed to feel just *something*, nor are they supposed to be simply shocked or shaken by what they see. Rather, the experientiality of In-Yer-Face Theatre relies on a kinship between (re-)presented and experienced emotions, and even though it is unlikely that a performance will evoke the *same* emotions that are depicted, the emotional effect experienced by the spectator is not independent from the play's content. In-Yer-Face Theatre, in other words, does not shock or move simply for the sake of rousing the audience from slumber or apathy but in order to reinforce the perception of its depiction of extreme emotional states. It seeks the most direct way of conveying the intensity of affects and emotions, which is not through language and rationality but through images and the evocation of strong feelings that are, if not identical, at least comparable to those depicted. The extreme emotional state that connects *Shopping and Fucking* and *Cleansed* with Kelly's *Love and Money*, and the different theatrical realization of which can sharpen our awareness of the aesthetic peculiarity of In-Yer-Face Theatre, is love and, particularly, its precarious nature. All three plays have a focus on how love casts the partners into states of dependency and, at the same time, threatens each lover with the uncontrollability and potential unattainability of the other, but they convey this "message" in strikingly dissimilar ways.

Experiencing Precariousness: Love in *Shopping and Fucking* and *Cleansed*

In Mark Ravenhill's merciless 1996 portrayal of a consumerist society where everything and everyone is on sale, love is a central but often overlooked topic. Throughout, it is linked up with the play's dominating motif of dependence. Most notably, Mark starts out as a drug-addict, then undergoes a rehab program and tries to rid himself of all sorts of dependencies, only to become emotionally dependent on rent boy Gary with whom he wanted to have a purely "transactional" relationship. In typical In-Yer-Face fashion, the play does not bother with long explanations, subtext, or figure characterization to arrive at one of its most important metaphors which equates drugs and love. In a blunt parody of "therapy speak"[9] Mark declares all forms of dependence equally harmful to his personality:

> I have this personality, you see? Part of me that gets addicted. I have a tendency to define myself purely in terms of my relationship to others. I have no definition of myself you see. So I attach myself to others as a means of avoidance, of avoiding knowing the self. Which is actually potentially very destructive.[10]

Mark's self-analysis as a person who tends to get addicted and for whom emotional relationships are therefore as dangerous as drugs corroborates Dominic Dromgoole's observation that, quite often, Ravenhill's "characters look into themselves, and at their peak, find a way of describing themselves, " a property that Dromgoole finds "compelling, but not alive. It's perilously close to soap, where everyone knows and describes what they are feeling."[11] In the same straightforward manner, the play stresses love's uncontrollability when Mark, despite himself, falls in love with the very first person he approaches after his resolution to have only transactional relations. His declaration of love to Gary is a prime example of verbal directness, of the kind of declarative speech typical of In-Yer-Face Theatre. With surprising outspokenness Mark separates love from sexual desire and puts his feeling of love in the longstanding tradition of the romantic myth of merging into completion, the ancient idea, dating back at least to Platonic philosophy, that love compensates for a fundamental loss or void by restoring the insufficient individual to a (consciously or unconsciously) desired state of wholeness:

Gary: Do you love me? Is that what it is? Love?
Mark: I don't know. How would you define that word? There's a physical thing, yes. A sort of wanting, which isn't love is it? No, That's well, desire. But then, yes, there's an attachment I suppose. There's also that. Which means I want to be with you, Now, here, when you're with me I feel like a person and if you're not with me I feel less like a person.[12]

Gary, who refuses Mark, is himself haunted by unfulfilled desire. His fantasy of a "big" and "rich bloke"[13] who will take both care and possession of him amounts to a quasi-religious yearning for security. His wish—"I want a dad. I want to be watched. All the time, someone watching me"[14]— evokes the concept of a watchful deity to which he would surrender completely in return for a sense of complete belonging. When Gary, who is deeply traumatized by the sexual abuse through his violent stepfather, comes to accept that this father-figure of hope is "not out there,"[15] his desire definitely takes on an otherworldly dimension. Bruised and wounded by this world, his desire develops into a death wish and he asks for the fulfilment of his sexual fantasy, in which the mysterious "bloke" rapes him with a knife. Hesitating first, Mark is eventually prepared to do it, forced by his emotional dependence and Gary's last words, "Do it. Do it and I'll say 'I love you.'"[16] The precarious dependence of love could hardly find a more direct expression than in this willingness to kill the beloved for the sake of being loved in return. And even though Gary's probably fatal penetration happens offstage, the play up to this point did not stint on graphic imagery to visualize love's precariousness. Mark's bloodstained mouth after stimulating Gary anally in an earlier scene or the violent joint rape of Gary during the consensual but still disturbing role play moments before he is probably killed offstage are powerful images that stay with the spectator. They create an atmosphere of pain and violence that lends force to the play's open declarations about the distress of emotional dependence, feelings of incompleteness, and unfulfilled desire. In combination with the guiding metaphor equating love and drug addiction, the recurring sexually charged "shopping story" about the purchase of people which echoes Gary's wish to be possessed, Mark's futile attempt to become emotionally invulnerable which, ironically, plunges him into a state of dependence in which he is prepared to grant Gary's every wish, and the habit of the characters to voice their thoughts and feelings with remarkable clarity and straightforwardness, this adds up to an aesthetics of directness that, regarding at least the subject of love's precariousness, arguably aims more at experiential perception than logical comprehension of an intricate storyline.

Sarah Kane's *Cleansed* (1998) differs considerably from the vast majority of In-Yer-Face plays as it largely abandons dramatic realism.[17] There is hardly a coherent storyline but rather a series of interwoven plotlines; there is a given setting—often perceived by critics as a "fascist institution designed to rid society of its 'undesirables'"[18] and described as a university in the stage directions—but it remains obscure and mysterious as no context explains why the inmates are there and why they are exposed to Tinker's tyrannical regime; there are clearly distinguished characters but their backgrounds and motivations remain mostly unexplained; and the different plotlines are full of improbabilities which testify that the play is neither meant to be performed nor interpreted as a naturalist play but rather as a highly metaphorical and symbolical piece.[19] And yet there is an aspect of its aesthetics that connects it firmly to the category in question. In terms of directness and declarativity, the play is as much In-Yer-Face as it can get. As Sierz writes, "the play's themes came at you with their pants down, defying criticism by being over-the-top."[20] Similarly, Susannah Clapp argues "that the piece wears its heart on its many limbless sleeves"[21] and, regarding figure conception, Ehren Fordyce observes that "from *Cleansed* onwards, Kane abandons subtextual characterisation" in favour of "straightforward declaration" in her characters' voicings of the "blunt emotional appeals"[22] distinctive of all her plays.

Carl and Rod, for instance, are never depicted as complex characters but are introduced right away as representatives of divergent attitudes towards love: the romantic idealist promising eternal love and fidelity (Carl) and the cynical realist rejecting this promise as ridiculous and impossible (Rod). Tortured and threatened with impalement by Tinker, Carl indeed betrays Rod, who immediately *"falls from a great height and lands next to* Carl"[23] to emphasize unmistakably Carl's act of "dropping" his lover. However, the betrayal does not kill their love, which is indeed immortal and invincible in this play. Even after Tinker has cut off his tongue, Carl keeps asking Rod for forgiveness, first by writing in mud and, after Tinker has cut off his hands, by dancing a *"dance of love,"*[24] which is followed by an amputation of his feet. In view of Carl's enduring suffering, the sceptical Rod eventually accepts the possibility of eternal love, repeating almost exactly Carl's words that he had ridiculed earlier: "I will always love you. / I will never lie to you. / I will never betray you. / On my life."[25] To be sure, while their love may be immortal, the lovers are not. This inevitable aspect of precariousness, which always terrifies the lover with the potential death of the beloved, is put into effect by Tinker, who cuts Rod's throat after his declaration of love. The plotline about Carl and Rod at no point asks for speculations about their background stories or the reasons for their imprisonment in Tinker's institution, which remain both unknown and irrelevant. The focus is entirely on the connection of a plainly declared subject—the precariousness of love, its potential painfulness, the limits of its expression, the uncertainty concerning the availability of the other and his love—with shattering images affecting primarily on a pre-discursive level.

In the plotline about Grace and Graham, their incestuous love even survives physical death. Although Graham has been killed by Tinker through an overdose of heroin in the first scene, he remains visible and tangible to his sister Grace. Even more than Mark's desire for wholeness in *Shopping and Fucking*, their love is a powerful longing for fusion. When they make love, their mutual desire for merging into oneness is visualized, as a series of stage directions indicates: they discover that "*each other's rhythm is the same as their own,*" they "*come together*" and "*hold each other, him inside her, not moving,*" while "*[a] sunflower bursts through the floor and grows above their heads,*"[26] symbolizing the rightness and metaphysical nature of their love. Shortly after, Grace also verbalizes this longing for union. Asked what she would like to change in her life, her answer is "My body. So it looked like it feels. Graham outside like Graham inside."[27] After she has already put on Graham's clothes and started to imitate his manner of moving and speaking, it is Tinker of all people who helps Grace to achieve the total union she desires. The merciless torturer, who has meanwhile given up his unrequited love for Grace and has found a lover in the unnamed stripper on whom he had hitherto projected his desire for Grace, agrees to assist in Grace's quest for merging and performs an operation after which she "*looks and sounds exactly like* Graham"[28] and is called "Grace/Graham" in the final scene of the play. Interpretations of the episode diverge regarding the question whether Grace's transformation is a happy ending to her desire or rather a lamentable loss either of selfhood[29] or of the beloved as a distinct other to whom love can be directed.[30] But that the play seeks to visualize the romantic longing for fusion—and the precariousness of this longing, as its fulfilment seems to presuppose the death of one of the partners (Graham), depends on external help (Tinker), and happens in an environment of horrible violence and pain—is unambiguous. In general, there is hardly another contemporary play that addresses and represents love's precariousness with such verbal and visual directness.

Understanding Precariousness: *Love and Money*

Dennis Kelly's *Love and Money* (2006) is in a double sense oppositional to Kane's *Cleansed*. In an interview, Kane had once declared that "[i]f you want to write about extreme love, you can only write about it in an extreme way. Otherwise, it doesn't mean anything. So I suppose both *Blasted* and *Cleansed* are about distressing things which we'd like to think we would survive. If people can still love after that, then love is the most powerful thing."[31] Kelly's play, in contrast, tells the story of a love that was not strong enough to survive "distressing things." Moreover, as if to disprove also the first part of Kane's statement, it is a play about extreme love that is not written in an extreme way. In fact, the play does entirely without any graphic stage images. What puts the play in contrast to In-Yer-Face theatre, however, is not only, and not so much, the absence of visual shock effects but the fact that it replaces the aesthetics of experientiality and directness with a subtler approach that asks for a more cognitive processing of information.

Interspersed with a few glimpses at the lives of minor characters, the play portrays the corruption of Jess and David's love in a capitalist and consumerist society. To pay for her shopping addiction, Jess takes out a loan with extortionate interest repayments and soon the newly married couple is encumbered with debts. When David finds out, he relinquishes his dignity and self-respect in attempts to raise the needed money—he takes on a sales job in telecommunications that he detests and even prostitutes himself at least once—but he cannot save their relationship from deteriorating emotionally. David's distrust concerning his wife's willingness and ability to control her shopping addiction damages their emotional connection and, moreover, once sucked into the maelstrom of capitalism through his new job, the former idealist teacher and amateur writer has developed a profound consumerist desire which makes him resent the money troubles caused by his wife all the more.[32] When he comes home one day and finds Jess unconscious after an unsuccessful suicide attempt with an overdose of anxiolytics, he feeds her vodka to kill her, getting rid of her debts, and fulfilling his consumerist dreams such as a new car.

Thematically, in its treatment of the precariousness of love, *Love and Money* has striking parallels with *Cleansed* and *Shopping and Fucking*. Like the story of Carl and Rod in Kane's play, it presents a situation where the limits of love are tested, exploring its durability and the lovers' readiness to make sacrifices. The parallel with Ravenhill's play lies in the use of a similar metaphor. Whereas in *Shopping and Fucking* the loss of control and total freedom that comes along with love is equated to drug addiction, Kelly uses the image of debt to express this form of precariousness. As her lover and partner, David is "indebted" to Jess. Out of love and because they share a life together, he feels responsible for her, accepts her financial debts as his own, and resolves to get them both out of a crisis that affects him as much as her due to the bond of love. But how much, the play asks, does a lover owe the beloved? How far will he go in making his happiness depend on hers? What will he do if what he pays into their relationship exceeds the return? As Zygmunt Bauman polemically writes with regard to the lack of commitment in a society infused with the logic of the consumer market:

> A relationship [...] is an investment like all the others: you put in time, money, efforts that you could have turned to other aims but did not, hoping that you were doing the right thing and that what you've lost or refrained from otherwise enjoying would be in due course repaid—with profit.[33]

For David, obviously, the relationship to Jess has become a profitless investment that does not "repay" the effort he puts into it. The values of the world of business and profit calculation, which he has only entered to save their marriage, get the better of him and eventually turn him into a murderer.

With these thematic similarities in mind, the aesthetic differences between *Love and Money* and the examples of In-Yer-Face Theatre become even more visible. While the latter visualize the precariousness of love in vivid stage images (the rape of Gary, Tinker's torture of the inmates of his institution), Kelly's play provides no shock images to elicit an experiential effect. In fact, *Love and Money* is downright minimalistic in its use of stage imagery and only little of the story is actually presented in action. Instead, the play relies almost exclusively on language and the two most shocking instances—a man being stabbed to death for a triviality and David feeding alcohol to his dying wife—are reported narratively. Moreover, the play presents the events and actions of the story in more or less reversed order, beginning with David confessing his crime via email to a new love interest and ending with Jess delivering an extended monologue in which she describes her deep love and her feeling of joy in view of the upcoming marriage with David. As Vicky Angelaki argues, the reversed chronology is a form of Brechtian *Verfremdungseffekt* that creates "critical distance"[34] just as much as the "open, fluid exchange of voices" in scene four, where unidentified speakers "gradually assume a narrator's role [...] summing up the events of this contemporary tragedy."[35] These epic elements and the play's tendency to convey information through narration produce an effect that is clearly less experiential and more speculative or cognitive. Through its analytic structure, the play constantly asks the spectator to combine the clues that are successively provided and finally add up to a coherent story that explains the initial situation.

The reversed chronology also endows Jess' final monologue, in which she revels in the joyful feeling that love has supplied her life with meaning and metaphysical security, with a bitter irony. As the audience knows how the story ends, the following words, for instance, appear like a form of tragically naïve idealism.

> [...] what is wrong with purpose, what's wrong with, you know, fucking belonging or
> or
> or just, you know, having an ideal that there is something, that there is a point and that maybe it's about more than just I have this pot of stuff here and that's got more in it than your pot of stuff over there, but I'm just talking about, maybe, I dunno, choosing a world that is more than numbers and quantities and saving and choosing a world that is flesh and bone and
> love or,
> more than just
> isn't it more than just
> money, mathematics, numbers, values I don't know[36]

While in *Cleansed* Carl's idealism concerning his unfaltering love is immediately countered by Rod's scepticism and tested and disproved through Tinker's torture only moments later, Jess' tentative idealist belief in a nonmaterialist meaning of life is preceded by the story of its gradual frustration. The entire play is dedicated to conveying the improbability of an idealized concept of love that heroically withstands both the temptations and necessities of the world of money. Neither Jess nor David are freed by love from materialist desires. Tragically, the death of love in the battle against consumerism is already "retrospectively foreshadowed" in Jess' liability to fall prey to the lure of everyday luxury omnipresent in a society saturated with media and advertisement. As she adds after having elaborated on her metaphysical belief in love as the guide to existential happiness:

> Not saying that I don't want things though.
> *She laughs.*
> I do. I do want things. I want things for us. [...]
> I want it to be a bit like
> *She laughs.*
> a bit like it is on the telly.
> *She laughs.*
> I know, I know. What a cunt.[37]

The speech gives the play a tragic atmosphere as it reveals that the materialist desire which eventually was to become the cause of the catastrophe had been present from the start. The embarrassed self-awareness regarding her television-induced materialism does not prevent her from developing the shopping addiction that would cause their enormous debts and thus, eventually, her death. Holding back this revelation until the end of the play, Kelly shifts the focus of attention from David's crime to its original seed. Equally, the reversed order of the play asks for a successive re-evaluation of David's character, whose deed turns from appalling and incomprehensible to still appalling but more understandable in the light of the trials he had undergone before. Clearly, the play aims not at the creation of immediate, visceral, affective reactions but invites slow, analytical thought processes. Instead of addressing the affective apparatus with a combination of shocking imagery and declarative speech, it requires rational activity to precede its emotional effects.

Conclusion

The thematic correspondence between Kelly's play and those of Ravenhill and Kane helps to foreground their aesthetic difference. All plays are concerned with the precariousness of love in a hostile environment, but Kelly's play abandons the directness that has characterized In-Yer-Face theatre. Where Ravenhill and Kane provide gripping stage images connected to the declarative speech utterances of their characters, Kelly's approach is less immediate and more subtle. Neither are his characters voicing the content matter of the play with In-Yer-Face Theatre's typical straightforwardness, nor is their discourse linked to visually shocking scenes. The directness of In-Yer-Face Theatre relies on the attempt to make its content experiential. The spectator is not tasked with discerning or understanding the play's major theme (i.e. the precariousness of love), which is plainly given away in speech utterances anyway, but is instead forced to perceive the thematic content together with the visceral effects evoked by the play's imagery. Kelly's play, on the other hand, prompts a completely different perception. Although it treats the same major subject and its story elements would easily yield a paragon of In-Yer-Face Theatre—there is humiliation, sexual exploitation, the desecration of a grave, a man stabbed to death, and a wife killed by her husband—the transformation of this story into a plot refrains from any "aesthetics of extremism."[38] Apart from David's humiliation during the job interview, none of it is presented directly on stage but reported narratively. The narratives may still be shocking, but they lack the experiential dimension of visual imagery. Moreover, what is really most shocking in Kelly's play is the realization how the tragedy of Jess and David proceeded from the absolutely ordinary and seemingly harmless element of materialist desire they both share and of which Jess is so articulately aware in the last (i.e. chronologically first) scene. The shock value of this realization, however, is of a rational, cognitive nature as it builds up on all the information the play has provided until this point. It is precisely such cognitive processes which In-Yer-Face Theatre circumvents with its aesthetics of directness and it is here, much more than merely in the presence of shocking images per se, that it has its defining feature. Admittedly, the "menu of ingredients"[39]—the scenes of explicit sexuality and violence, the breaking of taboos, the provocation—can be found to some extent in all plays belonging to the category, but the shocking scenes are not in themselves what defines the aesthetics of In-Yer-Face Theatre. They are so only insofar as they are used in an attempt to transmit their thematic concern to the spectator in the most immediate way, with a directness that is supposed to avoid the detour of cognitive processes and rational understanding, an approach that is "experiential, not speculative."

Notes

1. Aleks Sierz, *In-Yer-Face Theatre: British Drama Today* (London: Faber and Faber, 2001), 4.
2. Ibid. In an interview, Kane had suggested that, regarding the hostile reactions to *Blasted*, "the press outrage was due to the play being experiential rather than speculative" (qtd. in Sierz, *In-Yer-Face*, 98).
3. Ibid., 5.

4. Ibid.
5. Aleks Sierz, "'We All Need Stories': The Politics of In-Yer-Face Theatre," in *Cool Britannia? British Political Drama in the 1990s*, ed. Rebecca D'Monté and Graham Saunders (Basingstoke: Palgrave Macmillan, 2008), 29.
6. Ibid., 30.
7. This feature of In-Yer-Face theatre to transcend the limits of language and to aim for a pre-discursive and bodily perception instead of or in addition to cognitive understanding is minutely examined in the theatre of Sarah Kane by Laurens de Vos, who emphasises the parallels of this aesthetics with that of Antonin Artaud's "theatre of cruelty" in *Cruelty and Desire in the Modern Theatre: Antonin Artaud, Sarah Kane, and Samuel Beckett* (Plymouth: Fairleigh Dickinson University Press, 2011).
8. Aleks Sierz, "Theatre in the 1990s," in *Modern British Playwriting: The 1990s. Voices, Documents, New Interpretations*, ed. Aleks Sierz (London: Methuen, 2012), 58.
9. Sierz, *In-Yer-Face*, 137.
10. Mark Ravenhill, *Shopping and Fucking*, in *Plays: 1*, by Mark Ravenhill (London: Bloomsbury, 2001), 32–33.
11. Dominic Dromgoole, *The Full Room: An A–Z of Contemporary Playwriting* (London: Methuen, 2002), 236.
12. Ravenhill, *Shopping and Fucking*, 55–56.
13. Ibid., 26.
14. Ibid., 33.
15. Ibid., 85.
16. Ibid.
17. Catherine Rees, "Sarah Kane," in *Modern British Playwriting: The 1990s: Voices, Documents, New Interpretations*, ed. Aleks Sierz (London: Methuen, 2012), 113.
18. David Benedict, review of *Cleansed*, by Sarah Kane, *Independent*, May 9, 1998, reprinted in *Theatre Record* 18, no. 9, 564.
19. Kane herself has stressed the metaphorical use of violence in *Cleansed* in an interview with Nils Tabert (February 8, 1998, in *Playspotting: Die Londoner Theaterszene der 1990er*, ed. Nils Tabert [Reinbeck: Rowohlt, 2001], 20). Regarding the metaphorical character of the play, see also Paula Deubner, "'Into the Light': Selbst und Transzendenz in den Dramen Sarah Kanes" (Trier: WVT, 2012), 123 and 127–128; and Heiner Zimmermann, "Theatrical Transgression in Totalitarian and Democratic Societies: Shakespeare as a Trojan Horse and the Scandal of Sarah Kane," in *Crossing Borders: Intercultural Drama and Theatre at the Turn of the Millennium*, ed. Bernhard Reitz and Alyce von Rothkirch (Trier: WVT, 2001), 179.
20. Sierz, *In-Yer-Face*, 114.
21. Susannah Clapp, review of *Cleansed*, by Sarah Kane, *Observer*, May 10, 1998, reprinted in *Theatre Record* 18, no. 9, 566.

22. Ehren Fordyce, "The Voice of Kane," in *Sarah Kane in Context*, ed. Laurens De Vos and Graham Saunders (Manchester: Manchester University Press, 2010), 111.
23. Sarah Kane, *Cleansed*, in *Complete Plays*, by Sarah Kane (London: Methuen, 2001), 117.
24. Ibid., 136.
25. Ibid., 142.
26. Ibid., 120.
27. Ibid., 126.
28. Ibid., 149.
29. See for example Clare Wallace, "Sarah Kane, Experiential Theatre and the Revenant Avant-garde," in *Sarah Kane in Context*, ed. Laurens De Vos and Graham Saunders (Manchester: Manchester University Press, 2010), 94; David Greig, Introduction, in *Complete Plays*, by Sarah Kane (London: Methuen, 2001), xiv; and Christine Quay, *Mythopoiesis vor dem Ende? Formen des Mythischen im zeitgenössischen britischen und irischen Drama*, CDE Studies 16 (Trier: WVT, 2007), 274–276.
30. Sean Carney, *The Politics and Poetics of Contemporary English Tragedy* (Toronto: University of Toronto Press, 2013), 277–278.
31. Qtd. in Graham Saunders, *About Kane: The Playwright and the Work* (London: Faber and Faber, 2009), 74. Original source: Interview with Claire Armitstead, "No Pain, No Kane," *Guardian*, April 29, 1998.
32. Elżbieta Baraniecka, "Precariousness of Love and Shattered Subjects in Dennis Kelly's *Love and Money*," in *Of Precariousness: Vulnerabilities, Responsibilities, Communities in 21st-Century British Drama and Theatre*, ed. Mireia Aragay and Martin Middeke (Berlin: De Gruyter, 2017), 173.
33. Zygmunt Bauman, *Liquid Love: On the Frailty of Human Bonds* (Cambridge: Polity, 2003), 13.
34. Vicky Angelaki, *Social and Political Theatre in 21st-Century Britain: Staging Crisis* (London: Bloomsbury, 2017), 83.
35. Ibid., 88.
36. Dennis Kelly, *Love and Money* (2006), in *Plays One* (London: Oberon Books, 2009), 284.
37. Ibid., 286.
38. Sierz, *In-Yer-Face*, 5.
39. Sierz, "'We All Need Stories,'" 29.

CHAPTER 15

The Echo Chamber: Theater in a "Post-Truth" World

Shane Kinghorn

The "post-truth" era poses a threat to the relevance, if not survival, of a form of theater to which the concepts of "truth" and "authenticity" stubbornly adhere. The vexed status of "authenticity" within verbatim theater practice is frequently questioned in critical discourses responding to the decade of intense activity that followed its revival in the United Kingdom. Academic criticism frequently rebukes verbatim artists' compositional strategies—especially the contrivance of narrative coherence—for somehow belying the documentary impulse, as if factual integrity must be compromised by overtly "creative" intervention.[1] In this chapter, the term "verbatim theatre" indicates that the material will emphasize the assemblage of "testimony," by which I mean the stories told through the words of individuals—the "private narratives" that, according to Carol Martin, infer "great authority to moments of utterance"[2]—gathered by practitioners through interview processes prior to production.

S. Kinghorn (✉)
Manchester Metropolitan University, Manchester, UK
e-mail: S.Kinghorn@mmu.ac.uk

IN-YER-FACE: A RETROSPECTIVE ASSESSMENT

Sarah Kane and Mark Ravenhill, the leading playwrights among the "disaffected group of dramatists" clustered under a series of monikers, including "'the Britpack' and 'the New Brutalists,'"[3] both resisted their categorization as "In-Yer-Face" writers. Kane's statement that movements "define retrospectively and always on grounds of imitation [...] the writers themselves are not interested"[4] reverberates in Ravenhill's later reflection on the mid-nineties moment when his hit play *Shopping and Fucking* (1996) "marked him as a potential 'pack leader.'"[5] Similarly reluctant, at the time, to "label," or even acknowledge, this "phenomenon," Ravenhill found "the diversity of [the writers'] voices ... more striking than the similarities"; although "a series of unique, strong voices all emerged at the same time," they should not be "linked as a movement or school."[6] In his conclusion to *In-Yer-Face Theatre*, Aleks Sierz's retrospective assessment of the nineties new wave (to which his own, paradigmatic epithet has famously, and persistently, adhered) articulates a sense of purpose and optimism that prompts interrogation of its reputation for "uncompromising sensationalism"[7]:

> It was also a powerful reminder that culture is a place of half-truths, contradictions and ambiguity. Those searching for absolute truths and simple answers didn't find them in theatre [...] [T]here was also a sense of hope that by facing such extremes we might all grow more able to bear the real world of which they were a lurid reflection.[8]

Extolling Ravenhill's *Shopping and Fucking* (1996) as an "impeccable social document"—one that "captured the public mood"—Michael Billington recalls also his hunger for "remedies for the characters' urban angst."[9] That the plays of the nineties "lacked ... any vision of Utopia" was, he concedes, the fundamental idea: "In the drifting, desolate Nineties ... there were no ready-made Utopias and no grand narrative schemes. The best we could hope to do was construct our own private dreams and tell each other stories."[10] Billington's emphasis on storytelling anticipates the intrinsic "promise" of documentary practice[11] that is problematized, argues John F. Deeney, in Ravenhill's work.

Rather than propagate absolute faith in the veracity of lived experience, Ravenhill's plays "question the reliability of narrative (and its manifestations in memory and history)."[12] *Shoot/Get Treasure/Repeat* (2007)—"a complex contemplation on the relationship between a real world epic narrative of recent history, and how individual life stories operate within"—is, argues Deeney, framed "as a retort to the preponderance of contemporary verbatim or documentary theatres,"[13] allowing for poetry, metaphor even, to supplant the journalistic pragmatism of the genre.

Steve Waters' thesis, ten years on from the debut of *Blasted* (1995), separates Sarah Kane from "the *enfants terribles* of the mid-1990s."[14] Drawing parallels between artistic and actual "terror," Waters argues that although "Kane did not live to see the events of 9/11 and the ensuing open-ended 'war on terror,'" her plays "resisted ideology ... in response to political conflicts enacted in the name of fixed identities and categories."[15] While "the post-ideological dramatists of the 1990's ... shook themselves loose from the constraint of 'grand narratives,'" Kane's formal innovation in *Blasted* anticipated "the politics that would occupy the ensuing vacuum—post-humanist, experiential, non-consensual."[16] Into this "vacuum," then, came the preoccupations that would inform the revival of verbatim practice in the United Kingdom, an epoch ostensibly triggered by the events of 9/11.[17]

Lib Taylor, examining the parallels and distinctions between In-Yer-Face drama and the "fact-based" theater that followed on its heels, argues that the former "sought its politics through shock and disgust," while the latter "addressed events and issues that belonged squarely in the realm of political discourse, but treated these things by engaging the audience ... *emotionally* in the detail of real stories."[18] Taylor's central thesis—that the "strategies of immediacy and directness" found in the nineties new wave are cultivated, in verbatim theater, into strategies of "emotional enlistment"[19]—will be revisited later in this chapter, when Taylor's emphasis on subjective attachment to political mindsets is reexamined in light of current cultural forces.

What Has Happened to Truth?

Verbatim theater experienced its resurgence in the United Kingdom at a time bereft of trust in political discourse, when theater was challenging the ways audiences took meaning from stories. Spectators sought not "simple answers" (and surely not Utopias), but a greater sense of certainty, of factual accuracy, or even *truth*, than could be found outside the auditorium. Live encounter with testimony offered temporary communities privileged access to a reflection of the real world that seemed impulsive, unmediated, and *authentic*.[20] Viewed from a present-day perspective, the expectation that theater predicated on its truth claims could offer a welcome corrective to the realities it purports to reflect looks nostalgic at best.

Now that it has become hugely challenging to fish through the ceaseless stream of social media for unprocessed, unbiased information, can audiences still expect to find, in live encounters with verbatim testimony, portals to "an urgent 'truth'"?[21] The Brexit debacle in the United Kingdom and the lurid theatrics of Donald Trump have weathered our trust in government and the business of politics to the verge of erosion. In an age when elected representatives and influential commentators brazenly rebrand blatant lies as "alternative facts," the demand for genuine facts should be more urgent than ever. But the defining casualty of this extraordinary "post-truth" era has been the steady decline of faith in their authority. What has happened to truth?

While the significant characteristic of postmodernism is recognized by both supporters and critics as "a Socratic impulse to question truths,"[22] in an ever more socially and behaviorally fragmented world "the lines of force and meaning are more dispersed, more conflictual, more partial than [the] term … conveys."[23] Douglas Kellner draws attention, however, to a transformation in the current age "comparable in scope to the shifts produced by the industrial revolution."[24] Predicting "a postindustrial, infotainment and biotech mode of global capitalism, organized around new information, communications, and genetic technologies,"[25] Kellner posits that our social and cultural situation is hard to comprehend "in a hypercapitalist culture of spectacles, simulacra and disinformation."[26] Thus, we are pivoted between the postmodern and the modern, "in an interim period between epochs,"[27] an ambiguous situation foundational to Daniel Schulze's conception of the search for authenticity as a riposte to fragmentation and uncertainty.[28] In postmodern life, posits Schulze, the notion of authenticity has been replaced by that of multiple and constructed identities.

Within pluralist models of twenty-first-century verbatim theater (see, e.g., Robin Soans's *Talking to Terrorists* [2005]),[29] the assembled presence of individual testimonies entwines a number of competing, subjective "truths," disguising any thread that might be identified as a "master" narrative. While the exposure of unreported voices intends to challenge the authority of the "official" narratives that have conspired, through various operations of power, to exclude them, the potential for authorial or political bias in the construction of "narratives of opposition"[30] has called into question their potential for offering more "truthful" accounts.

Schulze's characterization of authenticity can be applied to the realms of theater and performance in the sense that it can be *constructed* and commoditized in contemporary culture: it is "created, performed and developed, and once it is established it becomes a social (unquestioned) reality."[31] Carol Martin argues that the "provocative" element of documentary theater "is the way in which it strategically deploys the *appearance* of truth while *inventing* its own particular truth through elaborate aesthetic devices."[32] In Schulze's discussion of reality, the "real" materializes as the original, unmediated object.[33] Benjamin's distinction is useful in that it sets up a qualitative difference in "object" and "facsimile." Applied to verbatim strategies, these terms can be understood as the source material and its adaptation into theatrical presentation.

Citing *My Name Is Rachel Corrie*[34] as her primary example, Martin investigates the various types of "evidence" presented by documentary theater (the presence of documents, film clips, and so on) that act as surrogates for absent subjects. Here, those "surrogates" may be seen as the "original, unmediated objects" that trigger, in the audience, a temporal awareness of mortality through the idea that absent subjects might be "ghosted" by performers. If audiences then "create their own version of an (imagined) authentic past," it follows that reality must be "experienced as *staged, a mere representation* that has no depth."[35] Viewed from the perspective of our current, "post-truth" era, Schulze's troubling notion that reality has no more depth and substance than a projection screen demands scrutiny. Such an inquiry leads the discussion of postmodernity and authenticity into confrontation with the cultural forces influencing the present-day sense of dysphoria. It brings us to the defining questions of our age: how did the truth become an endangered species in the West? How did subjectivity come to trump factuality?

The "Echo Chamber": Theater in a "Post-Truth" World

Are we living in a post-truth world? The answer to that question requires looking at definitions of the term, its origins, and applications, and then asking how it applies to theater. In a post-truth era, documentary and verbatim's contested relationship to truth becomes even more problematic.

Does the widespread erosion of trust in sources of information, seen in the proliferation of phrases such as "fake news" and "alternative facts,"[36] extend to the realms of theater and performance? If so, verbatim theater is obsolete, because it is driven by a quest to expose the truth; without even a vague collective sense of *belief in*, let alone what we *mean by* "truth," the quest becomes futile. But if post-truth is more about contemporary information overload, an avalanche that is burying truth alive, then the task of verbatim practice—to clear away the debris of cascading falsehoods—becomes more urgent, more necessary than ever.

Is a stable definition of post-truth possible? *Oxford Dictionaries* selected "post-truth" as its word of the year in 2016, defining it as shorthand for "circumstances in which objective facts are less influential in shaping public opinion than appeals to emotion and personal belief."[37] This is an intriguing definition that does not quite substantiate the hazy concept of a "post-truth era" but does offer a tentative rationale for the word that appears to cast subjective—personal—feelings as being "untruthful." The definition could serve perfectly well if the word was "post-fact." It is hard to comprehend the death of truth; intrinsic to the discourses and belief systems foundational to an operative society, it is "a cornerstone of our democracy."[38] Postmodern discourse invites scrutiny of the concept but has never entirely rejected "truth."

The technologies we rely on and their uncanny powers of silent observation draw us into a quest for the truth condemned to perpetual deferral. Technology can—and does—construct versions of ourselves made entirely of algorithms designed to detect what we like to look at and lead us to similar content. Thus, as I access the Internet, filters target my virtual self, leading me to information I believe I have found and selected autonomously. Through that monitored interaction with technology, my real and virtual selves become somehow fused, the consequence being that I am guided from any opinions that may substantially challenge my own.

This development implies a loss of autonomy that Kellner, in his conception of a new technoculture as a postmodern phenomenon, did not foresee; his prediction of "a more decentralized, individualist and variegated culture"[39] enables the subject to "generate postmodern selves—multiple, fragmented, constructed and provisional, subject to experiment and change," the result being "awareness of the variety of roles we play and dimensions to our subjectivity."[40] Kellner, writing in 2007, had not anticipated the commodification of online activity that has undoubtedly played a substantial role in the movement toward post-truth and has profound political implications. As Matthew d'Ancona states:

> We have entered a new phase of political and intellectual combat, in which democratic [values] and institutions are being shaken to their foundations by a wave of ugly populism. Rationality is threatened by emotion, diversity by nativism, liberty by a drift towards autocracy. [...] At the heart of this global trend is a crash in the value of truth, comparable to the collapse of a currency or a stock.[41]

In light of this apparent deficit it becomes necessary to expose the ways truth is obscured, and ignored, and fabricated; and consider whether, and how, we can get anywhere near to glimpsing, or grasping it.

As we increasingly receive our news through our mobile phones, it follows that social media profoundly influences the way we see the world. Michiko Kakutani observes a landscape in which "people live in increasingly narrow content silos and correspondingly smaller walled gardens of thought."[42] D'Ancona states that between them the "big five" providers—Google, Microsoft, Apple, Facebook, and Amazon—"outstrip ... all the databanks, filing systems and libraries that have existed in human history"; information about all of our online transactions "has become the most valuable commodity in the world."[43] Further,

> This technology has also been the ... engine of Post-Truth. [...] [While] it was optimistically assumed ... [it] would ... smooth the path to sustainable cooperation and pluralism ... the new technology has done at least as much to foster online huddling and general retreat into echo chambers.[44]

The terms "fact" and "truth" are not interchangeable: truth is more subjective. This does not mean either that people do not believe in or that they would necessarily dismiss facts; the point is that they are not *emotionally* invested in them. Facts may have lost their currency because areas of life that are not really about facts, but *values*, are no longer considered to be the monopoly of politicians, intellectuals, and self-appointed authorities. Indeed, one of the casualties of the post-truth era has been the discrediting of so-called experts, a situation that confinement to the echo chamber can only perpetuate and amplify. Facts, informed debate, even science "is under attack, and so is expertise of every sort."[45] In this climate, the term "post-truth" is misleading: the issue becomes a matter of who is qualified, or entrusted, to speak the truth. The danger comes when people decide to trust a narrative that cannot be—or, worse, does not ostensibly *need* to be—supported or verified by facts. Reinelt, stating that audiences seek reassurance in "the assertion of the materiality of events, of the indisputable character of the facts,"[46] implies that verbatim theater establishes trust through blending subjective truths with factually sound archival evidence; d'Ancona sees, in recent political narratives, that facts have lost their sovereignty.

Both Kakutani[47] and d'Ancona[48] find the possibility that postmodernist texts, by questioning the very notion of objective reality, augured the "post-truth" phenomenon. While postmodernists did not entirely dislodge the consensus that truth was a sacrosanct value, we have arrived at the moment when "that consensus has collapsed."[49] The US president's unlikely ascent may be indicative of its demise: "His rise to the most powerful office in the world, unhindered by care for the truth, accelerated by the awesome force of social media, was the ultimate post-modern moment."[50] This discussion alludes not only to Donald Trump but also to another defining moment of the post-truth era: the United Kingdom's vote to leave the European Union in 2016. In her analysis of the Brexit campaign, the journalist Katherine Viner[51] highlights the most persuasive, emotive claims made by the key strategists (Gove, Farage, and Ukip donor Arron Banks) that were subsequently revealed to have had no factual basis.

In light of these troubling developments, can verbatim theater offer a meaningful intervention? Anderson and Wilkinson see the explicit advantage of *empathetic* engagement with testifiers. They argue for "[a] community's need ... to be informed, engaged and transformed"[52] in ways that invite them to respond to performances both intellectually and emotionally, a process further emphasized by Lib Taylor's notion of "emotional enlistment."[53] Their analyses posit that verbatim practice offers a corrective forum for marginalized expressions of dissent: the authentic storytelling of those individuals whose stories have been somehow consigned to the margins, forgotten by history, or silenced by regimes of power. In a skeptical (postmodern?) age, the audiences are, according to Anderson and Wilkinson, attuned to the duplicitous nature of political spin, so that they are "asked to examine what playwrights and performers consider as *inauthentic*."[54] But an uneasy affiliation can be detected, here, between falsehoods in political ideologies (the "inauthentic" narratives) and the stories gathered from the testimony of real people that are somehow deemed worthier of trust (the "authentic" narratives).

If we are indeed living in a "skeptical" age—or even in a post-truth age—there is no compelling reason to believe that we should be more inclined to accept each other's words than those of our elected representatives. Such an assumption homogenizes testimony, not just to a flatly oppositional narrative, but as somehow untethered to *any* form of external political influence, because it implies that the recounting of subjective experience is entirely free, in its articulation, from the biased expression of political affiliations. D'Ancona and Kakutani argue, however, that we are now being led to online content that closes off anything that may cast doubt upon, or oppose, content to which we have already expressed an affiliation. This is a form of "enlistment" that denies the agency advocated (below) by Lib Taylor.

In response to technological developments, our definition of "community" has changed: communities exist online, can be built through campaigning action, shared enthusiasms, obsessions, or political allegiances. The work of pioneering United Kingdom verbatim practitioner Alecky Blythe exhibits her fascination with journeys from division to cohesion in particular communities (see, e.g., *London Road* [2011],[55] *Little Revolution* [2014]).[56] While it is fastidiously observed and recorded, it is precisely that affinity to localized issues that gives the work its pervasively parochial accent, but also its optimism. The current "global community" now that it has shifted to an online collective owned and monitored by the "big five" expresses a conception of connectivity—the "echo chamber"—that taints the positive idea of unity. The question, now, must be whether the stories heard in verbatim theater—if they do encourage empathetic connection—also encourage an emotional affinity to subjective truth. D'Ancona sees this possibility, in the context of online "clusters," as one of the contributory factors in the movement toward "enlistment" to narratives with *no factual* credibility. This development, seen in the context of recent political upheaval, is a threat to democracy. Is there any political agency in subjective reception?

Taylor does not explain precisely how the shift, in the spectator, from "a position of passive sympathy" to "active participation"[57] is actuated, but would seem to confirm Tomlin's apprehension of pluralistic strategies in verbatim practice that ostensibly replace the single protagonist, consigning audiences to biased "narratives of opposition."[58] D'Ancona has argued that, far from triggering oppositional activism, (online) emotional enlistment has a perilous tendency to silence opposition, and thus to play straight into the hands of the opponent. Taylor's optimistic expectation is that audiences will be directed to channel their "emotional enlistment" toward meaningful activism, demanding reform, if not revolution. Allowing for this possibility, the emphasis upon "authenticity" as securely residing in *factual* material loses some of its authority, but in a post-truth era, the erosion of any factual basis to the perception of authenticity is a troubling prospect. Can viable alternative strategies in verbatim practice be evidenced?

INTO THE BREACH: IN SEARCH OF "AUTHENTICITY"

The truth claims made in, and of, verbatim theater have, according to Amanda Stuart Fisher, been overemphasized because they place "limitations on theater's capacity to respond *authentically* to real stories of trauma."[59] Stuart Fisher proposes "a more existentially nuanced articulation of truth grasped as 'authenticity,'"[60] informed by Martin Heidegger's account of being-toward-death, which looks beyond pedestrian fidelity to *factual accuracy* to consider "fidelity to the very conditions of our own existence."[61] The context of a post-truth era must acknowledge Stuart Fisher's call for a shift of emphasis, in the assessment of verbatim practice, from its supposed obligation to generate "technical" and "factual" truth.

If the faithful replication of verbatim accounts can only touch the surface of traumatic experience, how else might such profoundly subjective depths be explored or "authentically examined"?[62] An "authentic" methodology should break through the constraints imposed by factual legitimacy and reach for different dramaturgical strategies capable of locating and inhabiting this liminal space. What does this "space" look and sound like? Arguably, we have already encountered it, in the tangential environments imagined by the mid-nineties playwrights cited. Stuart Fisher looks closely at the impact of trauma upon the subject: it can be perceived "as a 'breach' in the processes of cognition with which we ordinarily experience and make sense of the world."[63] There are clear links to be found here, in subject and form, with the experiential theater of Kane and Ravenhill: if trauma cannot be assimilated into experience, it may therefore "stand radically beyond language and communicability."[64] The authors of "in-yer-face theatre," in their articulation of "the experience of absence and dislocation,"[65] captured the veracity of lived experience as defined by Stuart Fisher; verbatim theater, in its phlegmatic reliance on the spoken word, might actually foreclose communication of that which it seeks to disseminate.

It should be acknowledged that Stuart Fisher is not concerned with forms of verbatim theater that *necessitate* the presentation of facts. The foremost example, in the United Kingdom, of "tribunal theatre," *The Colour of Justice*[66] did not set out to investigate "what it *means* to speak of the truth"[67]; rather, it intended—successfully, as it transpired—to *evidence* institutional racism within the Metropolitan Police. The hyperreal tribunal theater form offers no juncture at which a radical departure from mimetic modes of delivery might occur. There is a more convincing link to be found with Stuart Fisher's call for a poetic dimension to the presentation of lived experience in Lloyd Newson's dance-theater piece, DV8's *John* (2014), the third in a sequence of verbatim pieces, following *To Be Straight With You* (2008) and *Can We Talk About This?* (2012).

Director Lloyd Newson's intention in making *John* was to allow the company's improvisational process—that is, the expression of their individual encounters with verbatim texts—to inform the somatic score. Thus, *John* offers a definition of authenticity that can be understood as "authentic" to *their* process, *their* experience, as much as to the traumatic experience of the testifiers. Arguably, the autobiographical content in DV8's *John*, and the work's extension, beyond spoken language, into physical expression of its extremities, force us more directly into contact with explicit experiences of trauma; into close proximity to mortality. Stuart Fisher is calling for verbatim strategies that somehow embrace and convey this dimension, and in doing so reveal a degree of "truthfulness" that factual accuracy and mimetic performance styles fail to disclose.

In DV8's *John*, the titular protagonist's narrative function oscillates between telling *and* reliving his own story, which is structured as a relentless chronology of trauma. The piece achieves a disorienting temporal trick through the juxtaposition of the "storied" John's past tense, verbatim text, and its immediate, "here-and-now" enactment; the character is both interlocutor and participant, inhabiting a space located somewhere between detached reportage and embodied, integrated reconstruction of the past. Trauma, posits Stuart Fisher, "returns unbidden to disrupt the present while also radically re-aligning the subject's vision of the future."[68] DV8's piece conveys this view: John is shown to have no control over the sequence of occurrences that make up his story, has limited control over their recollection and no control over their consequences.

While it has not proven possible to circumvent entirely the preoccupations with "truth" and "authenticity" that informs the critical landscape, I have drawn attention to one example of work that has pushed the form from familiar treatments of verbatim material toward the formulation of dramaturgies that expand the definitions of these terms. Finding innovative ways and means to engage with urgent, real-world issues and debates, Newson is a contemporary practitioner that still "authenticates" material through the veracity of verbatim testimonies, discovering that he need not adhere to verbatim performance conventions in devising interpretative strategies. The imitations of "authenticity" apparent in DV8's work can be seen in the utilization and exposure, within the formal properties of the work, of their processes of making.

Newson's work is not at all times crafted in service to the text: the primacy of the verbatim material is subverted by an elliptical, often cryptic somatic score, by images and impressions gathered from somewhere outside and later imported. While those imported elements, being unrelated to the spoken words, cannot always be read (in performance) with any certainty of their precise meaning, what DV8 is doing with the text is opening up a space for interpretation, making the audience work to connect action and image to their speech acts (or leaving them free to accept this lack of correlation). Rarely seen in the treatment of verbatim material, this is arguably one of the foremost tenets of the In-Yer-Face aesthetic. Such innovative treatment both suggests a way forward for the practice and brings us full circle to Ravenhill's rebuttal of verbatim theater's dogmatic adherence to factual accuracy, to the need for "a poetic and therefore ... more political sensibility than 'journalism' allows."[69]

Conclusion

If indeed we are in a "post-truth" era, living in the era of "alternative facts" and "fake news," it is significant—perhaps inevitable—that the art being talked about now is dystopian fiction: it is worth noting that Orwell's *Nineteen Eighty-Four* rose to the top of the bestseller charts days after Americans were encouraged to embrace "alternative facts." Fictional dystopias can invite queasy recognition of our current circumstances; not through facsimile, or Baudrillardian simulacra, but rather, through elements of allegory: the celebrated television adaptation of Margaret Atwood's *The Handmaid's Tale*, for example, exhibits recognizable parallels with the real world that seem to confirm our worst presentiments. I had anticipated a second resurgence of verbatim theater in response to the current political and cultural climate, but we are turning to work that reflects a kind of foreboding, perhaps because we are resigned to a world in which the moderate, putatively liberal territory known as the "middle ground" has been squeezed out by the bellicose populism of recent political upheaval. The relationship of the genre to journalism has been undermined by the diminishing status, in the real world, of print journalism and the shift to online content. Fueled by rapid technological advances, and with astonishing rapidity, the persuasive influence of the "media," as we knew it—the reportage and opinion of paid professionals—has been all but eclipsed by the ceaseless chatter of social media. This is not to pretend that print journalism is not possessed of a promiscuous relationship with truth, or that its readership is not divided along lines of politics, class, and income. Alongside the addictive distractions of Clickbait, there are positive aspects to this phenomenon: the secretive nexus of politicians and media moguls has been exposed and weakened; the voices of individuals in the public domain appear to have gained status and power. Yet the ownership and manipulation of social media by five supremely influential, global corporations raise serious doubts about where the power truly lies. The capacity of search engines to feed bogus news stories to our handheld devices has brought about unchecked assimilation of the fake and the real that Baudrillard could scarcely have conceived of.

The examples of verbatim theater cited consider the dissemination of marginal voices as a positive alternative, corrective or form of redress to the "master narratives" propagated by media corporations bound by their own political associations. Now, however, the proliferation of public opinion, expressive of more extreme, more reactionary, more polarized affiliation to online "clusters," *is* the master narrative. The claim that verbatim theater could offer a viable *alternative* is no longer so easy to make: a form of theater predicated on the veracity of individual testimony seems destined, in the current climate, to get lost in the maelstrom. In-Yer-Face Theater is historically placed as a forerunner to the form, but its dystopian stories, offered in resistance to "the unrelenting ideological monopoly of late capitalism,"[70] might now be reconsidered as premonitions of the "post-truth" era. While my fascination with verbatim practice, and belief in its capacity for meaningful political intervention and aesthetic innovation, has not diminished, I conclude with the awareness that the status of "authenticity" and "truth" as sacrosanct values has diminished even further than postmodern skepticism would dare to have anticipated.

Notes

1. See Stephen Bottoms, "Putting the Document into Documentary–An Unwelcome Corrective?" *The Drama Review* 50, no. 3 (2006): 56–68; Jenny Hughes, "Theatre, Performance and the 'War on Terror': Ethical and Political Questions arising from British Theatrical Responses to War and Terrorism," *Contemporary Theatre Review* 17:2 (2007): 149–164; Donna Soto-Morettini, "Trouble in the House: David Hare's *Stuff Happens*," *Contemporary Theatre Review* 15, no. 3 (2005): 309–319.
2. Carol Martin, "Bodies of Evidence," in *Dramaturgy of the Real on the World Stage*, ed. C. Martin (Basingstoke: Palgrave Macmillan, 2012), 23.
3. Graham Saunders, *Love Me or Kill Me: Sarah Kane and the Theatre of Extremes* (Manchester: Manchester University Press, 2002), 5.
4. Ibid., 7.
5. John F. Deeney, "Mark Ravenhill," in *Fifty Modern and Contemporary Dramatists*, ed. John F. Deeney and Maggie Gale (London: Routledge, 2015), 190.
6. Mark Ravenhill, "A Tear in the Fabric," *New Theatre Quarterly* 20, no. 4 (2004): 310.
7. Peter Billingham, *At the Sharp End* (London: Bloomsbury, 2007), 134.
8. Aleks Sierz, *In-Yer-face Theatre: British Drama Today* (London: Faber, 2001), 24.
9. Michael Billington, *State of the Nation* (London: Faber, 2008), 361.
10. Ibid.
11. See Janelle Reinelt, "The Promise of Documentary," in *Get Real: Documentary Theatre Past and Present*, ed. Chris Megson and Allison Forsythe (Basingstoke: Palgrave Macmillan 2009), 1–25.
12. Deeney, 193.
13. Ibid., 194.
14. Steve Waters, "Sarah Kane: From Terror to Trauma," in *A Companion to Modern British and Irish Drama 1880–2005*, ed. M. Luckhurst (London: Wiley-Blackwell 2010), 377.
15. Ibid., 373.
16. Ibid., 381.
17. See Chris Megson, "This is all theatre: Iraq Centre Stage," *Contemporary Theatre Review* 15, no. 3 (2005): 369–371; Carol Martin, "Bodies of Evidence," in *Dramaturgy of the Real on the World Stage*, ed. Carol Martin (Basingstoke: Palgrave Macmillan, 2012), 17–26; Liz Tomlin, "Representing the real: verbatim practice in a sceptical age," in *Acts and Apparitions* (Manchester, 2013), 114–142.

18. Lib Taylor, "The Experience of Immediacy: Emotion and Enlistment in Fact-based Theatre," *Studies in Theatre and Performance* 31, no. 2 (2011): 226, my emphasis.
19. Ibid., 224.
20. See Paola Botham, "From Deconstruction to Reconstruction: A Habermasian Framework for Contemporary Political Theatre," *Contemporary Theatre Review*, 18, no. 3 (2018): 307–317.
21. Taylor, 224.
22. Pelagia Goulimari, (ed.) *Postmodernism. What Moment?* (Manchester: Manchester University Press, 2007), 1.
23. John McGowan, "They Might Have Been Giants," in *Postmodernism. What Moment?*, ed. Pelagia Goulimari (Manchester: Manchester University Press, 2007), 94.
24. Douglas Kellner, "Reappraising the Postmodern," in *Postmodernism. What Moment?*, ed. Pelagia Goulimari (Manchester: Manchester University Press, 2007), 104.
25. Ibid.
26. Ibid., 120.
27. Ibid., 119.
28. Daniel Schulze, *Authenticity in Contemporary Theatre and Performance* (London: Bloomsbury, 2017), 25.
29. Robin Soans, *Talking to Terrorists* (London: Oberon 2005).
30. See Liz Tomlin, "Representing the real: verbatim practice in a sceptical age," in *Acts and Apparitions* (Manchester University Press, 2013), 114–142.
31. Schulze, 28.
32. Martin, "Bodies of Evidence," 19.
33. Benjamin, Walter "The Work of Art in the Age of Mechanical Reproduction," *Marxist.org* (1936), https://www.marxists.org/reference/subject/philosophy/works/ge/benjamin.htm.
34. Alan Rickman and Katharine Viner, *My Name is Rachel Corrie* (London: Nick Hern, 2005).
35. Schulze, 33. Author emphasis.
36. See Michiko Kakutani, *The Death of Truth* (London: William Collins, 2018), 13.
37. OED 2016: online.
38. Kakutani, 19.
39. Kellner, 106.
40. Ibid.
41. Matthew d'Ancona, *Post Truth: The New War on Truth and How to Fight Back* (London: Ebury Press, 2017), 8.
42. Kakutani, 117.

43. d'Ancona, 48.
44. Ibid., 49.
45. Kakutani, 23.
46. Janelle Reinelt, "Toward a Poetics of Theatre and Public Events," in *Dramaturgy of the Real on the World Stage* ed. Carol Martin (Basingstoke: Palgrave Macmillan, 2012), 39.
47. Kakutani, 60.
48. d'Ancona, 92.
49. Ibid., 96.
50. Ibid., 97.
51. Katharine Viner, "How Technology Disrupted the Truth," *Guardian*, July 12, 2016, https://www.theguardian.com/media/2016/jul/12/how-technology-disrupted-the-truth (accessed October 10, 2017).
52. Michael Anderson and Linden Wilkinson, "A Resurgence of Verbatim Theatre: Authenticity, Empathy and Transformation," *Australian Drama Studies* 50 (2017): 167.
53. Taylor, 223–237.
54. Anderson and Wilkinson, "A Resurgence," 155. Author emphasis.
55. Alecky Blythe, *London Road* (London: Nick Hern, 2011).
56. Alecky Blythe, *Little Revolution* (London: Nick Hern, 2014).
57. Taylor, 229.
58. Tomlin, 120.
59. Amanda Stuart Fisher, "Trauma, Authenticity and the Limits of Verbatim," *Performance Research* 16:1 (2011), 112. Original emphasis.
60. Ibid.
61. Ibid.
62. Ibid., 114.
63. Ibid.
64. Ibid.
65. Deeney, 194.
66. Richard Norton-Taylor, *The Colour of Justice: The Stephen Lawrence Inquiry* (London: Oberon, 1999).
67. Stuart Fisher, 113. Author emphasis.
68. Ibid., 116.
69. Deeney, 194.
70. Ibid., 190.

Index[1]

A
Aesthetics, 217–219, 221, 222, 224, 227–228
 dialectical, 72–73, 75, 79
Alternative facts, 234, 236, 242
Artistas Unidos, 12, 91, 93, 96–98
Arts Council of Great Britain, 25, 27, 37
Australian theater, 121–133
 Australian In-Yer-Face, 126–133
 In-Yer-Face in Australia, 122–125
Authenticity, 231, 234–235, 240–242

B
Baudrillard, Jean, 59–61, 64
Betzien, Angela, 124–125
 The Dark Room, 125
Bolito, Carla, 92
Bond, Edward, 13, 139–150
 accident time, 13, 142–150
 on *Blasted*, 141, 142
 Born, 148
 on *Cleansed*, 142
 Coffee, 144, 148
 "Commentary on *The War Plays*," 141, 144
 Crime of the Twenty-First Century, The, 145, 148
 on madness, 140–142
 on violence, 140–148
Bond, James, 7, 8
Boy George, 60–61
Brecht, Bertolt, 72–73, 143
 Epic Theatre (*see* Dialectical theater)
 historicization, 77–78
 post-Brechtian theater, 11–12, 71–83
Brexit, 234, 238
Butterworth, Jez, 6–7
 Ferryman, The, 6
 Mojo, 7, 38, 43, 46
 on movies, 7
 River, The, 6

---

[1] Note: Page numbers followed by 'n' refer to notes.

© The Author(s) 2020
W. C. Boles (ed.), *After In-Yer-Face Theatre*,
https://doi.org/10.1007/978-3-030-39427-1

C

Candide, 114
Cardoso, Nuno M., 94–96, 98, 99
Carnation Revolution, 90, 100n3
Carneiro, João, 96
Catharsis, 186–191, 194, 197
Cleverly, Jess, 41, 48, 50
Community, 191, 194, 197, 204, 207, 239
Connery, Sean, 8
Cool Britannia, 10, 51, 57, 76, 83, 126
Corner Boys, 27, 30
Crimp, Martin, 156–162
    Attempts on Her Life, 160–162
    Fewer Emergencies, 157
Cruel Britannia, 172, 182
Cruise, Tom, 7

D

Daldry, Stephen, 21, 23–24, 27–31, 35n47, 37–40, 45, 49, 51
De Angelis, April, 31
Dialectical theatre, 72–83
Documentary theater, *see* Verbatim theater
Dodgson, Elyse, 24–25
Dromgoole, Dominic, 34–35n39, 69
Dudley, William, 50–51
DV8, 241–242
    John, 241

E

East is East, 24, 33n15
English Stage Company (ESC), 37–46, 49–52
Ethics, 139, 140, 144, 145, 147–150, 172, 177–178
Evans, Daniel, 13, 126–133
    comparison with Sarah Kane, 132–133
    Oedipus Doesn't Live Here Anymore, 132–133
    Tragedy of King Richard the Third, The, 129–133
Experiential theater, 80–82, 89, 99, 143, 164, 219, 224–226, 228, 240

F

Fatherhood, 204–213
Fox, James, 46
Frazão, Francisco, 91

G

Genet, Jean, 177
Grosso, Nick, 30, 31
    Peaches, 27, 28, 30
    Sweetheart, 38, 46
Gulf War, 59–60

H

Handley, Paul, 40, 43–44
Harvey, Jonathan, 32, 35n49
Heywood, Vikki, 50

I

Inspector Calls, An, 30
In-Yer-Ear theatre, 157–159
In-Yer-Face Conference (Bristol), 4
In-Yer-Face Sessions (Comparative Drama Conference), 10
In-Yer-Head theatre, 13–14, 155–166

J

Jeremy Kyle Show, The, 186, 195, 199–200n46
Jerwood New Playwrights (JNP), 28, 34n28

K

Kane, Sarah, 12, 13, 39, 89–100, 126–127, 132–133, 139–150, 159–162, 168n21, 217–219, 227, 233
- *Blasted*, 23, 27, 33n15, 46–47, 70n38, 91, 92, 125, 145, 146, 148–149
- *Cleansed*, 4–5, 38, 47–48, 89–90, 94–96, 146, 149, 222–224
- correspondence with Pinter, 48–49
- *Crave*, 93–94
- on Edward Bond, 141
- *4.48 Psychosis*, 96, 97, 125, 146, 149, 159–162
- on madness, 140–142
- *Phaedra's Love*, 97
- reviewing *Ashes to Ashes*, 55n54
- on violence, 140–149, 229n19

Kelly, Dennis, 14, 15, 218–219, 224–228
- *Love and Money*, 14, 224–227

L

Lacan, Jacques, 144
Lad culture, 209
Language, 217–228
London New Play Festival, 30–31
Love, 62, 64–65, 68, 80, 91, 220–228

M

MacDonald, James, 51
Madness, 164–166
- *See also* Kane, Sarah; Bond, Edward
Masculinity, 58, 63–64, 209–213
Materialism, 226–228
McDonagh, Martin, 7–8
- *Beauty Queen of Leenane, The*, 2–3, 7
- on movies, 8

Pillowman, The, 8, 16n2
Very Very Very Dark Matter, A., 8
Miller, Arthur, 48
Miller, Carl, 31, 35n47
Mitchell, Katie, 4–5

N

National Theatre (NT) Studio, 27–28
Neilson, Anthony, 4, 57–69, 155, 162–166
- adaptation of his texts, 67–69
- depiction of family, 65–68
- depiction of homosexuality, 62–64
- depiction of masculinity, 59–65
- *Marat/Sade*, 4
- *Penetrator*, 11, 57–69
- *Wonderful World of Dissocia, The*, 155, 162–165

Newson, Lloyd, 241–242

P

Pallasmaa, Juhani, 157
Penhall, Joe, 9–10, 14, 30–31, 201–213
- *Birthday*, 208–213, 214n23
- *Blue/Orange*, 9, 208, 213n5, 214n18
- on fatherhood, 203
- *Haunted Child*, 204–207
- *Landscape with Weapon*, 202
- *Last King of Scotland, The*, 10
- *Mood Music*, 212–213
- on movies, 9
- on National Health Service, 208, 212
- *Road, The* (screenplay), 9, 10, 204
- *Some Voices*, 9, 27, 28, 30–31, 35n39
- *Sunny Afternoon*, 9

Pinter, Harold, 7, 39–44
  Ashes to Ashes, 11, 40–44, 46–49
  correspondence with Royal Court staff, 40–43
  correspondence with Sarah Kane, 48
  history with Royal Court, 43
Polar Bears, 159
Political theater, 71–83, 112, 113
Portuguese theater, 89–100
Postmodern, 234–237
Post-truth, 14–15, 231–243
Prichard, Rebecca, 29–31, 34n35
  Essex Girls, 27, 30
  Fair Game, 31, 32
Psychopoetics, 154, 159, 163–165
Purple Clouds, 116

R
Ravenhill, Mark, 16n4, 71–83, 112–114, 126, 150, 218–221, 227, 232–233
  on Bertolt Brecht, 72–74
  Candide, 114
  Shopping and Fucking, 1, 11, 14, 23, 33n15, 40, 43, 113, 220–224, 232
  Some Explicit Polaroids, 11–12, 74–83, 113
Régy, Claude, 157–159
Rickson, Ian, 35n47
Ridley, Philip, 14, 171–182, 185–197
  Dark Vanilla Jungle, 181–182, 186, 187, 191–197
  Karagula, 180–181
  Leaves of Glass, 175
  Mercury Fur, 176–180
  Piranha Heights, 175
  Pitchfork Disney, The, 172–175, 177
  Radiant Vermin, 176
  on ritual, 177
  Shivered, 175
  Sparkleshark, 180
  Tender Napalm, 175–176
  Tonight with Donny Stixx, 181–182, 186, 187, 191, 194–197
  use of autobiography, 174–176
  use of violence, 174
  Vincent River, 186–192
Royal Court Theatre, 11, 21–33, 37–52
  avoiding prosecution, 44–45
  Coming on Strong, 27, 29–33
  productions of Russian writing, 109
  Sloane Square season (2000), 52n3
  start time squabble, 40–42, 52n10
  visit to Russia, 106
  West End advertising campaign, 37, 42
  West End seasons, 37–40
  Young People's Theatre (YPT), 22, 24–32
  Young Writer's Festival, 24–27, 38
  Young Writer's Programme, 32
Russian In-Yer-Face theatre, *see* Russian new drama
Russian new drama, 103–116
  compared with In-Yer-Face, 106–108
  government restrictions, 114
  political theater, 112
Rylance, Mark, 6, 201

S
Shame and Mold, 115, 116
Shepard, Sam, 201–205, 207
  Buried Child, 204–206
  True West, 201–203, 213
Sierz, Aleks, 4, 38, 51–52, 98, 217–218
Sigarev, Vassily, 111
  The Land of Oz, 111

Silva Melo, Jorge, 91–94,
    97–99, 101n6
Stafford-Clark, Max, 11, 21, 23, 41
Storytelling, 185–187, 191, 232, 238

T
Technology, 234, 236–237,
    239, 243
Thatcher, Margaret, 23, 61, 65–66
Tickell, Dominic, 24, 26–28,
    32, 35n47
Trump, Donald, 234, 238
Truth, 233–243

U
Upton, Judy, 31, 34n35
    Ashes and Sand, 27

V
Verbatim theater, 15, 233–243
Voloshina, Asya, 114–115
    Antigone: Reduction, 115
    The Man of Fish, 115
von Mayenburg, Marius, 123
    Fireface, 13, 52n3, 122–125, 134n8
Vyrypaev, Ivan, 110
    The Drunks, 110
    Oxygen, 110

W
"War Song, The," 60–61
Weir, The, 39
Whybrow, Graham, 21, 23–24, 29, 31
Williams, Roy, 6
Wynne, Michael, 30, 31, 35n45
    Knocky, The, 27, 28, 30

CPI Antony Rowe
Eastbourne, UK
October 22, 2020